10/98

The Making of the Alice Books
Lewis Carroll's Uses of Earlier Children's Literature

Analysing Lewis Carroll's Alice books in the context of children's literature from the seventeenth through the nineteenth century, Ronald Reichertz argues that Carroll's striking originality is the result of a fusion of his narrative imagination and formal and thematic features from earlier children's literature. *The Making of the Alice Books* includes discussions of the didactic and nursery rhyme verse traditionally addressed by Carroll's critics while adding and elaborating connections established within and against the continuum of English-language children's literature.

Drawing examples from a wide range of children's literature, Reichertz demonstrates that the Alice books are infused with conventions of and allusions to earlier works and identifies precursors of Carroll's upside-down, looking-glass, and dream vision worlds. Key passages from related books are reprinted in the appendices, making available many hard-to-find examples of early children's literature.

This new inquiry into the sources of the Alice books makes an important contribution to the study of both children's and Victorian literature.

RONALD REICHERTZ is professor of English, McGill University.

The Making of the Alice Books

Lewis Carroll's Uses
of Earlier Children's Literature

RONALD REICHERTZ

McGill-Queen's University Press
Montreal & Kingston • London • Buffalo

McGill-Queen's University Press 1997
ISBN 0-7735-1625-5

Legal deposit third quarter 1997
Bibliothèque nationale du Québec

Printed in Canada on acid-free paper

This book has been published with the help of a grant from the
Humanities and Social Sciences Federation of Canada, using
funds provided by the Social Sciences and Humanities Research
Council of Canada.

McGill-Queen's University Press acknowledges the support
received for its publishing program from the Canada Council
Block Grants program.

Canadian Cataloguing in Publication Data

Reichertz, Ronald, 1933–
The making of the Alice books: Lewis Carroll's
uses of earlier children's literature
Includes bibliographical references and index.
ISBN 0-7735-1625-5
1. Carroll, Lewis, 1832-1898. Alice's adventures in
Wonderland. 2. Carroll, Lewis, 1832-1898. Through
the looking glass. 3. Carroll, Lewis, 1832-1898 – Sources.
4. Children's literature, English – History and criticism. I. Title.
PR4612.R45 1977   823'.8   C97-900657-0

This book was typeset by Typo Litho
Composition Inc. in 11/13 Garamond.

For Diane, Marc, and Mathew

Contents

Acknowledgments

There are a number of people to thank for setting this book in motion and moving it along in a variety of ways. My friend and colleague David Williams demonstrated enthusiasm, encouragement, and critical interest throughout the process of my writing and preparing the manuscript for publication. William Booth listened patiently to my early speculations about establishing a context for Carroll's Alices and offered a number of interesting insights and criticisms.

My wife, Diane, was energetically supportive of my thoughts about Lewis Carroll and the Alice books over the long period from genesis through development and completion, and she was especially helpful during difficult times.

An earlier version of chapter 5, which considers *Through the Looking-Glass and What Alice Found There* in relation to the variety and functions of the "looking-glass book" in the years after it was co-opted by children's literature, appeared in *The Children's Literature Association Quarterly.* I am grateful to the editors for permission to reprint it here. I am also grateful to the Board of Trustees of the Victoria and Albert Museum and to the British Library for permission to use material.

I thank the McGill Humanities Research Grant Committee for funding related research and the Aid to Scholarly Publication Agency for a subvention to support the publication of my book.

Finally, my thanks to three concerned and careful editors – Joan McGilvray, Judith Turnbull, and Sarah Wight.

The Making of the Alice Books

· I ·

Introduction:
Carroll's Uses of "Litterature"

The extraordinarily large body of critical response to Lewis Carroll's *Alice's Adventures in Wonderland* and *Through the Looking-Glass and What Alice Found There* is wide-ranging in both critical methodology and focus. This is largely true, as Nina Demurova says, because "Carroll's fairy tales realize in most original and unexpected forms both literary and scientific types of perception. And this is why philosophers, logicians, mathematicians, physicists, psychologists, folklorists, politicians, as well as literary critics ... all find material for thought and interpretation in the Alices" (86).* One potentially important critical approach that has generally been overlooked relates to Carroll's use of the tradition of earlier children's literature in developing both the thematic and formal features of the Alice books.[1] The only major exception to date is the critical attention paid to Carroll's consistent fascination with parody, from his juvenilia through *Sylvie and Bruno*. Many editorial notes do in fact identify and comment on works Carroll parodies. Recently, a very ambitious book, John Docherty's *The Literary Products of the Lewis Carroll–George MacDonald Friendship*, argues for such very specific parodic and satiric literary relationships as those between *Alice in Wonderland* and *Phantastes*, "Cross Purposes," and an unpublished novel titled "Seekers and Finders" (109).[2]

This present volume develops a context for Lewis Carroll's *Alice's Adventures in Wonderland* and *Through the Looking-Glass and What Alice Found*

---

* See the section Works Cited for full bibliographical information for those works quoted or referred to in the text.

There in English-language children's literature from its self-conscious beginnings in the middle of the seventeenth century through the 1890s. The hypothesis is that Carroll's fantasies incorporate an extensive literary tradition that ranges from conventional kinds of children's literature (for example, moral and informational didacticism, nursery rhyme, and fairy tale) to general literary topoi and forms (such as the "world turned upside down," the looking-glass book, and dream vision) that had been assimilated into children's literature before the Alice books were written. Chapters 2–6 develop some of the possible relationships between particular earlier works and literary forms from earlier children's literature and Carroll's fantasies. Appendices relating to each of these chapters contain examples of such earlier work, each introduced by a short description placing it in a chronological literary context. In recent years some of these early children's books have been republished in expensive collections, but many representative works have been overlooked. At this time, there is no single gathering of children's books specifically related to Carroll's Alice books available.

Although the certitude in citing proven sources is attractive, many sources may very well be analogues whose evidence has been lost. To avoid getting caught up in and blocked by such distinctions, I adopt the tenets of intertextual criticism and link other texts to Carroll's Alice books through his open and covert citations and allusions, the assimilation of important features of earlier texts, and his use of a common stock of thematic and formal codes and conventions. Whether Carroll was familiar with specific earlier works will be noted when possible, but textual evidence from the Alice books will determine the basis for a number of the arguments developed.

This book does not replace or displace any other approach to Carroll's Alice books. For example, Stephen Prickett's *Victorian Fantasy* develops a context for the genre and a number of its differing directions by placing fantasy in the literary context of the Gothic, that is, in the general cultural context engendered by the discovery of prehistoric skeletal remains, especially those of the saurians, and the resulting debate between the creationists and the evolutionists. The context presented in my book is more exclusively literary and is especially concerned with Carroll's fantasy within the development of children's literature. Further, Carroll was not alone in working out the shape and variety of nineteenth-century fantasy. In the twenty years preceding Carroll's first version of *Alice's Adventures in Wonderland* (originally titled *Alice's Adventures under Ground* and produced in 1864), John Ruskin had produced *The King of the Golden River*, William Thackery had published *The Rose and the Ring*, and Charles Kingsley had published *The Water Babies*. Although Ruskin somewhat dismissively considered his book "a fairly good imitation of Grimm and Dickens, mixed with some true Alpine feeling of" his own, the "mix" is more complicated than he suggests. It includes a thematic and formal borrowing from mythology that shows how immorality and inhumanity transform "Treasure Valley" into a wasteland that is only restored through selflessness and sacrifice, as well as a *pourquoi* motif that accounts for two great black rocks that were once the heartless Schwartz and Hans. That is to say, Ruskin has made something new in the context of adult and children's literary material. Thackery creates another mix, borrowing from the pantomime, which had already borrowed from folk and fairy tale and nursery rhyme. And Kingsley's *Water Babies* concerns a chimney-sweep named Tom who is certainly a literary cousin of Blake's Tom Dacre; it contains a scene that attacks informational literature for denying the existence of fairies, and satirizes Peter Parley as "Cousin Cramchild" from Boston, US, based on his "Conversations" that champion informational literature over imaginative literature (35). Such attention to information is also satirized in the book's world of the "Examiner-of-all-Examiners," where examinations make children's brains grow while their bodies shrink, changing them into turnips (185).

Edward Lear and George MacDonald also incorporate specific thematic material and shaping elements from children's literature. MacDonald frequently includes brief fairy stories in his realistic novels to add an emotional counterpoint. More specifically, he uses the world turned inside out and upside down in *The Princess and the Goblin* and *The Princess and Curdie*. For example, he spends several pages describing the geological process that creates mountains by literally inside-outing them at the beginning of the latter book, preparing the way for Curdie's mining knowledge of the underworld to carry over into the mountains. Further, MacDonald has the elder Princess Irene prepare Curdie for major moral discriminations through the transforming "washing" of his hands in burning roses, a ritual that allows Curdie to "see" the true or inner nature of apparent beasts and beauties who are undergoing moral evolving or devolving. This specific elaboration of the necessity of the protagonist to discriminate between appearance and reality in folk and fairy tales speaks directly to a child reader with a background in children's literature.

Lear, who created a form of nonsense similar to but quite different from Carroll's, found a number of his forms and themes in children's literature. For example, his most used form, the limerick, came from a volume of children's poems, while many of his other poems take their form from the alphabet rhyme. Lear uses the world turned upside down in "The Chair and the Table," the cautionary tale in "The Seven Families that Lived by the Side of Lake Pipple-Popple," and the travel book in "The Story of the Four Children Who Went Round the World," a prose work that employs talking vegetables and elements of the Land of Cocayne, such as the availability of gourmet meals supplied by nature, with minimal or no work done by the children.

Although all of these writers work with material from children's literature in their own ways, they share an understandable impulse to reach an audience by playing with and against literary material that is already a potential part of the child reader's experience. I am especially interested in the contributions of such practice in Carroll's Alice books, since Carroll is a particularly rich and subtle user of thematic and formal material gathered from earlier children's books, especially those published in the first six decades of the nineteenth century. Further, aside from the obvious use of parodied children's works or works about childhood, there has been little acknowledgment of the great mass of material Carroll uses, consciously or unconsciously, to shape and elaborate his fantasies. For example, Carroll uses travel book conventions, the cautionary tale, the fairy tale, the nursery rhyme, children's poems, parody of moral and informational literature for children, and the conventions of the world turned upside down, the looking-glass book, and the dream vision.

Present collections of criticism, such as Robert Phillips's *Aspects of Alice* (1971) and Edward Guiliano's *Lewis Carroll: A Celebration, Essays on the Occasion of the 150th Anniversary of the Birth of Charles Lutwidge Dodgson* (1982), demonstrate that critics have attended almost exclusively to adult issues and concerns. For example, in the "As Victorian and Children's Literature" section of *Aspects of Alice*, there are but a few essays, the most relevant being a short one titled "*Alice in Wonderland* in Perspective" (by Elsie Leach), which makes connections with folk tales and the religious and moral didactic poems of Isaac Watts, and contrasts Alice's progress with Margery Meanwell's in *Little Goody Two-Shoes*. "The Alice Books and the Metaphors of Victorian Childhood," by Jan Gordon, also in *Aspects of Alice*, presents a characteristic "argument ... heavily weighted toward what [he thinks] to be a neglected view of Carroll's achievement: that these two companion volumes ... are decadent adult literature rather than children's literature" (94). The later *Lewis Carroll: A Celebration ...* includes but one essay concerned with children's literature, "Toward a Definition of Alice's Genre: The Folktale and Fairy Tale Connections," a very insightful generic study that catalogues a number of the "traditional" genre that Carroll employs while arguing that he alters them so completely that they no longer function as they generally do.

Donald Rackin's "Corrective Laughter: Carroll's *Alice* and Popular Children's Literature," published in *The Journal of Popular Culture* (1967), suggests a number of relationships between Carroll's work and earlier children's literature, but concentrates on the early Romantic writers' perception that imaginative children's literature had all but disappeared, having been replaced by the narrow and bleak moral and informational children's literature preceding Carroll's work. Rackin's article names few works of imagination before Carroll.

Finally, Carroll's references to the state of childhood and the difficulty of growing up in the rigid and unpredictable adult world are addressed frequently in the critical anthologies, but his uses of earlier children's books, other than as the ground of parody, are virtually ignored.

The child/adult-reader split behind the Jan Gordon statement quoted above and informing Alexander Taylor's *The White Knight* (1952) proves to be something of a critical red herring, as far as sophisticated sources and analogues go, in large part because adult forms, such as the topos of the world turned upside down and the looking-glass book, were incorporated into children's literature long before Carroll used them. One need not look to experiments in "light polarization in paratartaric acid" carried out by Pasteur or to Kant's speculations about asymmetrical bodies, as Taylor does in *The White Knight,* in order to discover possible sources of Carroll's fascination with and uses of reversal and asymmetricality. Reversal and asymmetricality, although indeed included among Carroll's adult interests, were present in children's literature at the beginning of the nineteenth century, making them equally accessible to both children and adults.

Another area that opens up if Carroll's work is placed in the context of earlier children's literature is his method of composition, an area that he found fascinating and wrote about in several places. In the preface to *Sylvie and Bruno* (1889), speaking specifically about the genesis of this later fantasy but generally about all of his own work, Carroll develops a theory of writing out of what he calls amassed "litterature": "litter"-ature or bits and pieces of "random flashes of thought," sometimes immediately traceable "to books one was reading," sometimes "struck out from the 'flint' of one's own mind by the 'steel' of a friend's chance remark," and sometimes simply as "effect[s] without a cause," such as those that frequently occur in reverie and dream (239). There is no doubt that, whatever else these flashes are and wherever else they originate, the books one has read, or those read by a friend and passed on in conversation or shaped and reshaped by dream, are a common element. Such an account of the composition of the Alice books jibes with Carroll's statement in "Alice on Stage" to the effect that the books "are made up almost wholly of bits and scraps, single ideas which came of themselves,"[3] and does not clash with his brief description of the genesis of *The Hunting of the Snark,* one that plays with confusion of fore and aft, with reversal, and elaborates a view of a composite reality that allows one to function safely in this curious and potentially destructive world. Reversal and portmanteau[4] are among the literary stuff referred to by Carroll in the *Sylvie and Bruno* preface.

Turning to close textual reading in a search for links to a network of children's books available in the 1860s, one soon discovers that the four annotated editions of the Alice books presently available – Martin Gardner's *The Annotated Alice* (Penguin) and *More Annotated Alice* (Random House), Roger L. Green's annotated edition (Oxford University Press), and Donald Gray's Norton Critical Edition – are generally, whatever their strengths, weak in recognizing literary material and allusion other than the obvious parodied works (for example, "The Star" by Jane Taylor and "Against Idleness and Mischief" by Isaac Watts) and incorporated works (for example, "Humpty Dumpty"). Green is the exception in this regard, being the only editor who notes, for instance, that "The King and Queen of Hearts" was not only printed in its entirety and together with poems on the other three card suits in *The European Magazine* (April 1782) but was the basis for Charles Lamb's book published in 1805 (note 1 to 98, 264).* Both the complete poem on the four suits and Lamb's book are included in Appendix 1, as they have possible connections with Carroll's description of the employment of the card suits. Moreover, John Tenniel's illustrations of the cards in *Alice's Adventures in Wonderland* may owe something to William Mulready's illustrations in Lamb's *The King and Queen of Hearts*.

Two further examples of how close attention to text (for instance, Carroll's use of pun and allusion) leads to larger issues of literary context are seen in Alice's attempt to locate herself during her fall and to regain a sense of certainty after her fall into Wonderland. Alice makes two speculations about her location and her destination while she is falling. The first speculation places her at the centre of the earth (a location traditionally accepted by Carroll's critics), but as Alice continues falling, she speculates that her destination is the other side of the world, the "world turned upside down" ("Down the Rabbit-hole," 11). Alice reveals her reading of both upside-down and geography books in this section: "I wonder if I shall fall right *through* the earth! How funny it'll seem to come out among the people that walk with their heads downwards! The Antipathies, I think ..." (10). Alice gives a textbook definition of "antipodes" here but mispronounces the word as "antipathies," which is precisely what the antipodes introduce in Wonderland, physical antipathies (opposites) that both amuse and confuse Alice, resulting in a frequently painful emotional antipathy. Further, she

---

* Since Green is the editor most alert to Carroll's use of children's literature, his edition is cited throughout this book.

connects all this with the then recent geographical discovery of the Antipodes when she says, "I shall have to ask them what the name of the country is, you know. Please, Ma'am, is this New Zealand? Or Australia?" (11). The place will, as the palindrome "Ma'am" suggests, turn reality not only upside down but backwards. Alice's speculation continues to develop in her reversal of "Do cats eat bats?" and comes to an abrupt end when she lands: "… thump! thump! down she came upon a heap of sticks and dry leaves, and the fall was over" (11). The final, and this time seasonal, pun in "the fall was over" reinforces the authenticity of Alice's speculation, since late spring, May 4th, in England is late fall in the Antipodes. This nest of pun and informational book material goes unnoticed in every critical or annotated edition of the Alice books, and the omission is significant because the series of related puns and allusions introduces the consistently developed overturning of Alice's expectations after she enters Wonderland, and connects to a number of similar allusions throughout.

A number of upside-down books for children are included in Appendix 3 as part of the argument presented in chapter 4. They range from geography to satire to philosophical romance to nonsense, and provide material for tracing the history of the topos of the world turned upside down and its movement into children's literature in the late eighteenth and early nineteenth centuries. Chapter 4 also develops some of the structural and thematic possibilities created by Carroll's incorporation of this tradition.

In "The Pool of Tears" Alice attempts to regain her sense of self in the midst of the Wonderland upheavals by reciting Isaac Watts's "Against Idleness and Mischief" from *Divine Songs Attempted in Easy Language for the Use of Children* (1715), a group of poems never out of print from its original publication through to the end of the nineteenth century, poems children were still expected to memorize in the 1860s. All the editors dutifully note this, but not one notes the possible source of the un-signifying multiplication tables or the confusion in set theory that leads Alice to err geographically in "London is the capital of Paris and Paris is the capital of Rome" (19). This is parody of informational books, such as William Pinnock's series of catechisms, and functions precisely in the same way as the parody of the morally didactic poems. Together, moral and informational didacticism dominated children's literature throughout most of the early nineteenth century, but the parody of informational didacticism in the Alice books has been ignored. In the first three decades of the nineteenth century, at a time when Jeremy Bentham was the "patron saint" of utility and anything "useless" or "silly" was thought to be a "sin" against reason, informational literature or the "history of realities" was read far more than nursery rhymes or fairy tales. A number of sections from Pinnock's catechisms on arithmetic, geography, perspective, etc., and from the informational work of "Peter Parley" (Samuel Griswold Goodrich) are included in Appendix 2 to help to clarify Carroll's parody of the genre, discussed here in chapter 3.

Sections from Goodrich's autobiography, *Recollections of a Lifetime* (1857), in which he explains why he is a champion of informational literature for children and how he developed the figure of his kindly old narrator, Peter Parley, will be set off against the attempt of "Felix Summerly" (Henry Cole) to place imaginative work – fairy tale and nursery rhyme and nonsense literature, etc. – at the heart of children's literature through his ambitious *Home Treasury* series. This tug of war between imaginative and didactic literature in the 1840s ended in the momentary victory of informational didacticism. That Carroll includes informational and moral literature for children, transforming both into their opposite, into nonsense, through the alchemy of parody, introduces yet another level of inversion in Wonderland while demonstrating Carroll's keen understanding of the forces working their way out in children's literature.

Chapter 5 is concerned with the looking-glass book, a form of which Alice herself mentions when she discovers "Jabberwocky" in *Through the Looking-Glass and What Alice Found There*. Again, just as with his use of the world turned upside down, Carroll borrows an ancient form that found its way into children's literature in the seventeenth century in Abraham Chear's *A Looking Glass for Children* (1673), a compilation of prose and verse narratives of children's lives meant to be either positive or negative models to the child reader. Once established in children's literature, the form was used in a succession of didactic ways, in religious, moral, and informational books, all of which were meant to teach by offering exemplary or admonitory models. Sections from such books are included in Appendix 4 in order to provide a context for Carroll's use of this tradition, which is at least as important as his use of the optics of the material looking-glass Alice passes through on her way to Looking-Glass Land. To date, there has been no recognition of Carroll's tandem use of the reversals of the material mirror and the form of the looking-glass book. None of the annotated or critical editions note how Alice's didactic play in "Looking-Glass House," the introductory chapter, builds to a key moment when her wish to teach through admonishment leads to the idea of passing through the looking-glass: Alice's kitten had been asked to model its posture on that of the Red Queen and had failed, "So, to punish [her kitten], she held it up to the Looking-glass, that it might see how sulky it was, '– and if you're not good directly,' she added, 'I'll put you through into Looking-Glass House. How would you like *that*?' " (127).

Carroll's use of the literary form of the mediaeval dream vision differs from the forms or types presented above in that there are no specific textual references that suggest conscious and playful use of the tradition. The dream vision is, however, a feature of both fantasies that Carroll discusses after the fact, and one that he uses to justify a claim of originality in the Alice books. In the preface to *Sylvie and Bruno*, Carroll stakes his claim to originality for *Alice's Adventures in Wonderland* by suggesting that while he was no conscious imitator in producing it, a number of succeeding works by others were written "on identically the same pattern" (241). The "pattern" Carroll refers to is made clear by a list of "books of the Alice type" that appears in his diary entry for 11 September 1891 (486). The list includes *Mabel in Rhymeland, From Nowhere to the North Pole, Wanted a King*, and *Elsie's Expedition*. The common denominator of these books is their use of a dream frame to enclose their fantasy worlds. Although other fantasists borrowed Carroll's pattern, none played off against each other the realities of wakefulness and dream so tellingly: for the imitators, the pattern became a simple vehicle for moving characters in and out of fantasy worlds.

Carroll's pattern is closer than that of his imitators to the mediaeval dream vision as developed by Chaucer and others, and he most certainly deserved to claim originality for using its elements – a discussion of dream, a May setting, a vision, the presence of guides (frequently helpful animals), personified abstractions, its promise of a vital connection between dream and wakefulness, and its formal divisions – to shape his fantasy. It is possible to catalogue these features in *Alice's Adventures in Wonderland* with some ease. There is discussion of dream in "A Mad Tea-Party": the Dormouse, seemingly talking in his sleep, says, "You might just as well say ... that 'I breathe when I sleep' is the same thing as 'I sleep when I breathe'" (61). Further, there is an entire theory of the relationship between dream and wakefulness suggested in the last chapter, in which Alice's sister re-experiences Alice's dream as day-dream by making allegorical connections between what is actually happening and what is being dreamed. Carroll's work meets the dream vision expectations in several other specific ways: May 4th is the day of Alice's dream; the White Rabbit, the Caterpiller, and the Gryphon all act as guides to some degree; and the King and Queen of Hearts and the Duchess are personified abstractions that work against the promised order of their roles as rulers and governness.[5] A similar case is made for *Through the Looking-Glass and What Alice Found There*, a fantasy that works against the formal expectations Carroll uses in *Alice's Adventures in Wonderland*.

Recapitulating, then, this book presents connections with the tradition of English-language children's literature by attending to a number of particular textual allusions, puns, and the like that create connections between the Alice books and other works, by demonstrating the clash between didactic and imaginative literature in the period immediately preceding Carroll's works, and through inclusion of various genre, such as world-upside-down books, looking-glass books, and the dream vision. All of the material presented in the appendices is meant to be taken as representative of the possible connections that may be made between Carroll's Alice books and earlier children's literature, with the rider that Carroll himself suggests the major connections (either within or without his texts) that are elaborated in this volume's last three chapters. A great deal of other material that may reinforce these connections and develop others remains to be gathered.

· 2 ·

Representative Specific Sources and Analogues

Any reader familiar with the three contemporary scholarly editions of Carroll's Alice books knows that Carroll frequently drew on prior children's literature or works about children in elaborating his fantasies. Martin Gardner has, following James Joyce's directive about reading, "wiped his glosses on what [he knows]" in *The Annotated Alice* and *The More Annotated Alice*; Donald Gray has recently published the second edition of his Norton Critical Edition of the Alice books (1992); and Roger Green has especially concentrated on uncovering and consolidating Carroll's sources and analogues from children's literature in his Oxford World's Classics edition. Any modest addition to this area presented here takes its lead from Green's work, and sometimes consists of supplying the actual texts he refers to (see appendices) as well as responding to and elaborating on some of his suggestions.

A close look at Carroll's sources and analogues from earlier children's literature reveals both a profusion of the expected didactic (rational/moral and informational) work for children and the increasing presence of imaginative work in the six or seven decades preceding Carroll's development of a new form of fantasy in the Alice books. A knowledge of this material, together with an understanding of how Carroll employs it generally and specifically, may help to clarify and expand present readings of particular parts of his fantasies. This material makes it possible to develop new readings and enriches understanding of how Carroll invented new forms by mixing several literary types together, that is, by creating portmanteau forms.

It is common knowledge that in *Alice's Adventures in Wonderland* Carroll parodies a number of other literary works for and about children. Further, it has been suggested that he uses an occasional adult work that has little or no prior connection to childhood or children's literature. For example, Roger Green says that "the idea of the talking-flowers is based on Tennyson's *Maud* (1855), Pt. 1, Section XXII, esp. stanza X: 'There was fallen a splendid tear / From the passion-flower at the gate, etc.' " (269). Donald Gray concurs and adds that "the flowers, and their announcement of the coming of the Red Queen are taken from a stanza in Tennyson's *Maud* (1855) in which a lover waits for his lady in a garden" (note 9, 120). Further agreement comes from Martin Gardner, who cites stanza X as a comparison to Carroll's description of the flowers (note 3, 205).

Talking flowers, however, have appeared for centuries in folk literature and predate Carroll's use of them in children's literature by decades. A comparison of the variety of flowers in Tennyson's and Carroll's gardens reveals that while Carroll's cast of live flowers is smaller than Tennyson's, it includes a daisy and a violet, not mentioned among Tennyson's flowers. In Tennyson's poem, the only really specific connection with Carroll's work is the line "She is coming, my life, my fate," delivered by the lover who is then joined by a chorus of flowers commenting on the beloved's expected approach. In *Through the Looking-Glass* the line is truncated to "She's coming" and spoken by the Larkspur, who adds, "I hear her footstep, thump, thump, along the gravel walk" (141). This not only is an accurate description of the Red Queen's authoritative walk, but is quite funny when compared to the "ever so airy a tread" seized on as evidence of the beloved's approach by the expectant lover in stanza XI of *Maud*. In any event, stopping with the connection with *Maud* is premature. Certainly Carroll knew Tennyson and his family, and just as certainly *Maud* is present in the Garden of Live Flowers. But the specific line parodied is at best a thin connective, leading to an esoteric joke that is, however clever, something of a dead end. Tennyson's flowers are affective projections of the lover's expectations and fears, and have little "life" of their own. It is more probable that the general presence of reified nature in children's literature gave Carroll what Green calls "the idea of the talking flowers." A likely specific candidate is *The Wedding Among the Flowers* (1808)* by Ann Taylor, a children's writer whose work Carroll uses in other parts of the Alice books. Taylor's work includes all the flowers Carroll employs and dozens more in its comic description of the marriage of Lord Sunflower and Lady Lily. This poem especially captures the haughtiness and superior tone that also characterize Carroll's flowers in their relation to Alice. Visually, a further possible source is

---

* See the appendices for reproductions, in whole or in part, of this and other works for or about children discussed in chapters 2–6.

Grandville's *Un Autre Monde* (1844) – a work that has stunning presentations of personified flowers.

Both of the Alice books are literally crammed with such parodies of and unaltered borrowing from earlier children's literature. Moral didactic works and informational works, all inverted by parody, dominate in *Alice in Wonderland,* while unaltered nursery rhymes, lullabys, counting songs, and riddles dominate in *Through the Looking-Glass.* One of the best ways to characterize the presence of this earlier literature in the Alice books is to borrow Carroll's own description of his use of "litterature" in the genesis of *Sylvie and Bruno.* He had, he says, "the possession of a huge, unwieldy mass of litterature – if the reader will kindly excuse the spelling – which only needed stringing together, upon the thread of a consecutive story" (239–40). In the case of the Alice books, the presence of a good deal of this "litterature" has been commented on many times and is well known. The student of Carroll's work knows that he parodies Jane Taylor, Isaac Watts, Mary Howitt, Robert Southey, and a number of other writers, and that he also incorporates material without parodying it, such as the nursery rhymes and riddles in *Through the Looking-Glass.* Since there is such a great number of parodied works present in the Alice books, including Carroll's own early parodies (e.g., "They told me you had been to her" and the Anglo-Saxon stanza that he elaborates into the poem "Jabberwocky"), it can be argued that the Alice books share the process of genesis Carroll describes in the introduction to *Sylvie and Bruno.* After all, Carroll did say in "Alice on Stage" that " 'Alice' and the 'Looking-Glass' are made up almost wholly of bits and scraps, single ideas which came of themselves" (*The Theatre,* 1887; reprinted in Gray's second edition, 281). There is no exact parallel here; as a matter of fact, the genesis of *Alice in Wonderland* seems the reverse of that of *Sylvie and Bruno* in that the later book grew out of a twenty-year increasingly conscious amassing of "litterature" that awaited a story, while Alice was (by the account of all present when it was first told) a rapidly produced story that provided an occasion for the immediate use of unconsciously amassed "litterature."

The "litterature" Carroll uses in the Alice books is of several kinds, and – turned around – there are several kinds of uses of earlier literature. *Alice in Wonderland* frequently parodies specific moral and informational work for children. For example, Carroll parodies one "divine" and one "moral" song by Isaac Watts. The divine song, "Against Idleness and Mischief," is parodied in the same episode of *Alice in Wonderland* as informational books, such as Pinnock's catechisms, are parodied. It is the absence of books with pictures and conversations that bores Alice and acts as a soporific at the beginning of *Alice in Wonderland.* In Alice's past she has had to commit both kinds of "official" children's literature to memory; later, when her sense of identity is questioned, she attempts to reassert herself through recitation of this socially approved material. Alas, as any reader of *Alice in Wonderland* knows, the comfortable moral and informational certitudes contained in these works are comically overturned and prove to be of no help to the distressed Alice.

Since the preface to Watts's *Divine Songs in Easy Language for the Use of Children* (1715) contains a serious and developed rationale for memorizing such songs, emphasizing – for one thing – their function as "mental furniture" to be used when one undergoes temptation or other spiritual duress, it is included in Appendix 1 to make the point that Carroll is upending more than a single poem, but rather an entire "philosophy" of reading and education. Further, this preface and Watts's introduction to the "Moral Songs" share a sense of the necessity to create acceptable literary work for children in order to provide antidotes for what Watts calls the "loose and dangerous sonnets of the age" (146–7) and the "idle, wanton, or profane songs, which give so early an ill taint to the fancy and memory" (253). The poems Watts so energetically attacks here are, I believe, snippets of adult songs that are the ancestors of or are themselves early versions of nursery rhymes, a form of children's literature Carroll uses unparodied in *Through the Looking-Glass*.[1]

Several further specific uses of earlier works are discussed here to demonstrate the variety of Carroll's sources and their employments. One, the parody of Jane Taylor's "The Star," presents a poem that does not seem to fit snugly with the other didactic work Carroll reverses through parody. Only Martin Gardner, of the three editors, includes the complete Taylor poem rather than only the well-known first quatrain, which had already gained a status approaching that of a nursery rhyme by the 1860s. The richness of the parody depends on a knowledge of the entire poem, which moves from the sense of wonder present in the first quatrain to a didactic assertion of navigational utility, a utility totally undercut by the version of the song sung by the Mad Hatter; the bat (star) is altered to a "tea-tray" (not an ornamental diamond) that has its ability to create a sense of wonder and lack of utility greatly enhanced by its new location (63).

The next two uses of earlier works are increasingly less specific. The first is found in the White Knight's song in *Through the Looking-Glass*: " 'I sometimes dig for buttered rolls, / Or set limed twigs for crabs' " (221). The humour of the first line results from the erroneous expectation of uncovering buttered rolls by digging in the earth. As such, it connects to the assertion delivered by Pat, the White Rabbit's servant in *Alice in Wonderland*, that he is "digging for apples" (34). Both of these statements are reversals, while the second also contains a hidden pun, *pomme/pomme de terre*; and both are of the same order as "limed twigs for crabs," which substitutes "crabs" for the proverbial "birds." All of the annotated editions cited here note this substitution, but none add that the expression also refers to the way enticing book elements can be used to draw the child reader into, however well meant, a didactic trap. Indeed, the Taylor sisters published such a children's book, an "early reader" entitled *Limed Twigs to Catch Young Birds*, in 1808.

The second of these less accessible uses is rather a textual stretch. Roger Green notes (266) a brief article by Kathleen Tillotson arguing that Carroll's opening paragraphs of *Through the Looking-Glass* are the result of an unconscious recollection of a parody of Dickens's *The Cricket on the Hearth* in "Advice to an Intending Serialist," written by William Ayton and published in *Blackwood's Magazine* in 1845. Tillotson lists the presence of the fireside scene, girl, cat, kitten, and the ball of worsted in both works, but she is especially interested in the similarity of the "half-mocking gravity of the debate over the *responsibility* of one cat or kitten rather than another" (137, my italics).[2] However, she leaves this insight altogether too rapidly as she moves on to other issues, missing the importance of the establishment of the didactic tone at the outset of *Through the Looking-Glass*. For example, there is a long cataloguing paragraph in which Alice fulfils her promise to the kitten – "I'm going to tell you all your faults" (125) – and this teaching by admonishment leads her to a game of "let's pretend" in which she tries teaching by positive modelling. It is through the actions that accompany Alice's didactic mood that she introduces the looking-glass as a corrective for bad behaviour (127). Concerning Alice's rather lengthy conversation with her kitten, a more specific analogue is found in Jane Taylor's "The Dunce of a Kitten" from *Rhymes for the Nursery*. In both works the kitten is called upon to do something extraordinary: to learn to read in Taylor's poem and to assume the posture of the Red Queen chess piece in Carroll's book. In both cases, the kitten fails, is thought to be uncooperative, and is called "sulky" by its mistress. The didactic tone of Alice's conversation with her kitten closely matches that of Taylor's poem.

Another possible specific source may inform the concluding poem to both Alices. The three editors all note that the first letters of the lines, if read vertically, spell out Alice Pleasance Liddell, but they overlook a possible source in the poem's last line, "Life, what is it but a dream?" William Madden, in his "Framing the Alices," a close analysis of the introductory and concluding poems to both Alices, also ignores the possibility and reads the concluding poem as the victory of "the golden gleam," of inspired narrative over the drift of the irreversible stream of time (370).[3] However, if the words "what" and "it" are extracted, the last line reads, "Life is but a dream," the refrain line of the song "Row, Row, Row Your Boat." The words of this song were written in 1852 by Eliphalet Lyte and were set to music in 1881.[4] The question asked in this last line connects it to the last chapter of *Through the Looking-Glass*, "Which Dreamed It?," as well as to the introductory poem to *Alice in Wonderland*. As Alice says, "This is a serious question" (244). Dream here differs radically from the use of dream in the conclusion of *Alice in Wonderland*. There, the "dream-child" of the introductory poem runs off to play after telling her dream to her sister and her sister tames the dream to a day-dream that anticipates Alice's control of story material as an adult storyteller, just as Alice and her sister "controlled" the storyteller in the introductory poem. In the concluding poem of *Through the Looking-Glass*, the wonder of the July boat trip that saw the dream born is momentarily recalled and then undercut by the failure of memory, since "Autumn frosts have slain July." As much as the poem claims the territory of the lingering "golden gleam," control of story is replaced by painful speculation that life may be beyond control, may be all drift, all dream. The "Row, Row, Row Your Boat" round, with its structure of eternal return and its suggested control through rowing, gives way to and underscores the melancholic drift and the assertion that all of life is but a dream. This material is developed further in chapter 6, on dream vision.

Carroll's uses of earlier children's literature are not always so particular. They sometimes get incorporated by contributing to the cast of characters, such as the playing cards in general and the King, Queen, and Knave of Hearts specifically. Here Carroll introduces the nursery rhyme "The Queen of Hearts," which supplies characters, a crime that necessitates a trial, the idea of hierarchy, and rules that are arbitrary. A look at the history of this rhyme in *The Oxford Book of Nursery Rhymes* reveals that Carroll was not the only one to have found it fascinating since its original appearance (together with three poems on the other suits) in the *European Magazine* in 1782. Charles Lamb used it as the basis of an extended story in *The King and Queen of Hearts; with the Rogueries of the Knave Who Stole the Queen's Pies* (1805) as did the author of *The New Story of the Queen of Hearts* (1845). And James Halliwell gave it full status as nursery rhyme in *The Nursery Rhymes of England* (1843). The original rhyme from the *European Magazine* and Lamb's variation on it (with illustrations by William Mulready) are included here to supply the background of the rhyme and to provide a ground of comparison for Carroll's (and his illustrator Tenniel's?) use of it. For example, Lamb retains the original rhyme by printing it, one line at a time, on the top of each page, while his own perhaps overly complicated version is developed in verses that run under each of Mulready's illustrations. Note that Carroll also grants the Royal Heart family many new experiences before organically introducing the stolen tarts and the rest of the story.

The final two analogues presented here have to do with the tone Carroll establishes through his use of the game of chess, a game that among many other things introduces romance literature into *Through the Looking-Glass*. Again, it is Roger Green who makes an important connection, this time between Carroll's *Jabberwocky* and a poem by a cousin, Manella Bute Smedley, titled "The Shepherd of the Giant Mountains," which appeared in *Sharpe's London Magazine* in 1846. This poem tells of a shepherd boy who, through courage in facing and destroying a griffin and its offspring, as well as consistent humility, rises to knighthood and, finally, marriage to the daughter of a duke. Carroll's poem condenses the story of the boy's courageous killing of the Jabberwock and his ultimate reward into five quatrains, positioned between identical opening and closing quatrains (originally written in 1855 and titled "Stanza of Anglo-saxon Poetry" in *Misch Masch*). While Carroll's "Come to my arms, by beamish boy" echoes Smedley's "Come to my heart, my true and gallant son," the knightly material (the shepherd/knight's joust to win his love, etc.) is absent here, hidden beneath the brilliant nonsense surface of seemingly non-referential language.

The romance material, introduced and altered by humour, in the quest for and slaying of the Jabberwock links with the introduction of the White Knight near the conclusion of *Through the Looking-Glass*. After the White Knight's original fight with the Red Knight as Alice's champion, any serious romance material is undercut by the White Knight's awkwardness, which so overshadows Alice's own that she soon finds herself taking care of him. It is of some interest that Carroll, writing during the period that saw the restoration of mediaeval romance and its appropriation by child readers, never uses romance material without comically undercutting it. Although critics have argued productively that Carroll is writing in the burlesque tradition of such works as Butler's "Huddibras," it is possible that an early-nineteenth-century children's book, *Sir Hornbook; or, Childe Launcelot's Expedition*, originally published in 1814 and reprinted in 1844 in Henry Cole's *Home Treasury* series, serves as well or better as a source of the tone of Carroll's White Knight character and his exploits. *Sir Hornbook's* comic mixture of the characters and events typical of romance literature with pedantic excess corresponds tellingly with the White Knight's well-developed pedantry and the burlesque of his expected knightly action presented through his physical awkwardness (he cannot sit a horse, for example).

Beyond such specific examples are three that are wider still in Carroll's application – the antipodes (the world upside down), the looking-glass book, and dream vision. The first two literally present the introductions of two earlier forms of children's literature (generated from the adult traditions) that provide *Alice in Wonderland* and *Through the Looking-Glass* with their respective overall fantasy structures, while the third provides the fantasy frame and numerous other features of both works. The first two are introduced textually, the world upside down by the antipodes/antipathies pun and the cluster of reversal material surrounding it (11) and the looking-glass book by Alice's imitation of admonitory and exemplary looking-glass books in her play at the beginning of *Through the Looking-Glass* (127 ff.) and in her labelling of "Jabberwocky" as a looking-glass book (134). The third, dream vision, is introduced "formally" through the frame of sleep and waking used in each fantasy. Carroll's use of a fourth example of children's literature, the clash between the literatures of information and imagination, is established in several textual episodes. By and large, however, this aspect is important as part of the vital history of children's literature that forms the backdrop of Carroll's developing fantasy. Since these four uses of earlier children's literature are important and complex, they are discussed in separate chapters.

The materials gathered here are simply a few of the types of sources and analogues from children's literature that inform the Alice books. They are chosen to demonstrate a range of use that begins with specific textual materials (frequently the basis of parody), includes characters and attitudes that are important throughout large sections of the works, and culminates in links with the prior children's works that provided the structures, themes, characters, and tone of both Alices.

· 3 ·

The Battle between Religious, Moral, and Informational Didacticism and Imaginative Literature for Children

The state of literature produced for children from the last decades of the eighteenth century through the turn of the century and on into the 1860s may be accurately characterized as a battle between several major kinds of literature: religious, rational/moral, and informational on one side and imaginative on the other. Although there were frequent antagonisms between the religious and rational/moral writers, the renewed religious didacticism – both Church of England and Evangelical (see, for instance, the work of Sarah Trimmer and Hannah Moore respectively) – shared a belief in the aesthetic of utility with both moral and informational didacticism, although these latter were sometimes a-religious and occasionally anti-religious. Religious didacticism employed the morally neutral and potentially explicable wonders of nature to attract the child reader, intermixing brief essays on natural wonders with religious essays. In *The Child's Magazine, and Sunday Scholar's Companion*, for example, exemplary and admonitory narratives of the lives of children were presented between essays on natural science. Similarly, writers concerned with the child's moral growth were keenly interested in using the wonders of nature (the Edgeworths, of this school, called these "the history of realities") to entertain and shape the child otherwise drawn to morally neutral or debilitating fancies. To their credit they sometimes emphasized the "story" part of "history" to produce compelling works for children; nonetheless, they hoped to eliminate or at least diminish the misleadingly "silly" and "useless" works of imagination. Informational literature, then, was one of the acceptable or "official" literatures for children and was incorporated, to some degree, in all of the other official literatures before the publication of the Alice books.[1]

Informational literature was so central in children's reading that it was shared by all official children's literatures and was the literature that supplied the aesthetic criteria of utility used against imaginative literature. Its dominance thus created a lively background of combativeness for the rise and consolidation of imaginative literature and, especially, of fantasy. Carroll wrote *Alice in Wonderland* in the context of this literary struggle, and it is possible that understanding the background will add to the understanding of Carroll's work. For example, Carroll creates imaginative worlds through the use of the world upside down, the looking-glass book, and dream vision, each of which is characterized by a central distorting element – reversal, inversion, and the replacement of waking consciousness, respectively. Carroll also creates complex mixtures of these distortions. And obviously such distortions are at odds with informational literature.

In keeping with the key place of informational literature in this short historical survey of the battle of children's literatures, a discussion of the representative informational literature used in each of the Alice books is presented here. For example, when Alice momentarily but very painfully has doubts about her identity, she not only uses Watts's "Against Idleness and Mischief" to attempt to reassert her sense of self, but also tries to recite the multiplication table and a catalogue of geographical facts. Earlier, during her fall into Wonderland, Alice had also turned to geography in her speculation concerning her location and destination. Her self-conscious use of words such as "latitude" and "longitude" ("grand" words which she thinks she pronounces properly but whose significance she doubts she understands) and her botched attempt to pronounce "antipodes" combine with her guess at the number of miles from pole to pole to suggest a good deal of reading in geography. All of this comes up again in *Through the Looking-Glass* when Alice attempts a description of her whereabouts at the beginning of "Looking-Glass Insects" (148). When this is taken in connection with her interest in and confusion about telescopes and mirrors and words and numbers, it is obvious that Alice has read widely in informational literature.

That informational literature had both a strong and enduring presence in children's literature is attested to by the work of a number of nineteenth-century writers who were opposed not so much to information as to its social aesthetic use as an attack on imaginative writing and the imagination itself. From Wordsworth's *Prelude* (Book v, 293–346), in which he uses common sense to "try this modern system [of factual education] by its fruits" (295), through Dickens's satire on Grandgrind's school and the schoolmaster, Mr McChoakumchild, in the "Murdering the Innocents" chapter of *Hard Times* (1854), to Charles Kingsley's attack on Cousin Cramchild in

Water Babies, a picture of the attack on imagination in education emerges that reveals the narrowness of factual education. Grandgrind is described at the beginning of "Murdering the Innocents" as a man "with a rule and a pair of scales, and the multiplication table always in his pocket, Sir, ready to weigh and measure any parcel of human nature, and tell you exactly what it comes to," a man who invariably uses a process that "is a mere question of figures, a case of simple arithmetic" (893). It is interesting that Dickens considered these two descriptions of life – "a mere question of figures" and "simple arithmetic" – as possible titles of his novel (note 2, 893). In sharp contrast with this wholesale use of rationality, as Harry Stone argues in *Dickens and the Invisible World: Fairy Tales, Fantasy, and Novel-making*, Dickens himself drew heavily on traditional children's literature in addition to horrifying stories told to him by his governess and his grandmother.[2]

In Catherine Sinclair's preface to *Holiday House* (1839), she addresses the same issues dealt with in the well-known attacks by Wordsworth and Dickens and Kingsley on informational literature. She links these issues directly to the necessity of making changes in the direction of contemporary children's literature:

In this age of wonderful mechanical inventions, the very mind of youth seems in danger of becoming a machine; and while every effort is used to stuff the memory, like a cricket-ball, with well-known facts and ready-made opinions, no room is left for the vigour of *natural* feeling, the glow of *natural* genius, and the ardour of *natural* enthusiasm. It was a remark of Sir Walter Scott's many years ago, to the author herself, that in the rising generation there would be no poets, wits, or orators, because all play of imagination is carefully discouraged, and books written for young people are generally a mere dry record of facts, unenlivened by any appeal to the heart, or any excitement of the fancy. The catalog of a child's library would contain Conversations on Natural Philosophy, – on Chemistry, – on Botany, – on Arts and Sciences, – Chronological Records of History, – and travels as dry as a road-book; but nothing on the habits of ways of thinking, *natural* and suitable to the taste of children; therefore, while such works are delightful to the parents and teachers who select them, the younger community are fed strong meat instead of milk, and the reading that might be a relaxation from study becomes a study in itself. (vii, my italics)

The informational children's library Sinclair describes meshes tellingly with the reading and memorization Wordsworth presents as having contributed to his precocious but flawed "model of a child" (*Prelude*, Book v, 294–336) as well as with the curriculum Dickens's McChoakumchild catalogues in *Hard Times*: " 'Orthography, etymology, syntax and prosody, biography, astronomy, geography, and general cosmography … ' " (31). Wordsworth, Scott, Dickens, Sinclair, and Kingsley are in obvious agreement about the harmful effects of a steady diet of informational books. All of them share the opinion that informational literature is allied with the machine, with industry, as opposed to the imagination, which is natural. In Wordsworth's famous passage alluded to above, he goes so far as to treat folk tales as parts of nature itself through his juxtaposition of woodland beds and flowers with folk tales:

> Meanwhile old grandame earth is grieved to find
> The playthings, which her love designed for him,
> Unthought of: in their woodland beds the flowers
> Weep, and the riversides are all forlorn.
> Oh! give us once again the wishing-cap
> Of Fortunatas and the invisible cloak
> Of Jack the Giant-Killer, Robin Hood,
> The child, whose love is here, at least doth reap
> One precious gain, that he forgets himself. (336–46)

The child of fact, full of fact and, therefore, himself, differs radically from the child able to lose self in wonder, in fantasy.

The materials for the child reader attacked by Wordsworth, Scott, Dickens, Sinclair, Kingsley, and others mesh closely with those defended as desirable by Samuel Griswold Goodrich in his "Prospectus" for *Parley's Magazine for Children and Youth* (1833), a list that contains the very subjects and educational theory that made Wordsworth's prodigy so inhumanly full of himself. Although there were many other suppliers of informational literature, Goodrich and William Pinnock (the publisher of dozens of books using the title formula of *A Catechism of …*) were so prolific and steadfastly informational that they are authentically representative. It is, as a matter of fact, highly likely that it is these two champions of informational books who are referred to in Sinclair's catalogue of "Conversation" books (Pinnock) and "travel" books (Parley) as writers who use these vehicles exclusively for the presentation of fact.[3] Henry Cole, a believer in the importance of imaginative children's literature and the editor of the ambitious *Home Treasury* series published in the 1840s, uses Goodrich's pseudonym, "Peter Parley," as a part for a whole to represent all such informational writing, which he labels "Peter Parleyism" in the prospectus for *Home Treasury*. Further, as the formula titles of Pinnock's books (*A Catechism of …*) and the rationale of Goodrich's books demonstrate, both of these producers of writing for children believed in teaching through conversation as a way of liming the literary twig to catch the young birds.

Darton believes that the catechism, with its mediaeval roots, and the narrative of the travel book created a type of nineteenth-century book that could be described as "dialogue instruction – amusement" (48). More accurately, the amusement was the lure and the instruction the goal. Goodrich, for example, was keenly aware of the appeal of both the narrative and an authoritative and caring narrator, and he says, in *Recollections of a Lifetime*, the autobiography of his literary life, that he learned to follow his natural inclination in his actual practice of writing for children informally: "I imagined myself on the floor with a group of children, and I wrote to them as I would have spoken to them." It was only later, he says, borrowing his terminology from Locke's theory of the acquisition of knowledge, that he understood that "their first ideas are simple and single" (308) and that he addressed this truth by using "images of things palpable to the senses" (309). Further, and somewhat to his credit, he not only developed the kindly grandfatherly narrative voice of Peter Parley but sought "to teach [children] history and biography and geography ... all in the way in which nature would teach them – that is, by a large use of the senses, and especially by the eye" (310). Travel, therefore, became a "natural" for Goodrich, since all these things could be taught in books in which Peter Parley guided the child reader through countries such as the United States and continents such as Africa, concentrating on the specific history and geography and biography of famous men in each.

Goodrich, imbued with the power of utility that Jeremy Bentham had introduced and solidified as the spirit of the time, answered Cole's encapsulation of the aesthetic of utility in the name of his fictitious narrator, Peter Parley, returning Cole's part for a whole "compliment" by attacking Cole's fictional narrator, Felix Summerly, the representative of what the self-styled radical, Goodrich, considered to be the "conservative," "silly," and generally destructive folk tale, nursery rhyme, etc. (311 ff.). By the second half of the 1840s Goodrich gleefully reported the bankruptcy of Joseph Cundall, the publisher of the books in Cole's *Home Treasury* series, compilations of the very literature Cole had thought would restore fancy and imagination to their proper central positions in children's literature. These books included tales such as "Beauty and the Beast," a collection of nursery rhymes titled *The Traditional Rhymes of England,* and *Puck's Reports to Oberon*, an original book concerned with the condition of the imagination and with ways to promote its centrality. All of the books in the series were illustrated beautifully with great care to appropriateness and aesthetic unity, and all were handsomely bound, unlike much of the inexpensive and ephemeral traditional imaginative material available since the latter eighteenth century.[4]

In *Puck's Reports to Oberon*, Cole wrote a long-verse preface tracing the distrust of "Fancy" to Jeremy Bentham's insistence on rational critique and the use of utility as the yardstick of value. Puck explains to Oberon that Fancy wants to return to earth, where for a number of years mortals had scorned her because they thought the "imagination was a useless, foolish thing" (6). Now a change of heart has taken place because the power of Jeremy Bentham, Fancy's major antagonist, is diminishing:

> There was one Jeremy Bentham;
> (Would they had sent him here,
> for us to make his brains a little clear,)
> A longheaded prosy fellow, who did nothing but bellow
> And rail at FANCY all day long,
> In country or in town
> He hunted her down,
> Till her small voice was heard no more, and
>   her reign seem'd o'er.
> And now a most strange change
>   Has come about,
>   For folks with a shout,
> In the north, south, east, and west,
> To extend her rule and region;
> Scarce a soul but agrees
> To join her legion of devotees,
> And unite to invite her back ... (7)

But, for the moment, Goodrich was right. Joseph Cundall did go broke publishing *The Home Treasury* series, dooming Felix Summerly's attempt, as Goodrich archly put it, "to woo back the erring generation of children to the good old orthodox rhymes and jingles of England" (312).

Goodrich then goes on to attack James Orchard Halliwell, the "popular antiquarian" who published scholarly books on topics ranging from Shakespeare's plays to nursery rhymes (*The Nursery Rhymes of England*), as well as Cole, for Goodrich finds Halliwell a co-conspirator in the attempted restoration of what he calls the "Homer to Mother Goose crowd" who found the Parley books "too utilitarian, too materialistic" (311). Goodrich attacks his enemies through a vignette he originally published in *Merry's Museum* in August of 1846 (313–17). In this piece a son corrects his mother's error by reciting a verse he has written based on the nursery rhymes in a book his mother had given him in a weak moment:

Higglety, pigglety, pop!
The pig's in a hurry,
The cat's in a flurry -
Higglety, pigglety-pop! (313)

The son-turned-rational-teacher-of-his-mother then delivers an ironic defence of the lack of sense in verse and rapidly turns out a number of what he considers to be equally silly verses to convert his mother to his "modern" view. What precisely this view is can be seen in Goodrich's memory manifesto: "As to books of amusement and instruction, to follow these, I gave them Parley's tales of travels, of history, of nature, and art, together with works designed to cultivate a love of truth, charity, piety, and virtue, and I sought to make these so attractive as to displace the bad books, to which I have already alluded – the old monstrosities, 'Puss in Boots,' 'Jack the Giant Killer,' and others of that class" (320). It is an interesting irony that Goodrich's spokesboy in this sketch creates a rhyme that joined the oral tradition and was picked up by Iona and Peter Opie for publication in *The Oxford Dictionary of Nursery Rhymes* in 1945, ninety-nine years later (207–8), and long after Peter Parley had ceased to be a household word. Maurice Sendak has done this fact magnificent creative justice in *Higglety Pigglety Pop! or There Must Be More to Life*, in which the "silly" verse that Goodrich had his boy improvise is celebrated for eternity by the cast of "The World Mother Goose Theatre." More importantly, the fault-finding Alice of "Looking-Glass House" is so emcumbered with the didactic baggage that she brings into Looking-Glass Land that she cannot understand nursery rhymes and confuses them with everyday reality, responding to them as such rather than understanding their spirit.

Carroll was born Charles Dodgson in 1832, the year of Scott's death, and he was the youngest of the writers – Scott, Sinclair, Dickens, and Kingsley – who protested or parodied the reign of informational didacticism. He was raised in the middle of this contentiousness by a mother who, from what biographers have gathered, was either an ally of imagination or benignly neglectful and a stern father who was capable of playfulness.[5] Judging from this and in light of the kind of work the Dodgson family produced in its magazines and other family publications, the young Dodgson had an uncharacteristic upbringing (he did not go away to school until he was twelve, first attending Richmond and then, when he was fourteen years old, Rugby

– this when the average Rugbian began attending at seven) that certainly may have put him in contact with the small but vital and sustained body of imaginative work dealt with in this book. I say "may have" because very little is known about Carroll's pre-Rugby education. He was also obviously familiar with books that taught through memorization. In *Victoria Through the Looking Glass: The Life of Lewis Carroll,* Florence Becker Lennon states that the academic education of children for some years "consisted in mere passive memorizing that ... fatigued the most active minds." The lesson books generally used, she adds, were "Mangnall's *Questions,* Joyce's *Scientific Dialogues,* Pinnock's *Catechism,* and Marcle's *Natural Philosophy*" (37). In offering a representative statement on education of boys from six to eleven in the 1830s, Lennon quotes from the recollection of G.G. Bradley, dean of Westminster: "Lists of kings, of metals, of planets, were repeated without interest and without discrimination ... I learned by heart the chief countries of Europe, and provided I said them in a sense correctly, was allowed to simplify matters by saying the columns separately or in pairs, Spain, Portugal, Madrid, Lisbon." This led to a confusion of countries and capitals very similar to Alice's recitation (38).

Proof that Carroll was familiar with the memorization of morally didactic material in his childhood is presented in the first of the Dodgson family magazines, *Useful and Instructive Poetry,* most of which was written and illustrated for a younger brother and sister circa 1845, and in the magazine that followed, *The Rectory Magazine* (1848–50). In *Useful and Instructive Poetry,* Carroll, at the age of thirteen, shows that he already understands the aesthetic of utility and instruction in children's books: he parodies maxims in verses such as "Rules and Regulations" and conveys the general negativity of admonitory verse in the poem "My Fairy," in which each quatrain ends with the formula "It said 'You must not _____ ' " and the summary moral reads, "You mustn't." There are also four instructive limericks, presented under the general title "Melodies" (22). The subtitle of *The Rectory Magazine – Being a Compendium of the best tales, poems, essays, pictures that the united talents of the Rectory inhabitants can produce –* demonstrates Carroll's knowledge of the works of early moral and informational didactic writers, such as Maria Edgeworth and the editors of *The Child's Magazine, and Sunday Scholar's Companion,* in the mixture of material presented. The essays, such as "Musings on Milk," "Twaddle on Telescopes," and "Rust," have titles that parody the informational essay and use both unrelenting alliteration or metaphor to undercut informational literature. For example, "Musings on Milk" (61–2) begins with "Marvellously [*sic*] many materials make milk" and continues until the unnecessary admission that it is meant to be funny and that care must be taken "lest our magazine merge into a monotonous, mouldy mockery of mirth." "Twaddle on Telescopes" (85–6) never once mentions telescopes; rather, it works off the metaphor that reading *The Rectory Magazine* "elevates" or expands the attentive reader through its presentation of "useful" and "entertaining" material, and goes a way towards the kind of "telescoping" Carroll performs in his Wonderland expansions and contractions of Alice (15). The verse "As it Fell Upon a Day" shows that Carroll's reversals were not reserved for informational and moral work. This poem uses the same irresistible "when/then" advance as the nursery rhyme "The Gay Lady that Went to Church," but it does a turn on the conclusion of the original rhyme, in which a lady is led inexorably from outside a church to witness a corpse on the altar within the church, substituting the stationary narrator's killing of a nameless "he" who is led inexorably to him.

In the frontispiece to *The Rectory Umbrella* (1850), Carroll offers another and opposing kind of utility, an emotional usefulness, to that intended by the moral and informational writers. The illustration shows an old poet sitting under an umbrella composed of a patchwork of tales, poetry, fun, riddles, and jokes, smilingly engaged with the spirits of good humour, taste, liveliness, knowledge, mirth, content, and cheerfulness. The umbrella protects them all from the rocks of woe, grossness, ennui, spite, and gloom hurled by evil spirits hovering above.[6] The psychological and spiritual protection offered by imaginative literature is Carroll's early answer to an informational didacticism that attacks imagination as "useless" and "silly." In *The Rectory Umbrella* Carroll parodies a number of moral and informational forms found in many children's books and magazines. His "Zoological Papers" take on imaginary figures in "The Pixies," and in their treatment of "The Lory," "angled and hollow fish [*sic*]," and "The One-Winged Dove," they parody the language, exotic subjects and scholarliness of essays on natural science. Carroll also parodies allegorical painting in the "Vernon Gallery" pieces and biography in a series connected with Emerson's "Representative Men," which were vehicles for moral and informational didacticism. He emphasizes the literalness of the democratic Emerson's figurative and honorific use of the phrase "little men." In "Cuffey, or The Chartist" (55, 66), Carroll uses variants of the word "little" twelve times in a brief paragraph to undercut the notion of a democratic levelling of men.

Carroll's juvenilia, then, proves not only that he was aware of the clash between imaginative literature and informational and moral literature, but that he was already engaged in developing his practice of upending or extending literary works through parody and other forms of reversal.

Similarly, Dickens, who grew up when the utilitarians had command of a great deal of the education system, not only survived his early and, thankfully, limited formal education with the help of stories he was told and read, but did a cutting satire of informational didacticism in *Hard Times*.

The visitor to Grandgrind's school envisions a governmental ministry of facts so rational and intimidating that his interrogation of Sissy Jupe concerning non-functional (but possibly beautiful) ornamentation leaves her thoroughly anxious and perplexed about the significance of life and her place in it (31). Carroll's Mock Turtle, judging on the basis of his weepy recollection of the curriculum he suffered as a "shrimp" growing up on the bottom of the sea, seems to have endured an education similar to that inflicted on Sissy Jupe.

Informational books such as those published by William Pinnock were as formulaic in their logic as the educator who interrogated Sissy Jupe. The Pinnock stable of writers took on almost every conceivable topic a child could understand in the slightest way and attempted to made it comprehensible. As the titles of all Pinnock books (and their "improvers") announce, their subjects, whether astronomy or British law or geometry, are presented through dialogue, a conversation between an expert and a pupil capable of framing very productive questions. These catechisms, initiated without a hint of condescension, always use the authentic vocabulary of a topic regardless of polysyllabic difficulty. After all, the adult present during most readings could always clear up any confusion. As the texts of the Alice books prove, Carroll knew books such as Pinnock's exceedingly well and could parody the formula with extraordinary effect. Judging from his interest in photography and many other inventions of his time, he was strongly drawn to information, especially technological information in and for itself and as the butt of satire, as is the case with the White Knight, where it is clearly but gently administered.[7]

As mentioned above, there are several specific places where informational books such as Pinnock's are clearly at work in the Alice books. In *Alice in Wonderland,* testing prior knowledge to reassure herself she has not been "changed in the night," Alice attempts to counter the primitive "logic" of imaginative literature with the certitudes of informational knowledge ranging from the arithmetical to the geographical to the moral (19). The arithmetical knowledge she chooses, a recitation of the multiplication table, fails to allow her to reassert herself, as Martin Gardner explains (note 3, 38), since it combines a "nonsense progression" and the tradition that the table "stops with the twelves": "Let me see: four times five is twelve, and four times six is thirteen, and four times seven is – oh dear! I shall never get to twenty at that rate!" (19). All of the ingredients of Alice's arithmetical confusion are found in Pinnock's note appended to "Case II" multiplication in *A Catechism of Arithmetic* (1826): "In working the sum I say, 5 times 4 are 20, in which are no units and 2 tens; I set down 0, and the 2 tens I carry to the place of tens, then I say 5 times 4 are 20, and the 2 I carry for 22, which are 22 tens; I then put down the 2 tens under the place of tens, and carry the 2 to the place of hundreds; I then say 5 times 1 are 5, and the 2 hundreds I carry are 7, which are 7 hundreds; I set down the seven and the work is done; and so on with all other operations when the number does not exceed 12" (33). Alice's recitation scrambles a good deal of the material in the Pinnock note, the most important being the numbers 4 and 5 used as multiplicand and multiplier (although in reverse order) and the substitution of the tradition of stopping at 12 by using 12 as the product of her multiplication operation.

Pinnock's *A Catechism of Geography* (1822) is used most frequently. When Alice attempts to recite knowledge of European countries and their capitals, she commits an error involving set theory. A typical entry in Pinnock's *A Catechism of Geography*, for instance, invariably includes a "what is the capital of [a particular country]" question. When Alice recites her geography, she picks up this pattern but confuses sets, improperly remembering capitals as capitals of capitals: "... let's try Geography. London is the capital of Paris, and Paris is the capital of Rome, and Rome – no, *that's* all wrong, I'm certain! I must have been changed for Mabel!" (19). Later in Pinnock's book, there is also a short chapter titled "Of Latitude and Longitude." As new geographical information was discovered, Pinnock's books incorporated it; thus, in the 1842 catechism there are entries on Australia and New Zealand that call the pair "the Antipodes." In *Through the Looking-Glass*, it becomes clear that Alice is using an acquired geographical formula to come to terms with the curiosities of a new place: "Of course the first thing to do was to make a grand survey of the country she was going to travel through. 'It's something very like learning geography,' thought Alice, as she stood on tiptoe in hopes of being able to see further. 'Principal rivers – there are none. Principal mountains – I'm on the only one, but I don't think it's got a name. Principal towns ...'" (148). Alice's geographical catalogue breaks down with the unstated "principal inhabitants" when her attention is drawn to anomalous elephant-sized bees: "... why, what are those creatures, making honey down there? They can't be bees – nobody ever saw bees a mile off, you know" (148). Once again Alice demonstrates that she has brought her everyday anticipations of and perspective on reality with her unchanged after passing through the looking-glass.

Other Pinnock books are used in less specific ways. For instance, although the information in Pinnock's *A Catechism of Optics* or *A Catechism of Heraldry* is never as specifically present in the Alices as that in his geography and arithmetic catechisms, it is at work just beneath the surface. The optics book spends a good deal of time on the reversibility of images on the surface of the retina and in mirrors, and speaks at length about telescopes and microscopes and magic lanterns and phantasmagorias. In the same way, although there are no direct or near-direct citations of material from the book on heraldry, the presence of kings, queens, knaves, knights, and lions and unicorns denotes links to such material as well as to the game of chess.

Carroll's parody of informational books involves books such as Pinnock's directly, but the Peter Parley travel books may certainly be at work here also. There are several sources for the use of travel in Victorian fantasy. The important adult travel books of the Middle Ages, especially *The Travels of Sir John Mandeville*, which reappeared in bits and pieces in eighteenth-century chapbooks that children had ready access to, offer an interesting model in that they play off the strangeness of the new lands against the comparative certainties of home. The philosophical romance also tests the known values of home against those encountered in such places as Voltaire's El Dorado (*Candide*) or Holberg's Nazur (*Journey to the World Underground*). Goodrich says that he uses travel to amuse while the true informational work is going on, and he includes an element missing from both Alice books: Peter Parley is an adult caretaker and knowledgeable guide in all the travel books and is present from beginning to end, while Alice, like Nicholas Klim and Candide, has only the occasional indigenous guide. More important, however, is the general doubleness of reality in the Alice books, a doubleness that creates the opportunity for critique. In Alice's conversations with herself, she is forever comparing and contrasting her everyday reality with the curiosities of Wonderland. The range of her relationship with her known world is wide: she is comforted or discomforted by the Wonderlanders' reactions to her statements about home, but she sometimes feels so shut off from home that she wonders why nobody responds to her loneliness.

It is one of Carroll's remarkable gifts that he is able to take material that is diametrically in opposition to fantasy, generically alien material, and give it a home in his fantasies. Instead of joining in the fray between the champions of antagonistic genres, Carroll absorbs or turns such material back on itself through parody, allowing the Alice books to transform the many attacks on imagination still current in the middle of the nineteenth century into fantasy.

· 4 ·

"The World Turned Upside Down"

When Lewis Carroll dropped Alice down the rabbit-hole, he sent her into a Wonderland shaped primarily through his use of the topos of the world upside down and its special antipodean geographical figuration, the principal example of radical inversion of perspective in Western literature. This ancient convention, altered but still in use in the middle of the nineteenth century (see, for example, George MacDonald's *The Princess and Curdie*), helped Carroll to work out the structural "logic" of his satiric fantasy by providing him with the means to compare and contrast (that is, a basis for a critique of reality), along with major themes, characters and a kind of characterization, and a strategy for parody and satire traditionally associated with the topos.

In order to establish the relationships between the topos of the world upside down, antipodes, and *Alice's Adventures in Wonderland,* the following discussions and surveys are presented in order. First, there is a brief survey of the criticism of the Alice books especially concerned with the themes of inversion and reversal and a discussion of specific textual evidence for Carroll's use of antipodes as the location of Wonderland.[1] This is followed by a survey of the history of the topos and in particular the uses of antipodes in seventeenth- and eighteenth-century satire. Following this, there is a discussion of the presence of – and a description of the functions of – the world upside down in early nineteenth-century children's books. Finally, there is a discussion of the formal and thematic features of the topos most clearly present in Wonderland and a demonstration of how these features unite to create a formal integrity that provides a generic context for reading *Alice's Adventures in Wonderland.*

Carroll's use of inversion and reversal as devices and themes in the Alice books is a central concern of Alexander Taylor's *The White Knight* (1952), Eric Rabkin's *The Fantastic in Literature* (1976), and Stephen Prickett's *Victorian Fantasy* (1979). Taylor reserves his most insightful discussion of inversion and reversal for *Through the Looking-Glass*, a book he believes to be totally concerned with Carroll's adult interests. In his discussions of the radical inversions and reversals in Looking-Glass Land, Taylor presents two groups of possible sources and analogues, one philosophical and scientific and the other literary. He links Kant's essay on space and asymmetrical bodies, Pasteur's experiment on light polarization in paratartaric acid, and the work on time and motion of the German physicist and nonsense writer Gustave Fechner ("Dr Mises") with three literary works – *The Water Babies, Erehwon,* and *Signor Topsy-Turvy's Wonderful Magic Lantern; or, The World turned upside down* – in order to discuss such features of reversal and asymmetricality as mirror images and the paradox of going forward by going backward (87–93).[2]

More recently, Eric Rabkin has argued that "fantastic" literary works rely on inversion and reversal: "The fantastic is a quality of astonishment that we feel when the ground rules of a narrative structure are suddenly made to turn 180 degrees. We recognise this reversal in the reaction of characters, the statements of narrators, and the implications of structure all playing on and against our whole experience as people and readers" (41). Rabkin's discussion of both Alice books is almost exclusively concerned with these features. Carroll's satire, parody, and burlesque are all linked with the fact that the Alice books "invert and reverse everything in sight" (111).

In *Victorian Fantasy,* Stephen Prickett locates inversion and reversal primarily in *Through the Looking-Glass.* Prickett goes so far as to distinguish between the Alice books on the basis of the degree of complexity and richness of these devices and themes as they are developed in each book: "The theme of inversion is thus taken up and explored at every level in *Through the Looking-Glass,* from the simple spacial reversals suggested by the mirror itself to a complete mathematical and linguistic scheme of things" (137). In Wonderland, contrarily, Prickett argues that "the laws of nature were the same as every day reality and it was merely the situation that was altered"(135).

The arguments presented here differ from those of Taylor and Prickett in that they suggest that inversion provides *Alice in Wonderland* with its fundamental structural unity. Further, although Rabkin's views are generally insightful, the arguments here go beyond his statement that inversion and reversal are found "everywhere" in the Alice books. The world upside down provides a singular and sustained structural ground for Carroll's Wonderland. This topos and its special figuration as antipodes inform *Alice's Adventures in Wonderland* with what Northrop Frye, in *Anatomy of Criticism* (1968), calls the "presentation of the world in terms of a single intellectual pattern" (310).

Carroll's spatial location of Wonderland is crucial to this argument. Compared to the frequently discussed location of Looking-Glass Land, the whereabouts of Wonderland have been somewhat ignored. In *Through the Looking-Glass*, Carroll announces the specific location of his fantasy world in the title itself. *Alice's Adventures in Wonderland* lacks this sense of particularity. "Wonderland" emphasizes the quality – rather than locality – of place, unlike the word it replaced in Carroll's original title – *Alice's Adventures under Ground*. These issues are ignored in all three of the critical editions of *Alice's Adventures in Wonderland*. Roger Lancelyn Green and Donald Gray say nothing about Alice's entry into Wonderland. Gray notes only the origin of the name of the Liddells' cat (9), while beyond that same observation Green only comments on the possible origin of "Do cats eat bats" (253–4). Those critics who do pay attention to the location of Wonderland take their direction from the first of the two speculations concerning her destination that Alice develops while she is falling: "Down, down, down. Would the fall *never* come to an end? 'I wonder how many miles I've fallen by this time?' she said aloud. 'I must be getting somewhere near the centre of the earth. Let me see: that would be four thousand miles down, I think …'" (10).[3] Taylor takes Alice at her initial word and places Wonderland at the centre or "hub" of the world (156–7), and Prickett follows his lead (132). Both critics use this location as evidence to explain the temporal curiosity of the Mad Hatter's watch.

But Alice falls for approximately a page longer and has ample time for a further speculation: "'I wonder if I shall fall right *through* the earth! How funny it'll seem to come out among the people that walk with their heads downwards! The Antipathies, I think –' (she was rather glad there *was* no one listening, this time, as it didn't sound at all the right word) '– but I shall have to ask them what the name of the country is, you know. Please, Ma'am, is this New Zealand? Or Australia?'" (11).

This passage is virtually the same in the original *Alice's Adventures under Ground* and *Alice's Adventures in Wonderland*. But the "Wonderland" version accounts for the change in title when it tellingly clarifies the location through the addition of "the Antipathies, I think … it didn't sound at all the right word" between Alice's description of the "people that walk with their heads downwards" and her display of geographical knowledge. The "right word" is obviously "antipodes," a word that applies equally to "people who walk with their heads downwards" and the combined land masses of New Zealand and Australia.[4] Donald Rackin noted this "prophetic pun" in "Alice's Journey to the End of Night" (1966) but did not develop an antipodean reading of the fantasy. In his recent rewrite of this essay for the book *Alice's Adventures in Wonderland and Through the Looking-Glass: Nonsense, Sense, and Meaning*, Rackin includes a brief discussion of the world upside down while curiously altering his original description of the pun to "an *unintended* but prophetic pun" (38, my italics). He fails to clarify precisely to whom he attributes the unintentionality of the pun (Alice? Carroll?); nor does he provide any argument for his inside knowledge of lack of intention. A close reading of the passage and a comparison with the earlier *Alice's Adventures under Ground* and the later *Nursery Alice* (1890) prove the pun to be both prophetic and developed to a degree that supports intention. Both Percy Muir (in *English Children's Books, 1600–1900*) and David Kunzle (in his chapter in *The Reversible World: Symbolic Inversion in Art and Society*) suggest the general presence of the world upside down in *Alice in Wonderland*. Kunzle, for example, writes: "It would be an amusing academic exercise to examine the work of [Lewis Carroll] in light of the inversion principle. Some of the most inspired passages clearly depend upon a cunning logical inversion or reversal" (note 13, 59). Kunzle's last sentence is true, but it should prove to be more than an "amusing academic exercise" to deal with the background of the use of reversal.

The use of the world upside down and, especially, of the antipodean location of Wonderland, for example, is further spelled out in the description of Alice's arrival in Wonderland. After Alice falls for almost another complete paragraph, while musing on cats and bats, her fall ends: "… thump! thump! down she came upon a heap of sticks and dry leaves, and the fall was over" (11). In *Alice's Adventures under Ground* Alice had landed on "sticks and shavings" (5). The substitution of "dry leaves" for "shavings" suggests a seasonal change that fits perfectly with the Antipodes and links with the seasonal pun in "the *fall* was over" (my italics). Although the date of Alice's journey in Wonderland is May 4th,[5] spring in England is fall in the Southern Hemisphere and this accounts for the heap of sticks and dry leaves. Carroll's use of the palindrome "ma'am" further emphasizes the centrality of inversion and its 180-degree shift. Later, in *The Nursery "Alice,"* Carroll dropped Alice's speculation about the "centre of the earth" and retained only the fall "through the earth" (7), suggesting that it was his intended destination from the beginning. The antipodean location of Wonderland is established within the text from the outset, then, and carries with it the great range of possibilities associated with the topos of the world upside down and the history of antipodean literature.

The world upside down is an antique, widely distributed, and protean device. Its forms range from the compact rhetorical topos to the expanded, thoroughly developed oppositions that shape entire literary works; its uses range from the sight gag to the serious. In his "The Antipodes," Thomas Traherne uses the idea with a religious seriousness comparable to St Paul's insight that Christians are seen as those who intend to turn religious life upside down. Romantic and transcendental writers such as Wordsworth, Emerson, and Thoreau establish the heart of their revolutionary enterprise through the use of the device. But most frequently, as Ernst Curtius notes about its uses in the Middle Ages, equally serious uses are accomplished through comedy, especially satire, burlesque, and parody.

In *Il Mondo Alla Rovescia*, Giuseppe Cocchiara locates the world upside down and discusses its function in Sumerian, Egyptian, and classical and mediaeval European cultures. Its most familiar presentation in Western culture grew out of Greek and Roman poetry and oratory, and was codified in classical rhetoric. The topos of the world turned upside down is the product of a special kind of hyperbole, a figure of exaggeration called "adynaton" ("not possible"). Adynata are connected to the inversion of both physical and social reality. The topos gained a specific sense of geographical place in early theories about a round earth, theories that reappeared with regularity in travel literature from the fourteenth century onward. (See, for example, chapter 20 of *The Voyages of Sir John Mandeville*.) "Antipodes" was the name given to the lowest part of the Southern Hemisphere and to its inhabitants who walked heads downwards and feet to European feet. The comparatively recent discovery and colonization of Australia and New Zealand, the Antipodes, in the eighteenth and nineteenth centuries certainly reintroduced and refreshened this classic inversion (see note 4).

Carroll's use of the world upside down and its special figuration in Antipodes connects his work to a long-established tradition in Western literature, one generally used in social comedy. There is another clearly developed political strain in which this topos creates a powerful subversive force that works to bring about actual social change. This strain is associated with carnival and is presented at length in Bachtin's *Rabelais and His World*. It is also linked to specific social and political upheaval by David Kunzle and others in *The Reversible World* and by Christopher Hill in *The World Turned Upside Down: Radical Ideas during the English Revolution*. In the Alice books, Carroll's presentation of the topos as a social corrective is more in tune with the spirit of Ernst Curtius's assertion in *European Literature and the Latin Middle Ages* that "comic motifs had more vitality than any other" use of the world upside down (96). These comic motifs, developed in burlesque, lampoon, and parody, were most frequently worked out in satire. If a writer wanted to support either side of an argument, such as the youth versus age debate (an argument central in *Wonderland*), he or she would undercut the opposite view by associating it with the world upside down. Curtius gives an example from *Carmina Burana* that begins as an attack on youth's premature claim to wisdom:

> Once it was good to understand,
> But play has now the upper hand.
> Now boyish brains become of age
> Long before time can make them sage,
> In malice too of age become,
> Shut wisdom out of house and home. (95)

The use of any individual figure of the world upside down acted as a kind of code key that signalled distortion, but individual examples could also be linked together, as they are in this poem, to create a sense of general dissatisfaction with a world where "everything is out of joint."

Within the general topos, individual impossibilities cluster together in terms of the kinds of exchanges involved. Impossibilities in nature, for example, work through exchange of environments: birds swim in the sea while fish take to the sky. Other groups form through exchange of accepted station or roles in society. In the man/animal group, an exchange of mastery creates inversions in which oxen lead men at the plow, fish angle for men, and game animals hunt hunters. A third group works out entirely in human society: wives husband husbands, masters serve servants, and children instruct and discipline adults.[6]

The topos of the world turned upside down was also established in visual art. Curtius briefly mentions Breughel's *Dutch Proverbs* as his sole example, but does not elaborate on how the topos is developed (97). This painting gathers a number of related impossibilities to create an overwhelming sense of general inversion. There are 118 individual illustrated proverbs joined together to produce a complex of deviations from the norm in human relationships.[7] The key to the general satire in the painting is the globe turned upside down in the far left centre, the detail that gave the painting its earlier title, *The World Turned Upside Down*. At about the same time in the sixteenth century, Giuseppe Porta (known as Salviati, after his teacher) depicted a series of individual impossibilities that anticipate the figures so abundant in European popular art of the seventeenth and eighteenth centuries and that are used in an early nineteenth-century English world-upside-down book. A number of anonymous woodcuts depicting the same inversions produced in French popular art during these centuries are gathered by Pierre-Louis Duchartre and René Saulniers in *L'Imagerie Populaire*, and Giuseppe Cocchiara includes prints from many countries in *Il Mondo Alla Rovescia*, as does the more recent *Le Monde à l'Envers* by Maurice Lever and Frederick Tristran (1980). These woodcuts and prints present standard inversions such as a horse riding a man, children disciplining adults, and a man stuck upside down through a globe.

This last figure, man upside down, had already become a summary human representation of the topos as early as the ninth century. In *Liber Monstrorum*, "antipodes" are described as monsters living on the other side of a round earth: "They say there is a human genus under the globe which they call antipodes and according to the Greek name, they tread the lowest bottom of the earth feet upwards to our own footprint" (103). This early presentation of the exotic geography of the other side of the world was elaborated in both actual and fictional travel books and was incorporated into comic literature from the sixteenth century forwards. It consolidates the essence of the topos of the world upside down and gives it substance and a place. Ian Donaldson describes the uses of antipodes in English theatrical comedy in *The World Turned Upside Down: Comedy from Jonson to Fielding* (1970). From the sixteenth through the eighteenth centuries, writers were stimulated by earlier accounts of travel such as *The Voyages of Sir John Mandeville* (a strange composite of eye-witness report, free imaginative play, and plagiarism – all attributed to a possibly fictional character) and actual accounts of exploration (for example, the works of Marco Polo, Christopher Columbus, and Walter Raleigh), both streams filling out in some detail another world in the Southern Hemisphere.

William Bullein's *Dialogue Against the Fever Pestilence* (1594), a work edited and republished in the late nineteenth century, presents Antipodes as a mirror world whose physical geography and social conventions were 180-degree opposites of those in England. This vision is elaborated by a character named Mendax (a liar, as his name suggests), who develops the idea of Antipodes by locating an anti-London in an anti–Great Britain, "Nodnol" in "Taerg Niatirb," and thereby establishes an inverted world (105). The exact symmetry of Bullein's exotic world is directly linked to Mandeville's description of Antipodes as a place where "alle the parties of see and lond han here appositees habitables or trepassables and [yles] of this half and beyond half" (134).

Richard Brome's play *The Antipodes* (1640) elaborates the structural and moral functions of the world upside down as place. Peregrin, a "thought-traveller," is so taken with the potentially superior world of Antipodes that he ignores his everyday life, even to the extent of failing to consummate his three-year-old marriage. Peregrin is cured through a play within a play arranged by Dr Hughball and a wealthy manipulator named Letoy. They drug Peregrin and convince him when he wakes that he is in Antipodes, complete with an anti-London, where social conventions are so repugnant that he is finally forced to accept the real world regardless of its faults. As Donaldson points out, Antipodes "provided a location from which to look back upon European manners with a quizzical and comparative eye ... [and] the antipodes, that traditional seat of absurdity, allowed for the sharpest and most spectacular of contrasts" (84). In social comedy, then, antipodes functions as a ground for comparison and contrast, a means to measure and evaluate the known or everyday world. When the ground is introduced, "reality" is either comically distanced and exotic as in Bullein's *Dialogue* or is critiqued and either confirmed (as in Brome's *The Antipodes*), subverted, or found to be flawed and requiring compensation.[8] In the Alice books, Carroll creates a tension between pure comedy and corrective satire to produce a fantasy with subversive elements that is, finally, compensatory.

An acute sense of doubleness is a constant feature of books that use antipodean travel. Everything that is seen and experienced is reported with the relish of comparative anthropology. Gulliver's reports of his trips contain hundreds of comparisons and contrasts that slowly chronicle his change from a boastful champion of European society to a humble believer in human inferiority in the Land of the Houyhnhnms. Swift may have used a standard adynaton, the horse who rides his master, and elaborated it into an antipodean land of rational horses in order to critique both human society and human nature itself. The following, from "A Meditation Upon a Broomstick," certainly solidifies his familiarity with the world turned upside down: "... and pray what is Man, but a topsy-turvy Creature, his Animal Faculties mounted on his Rational, his Head where his Heels should be, grovelling in the earth!" (*A Tale of a Tub with Other Early Works*, 240).

Perhaps the most thoroughly worked-out double structure in satiric literature that uses travel to another world, however, is presented in another eighteenth-century satire, Ludvig Holberg's *Nicolai Klimii Iter Subterraneum Novan Telluris Theoriam Ac Historiam Quintae Monarchiae Ahhuc Nobis Incognitae Exhibens E Bibliotheca B. Abelini* (1745). This satiric philosophical romance, originally written in Latin and translated into English in 1828, is a detailed account of the adventures of Nicholas Klim in a world (Nazar) that exists at the centre of the earth. During Klim's adventures in Nazar, he discovers a book written by Tinnian entitled *Supra-Terraneous Travels: or, A Description of the Empires, Kingdoms and Countries of the Earth and Particularly of Those in Europe* (206). This book within a book is an inversion of Klim's travels in Nazar and underscores once more the use of another world as a ground for comparison and contrast. A similar double awareness is at work in *Alice's Adventures in Wonderland* in both the narrator's and Alice's frequent comparisons and contrasts of Wonderland with the everyday world.

Holberg's book touches *Alice's Adventures in Wonderland* in several specific ways. Klim and Alice both speculate about destinations while falling into other worlds, and the worlds they enter are both inhabited by griffins, a clue to experience in antipodes since Mandeville's description of the griffins he encountered in Bacharia. More importantly, Klim's journey through Nazar brings him to places characterized by classic inversions. For instance, he is considered inferior by the anthropomorphized trees he first meets in Nazar. This encounter demonstrates his physical and social awkwardness. Frightened by a bull, Klim climbs a tree for protection only to discover that the tree is the sheriff's wife. After looking Klim over and judging his actions, the trees decide that he is an "extraordinary baboon." Further, Klim's experiences in other countries introduce him to cultures where women totally dominate men and where residents from birth to age forty rule over their "childish" elders. Quamboja, the land ruled by the young, is considered to be "inverted completely in its nature" (157). The law that states that "old men and old women shall be dutiful and obedient to their children" (160) is surely an instance of a classic youth/age inversion. Residents over forty are called "wild and impudent sauce-boxes," and they spend their time at hopscotch and prisoner's base until they are "lashed home to their children" by rational and "mature" youth (161).

Regardless of the fact that Nazar seems to be located at the centre of the earth, the satiric structure of Holberg's work is clearly antipodean. Nazar's curiosities most frequently result from individual figures of inversion. These same figures appeared in eighteenth-century English chapbooks and led directly to the use of the world upside down in early nineteenth-century children's books. In *English Children's Books, 1600–1900*, Percy Muir suggests some general relationships between world-upside-down chapbooks, Swift's horse/rider inversion in Book 4 of *Gulliver's Travels*, and children's books that appeared before the Alice books. Muir says that the Taylor sisters' treatment of the theme of the horse-turned-rider in *Signor Topsy-Turvy's Wonderful Magic Lantern; or, The World turned upside down* (1810) is one of the best treatments of a theme that "may have inspired Swift" earlier (99). The topsy-turvydom presented in chapbooks, Muir adds (without elaboration), was "later to claim the attention of another genius in the Lewis Carroll stories" (42).

The connection between chapbooks and children's books is most clearly demonstrated by Ann and Jane Taylor in *Signor Topsy-Turvy's Wonderful Magic Lantern*. In their preface, the Taylors recall their childhood wonder at the inversions presented in *The World Turned Upside Down: or The Folly of Man Exemplified in Twelve Comical Relations Upon Uncommon Subjects* (1750 and 1780). Although this eighteenth-century book was clearly not specifically intended for child readers (it presents references to adult sexuality and to crimes such as theft), it contains the type of material children traditionally appropriate in its exotic illustrated inversions while sometimes offering the type of material that adults thought suitable for children in its didactic correction of the pictured inversions within the accompanying narrative poems.

When the Taylors and others began to produce world-upside-down books especially for children, the traditional rhetorical elements threatened to transform into a kind of "pure" comedy, a comedy growing out of inversion and suggesting nothing beyond itself. Although their acknowledged chapbook source begins with a conservative attack on the realignments necessitated by an astronomy that displaced earth as centre, making it a "tennis ball for fools" (2), the Taylors' introductory poem accounts for inversion by describing a magic lantern show that is distorted by improperly placed "sliders," an occurrence signifying nothing more than human awkwardness. The audience immediately take delight in this altered perspective and, when "an envious fellow from college" attempts to make adjustments to right the world, demand that the inverted images continue, offering no rationale beyond their delight in the altered perspective. In the first narrative poem, "The Cook Cooked," animals normally eaten by humans roast the cook on his own spit and, by poem's end, the cook is basted, browned, and ready to serve. Correction of altered perspective and relationships, however, returns to dominate the majority of the stories. An important example of this, "The Boy Turned Giant," is a close analogue for some aspects of *Alice in Wonderland.* A boy becomes a giant after wishing to do so in order to retrieve his kite from a tree (compare this with Alice's key to her garden). He is successful but, in his accomplishment, is buffeted by strong winds and scratched by tree branches. Further, when he attempts to return home, he finds that "His knee was at the second floor / His foot alone block'd the door" (56). Turned inside out, this situation strongly suggests willed size changes and, especially, Alice swollen to fill the White Rabbit's house (32). The major difference rests in the appended moral: "What 'er thy station, be content, / Nor wish to change a good in hand, / For things you do not understand" (56). This conventional moral making is totally absent in Wonderland but so is pure comic distortion: Carroll married the two elements in his antipodean structural ground for satire, themes, and parody, normal features of adult works that employ the world upside down and are increasingly found in children's books from 1800 forward.

If the Taylors' work stood alone as an upside-down book for children, Carroll's connection with a tradition already present in English children's literature before he was born would be thin. But a number of individual poems, parts of books, and complete books that used upside-down material appeared throughout the nineteenth century: *The World Upside Down* (c. 1807); *Il Mondo Rovesciato; or, The World Turned Upside Down* (1822); two editions of *The World Turned Upside Down; or, No News, and Strange News* (1828 and 1830); "The Story of the Man Who Went Out Shooting" section of *Der Struwwelpeter* (1848); a panorama titled *The World Upside Down* (1860); Tom Hood's *Upside Down; or, Turnover Traits* (1868); Arthur Lilie's *The King of Topsy Turvy* (1870); E.C. Clayton's *The World Turned Upside Down* (1876) and *Topsy Turvy: or, Strange Sights to See* (1878); and Laura Lucie Finlay's *Philippa's Adventures in Upsidedownland* (1898). All of these demonstrate the popularity of the topos. Jean Jambon's (pseudonym) *Our Trip to Blunderland; or, Grand Excursion to Blundertown and Back* (1876), a book singled out together with others "of the Alice type" by Carroll in his diary entry of 11 September 1891 (486), not only borrowed his dream frame but signalled the characters' arrival in Blunderland by standard world-upside-down figures – a man sitting on his horse backwards and an aged man dressed as a schoolboy being controlled by a child dressed in adult clothing.

The early upside-down books share an exceptionally strong sense of play in their treatment of inversion: moral suggestion is either minimally present (introduced as an afterthought) or totally absent. As such, these books are anomalies in a period of children's literature dominated by moral, rational, and informational didacticism; they are part of what Darton terms an interim of levity, although one far richer than he suggests (198–218). In *Il Mondo Rovesciato*, Salviati's individual illustrations mentioned above (originally produced in 1564) are accompanied by explanatory verses that sometimes suggest a possible corrective by offering motives for inversion. "The son, imperious o'er the Sire forlorn, / Inflicts the beatings he so oft has borne," for example, provides a motivation for the child/parent inversion. Generally, however, the emphasis is on the bizarre world produced by inversion. The overturned world created by the twenty-seven individual illustrations and poems is consolidated and commented upon in the twenty-eighth offering:

> All lands have changed their latitudes; each breeze
> Has veer'd; and ships, reverted, plough the seas:
> O'er all things Magic seems to spread her robe,
> And powerful Laughter lords it o'er the globe. (22)

In the accompanying illustration, Africa and Europe have exchanged hemispheres and the name of each appears backwards and in mirror image. This illustration and verse sum up the general tone of the book.

In *The World Upside Down*, comic strangeness is the sole result of inversion. Here humanized animals appear in much the same spirit of amoral fun (although more zanily) as they do in William Roscoe's *The Butterfly's Ball and the Grasshopper's Feast* (1807):

> Here a monkey is shaving
> The head of a bear,
> And a dog puffs and powders
> Old pussy's grey hair. (10)

This book differs from Roscoe's, however, in that it lacks his use of a unifying narrative that frames fantasy with reality. Everyday reality is the assumed ground of comic contrast. Further, it includes materials that are simply incongruous, such as the above, in which basic antagonisms dissolve in the dog's attention to the cat's grooming, together with classic representations of the world upside down, such as the cook cooked and the animal turned butcher:

> Here's a sheep turned butcher,
> The man he has stuck,
> And a man being hunted
> By a fox on a buck.

The World Turned Upside Down: or, No News, and Strange News uses the formula contained in its title to juxtapose everyday and curious experience in order to create an exotic world. The frontispiece illustration and verse set the tone. Flanked by an upside-down tree and castle, a man is stuck upside down through a globe:

> Here you may see what's very rare,
>   The world turn'd upside down:
> A tree and castle in the air,
>   A man walks on his crown.

This synecdochical illustration of antipodes is a key to a number of new impossibilities totally innocent of moral intention. One example reveals the formula:

To see a man jump in a boat
is no news;
But to see a man jump down his own throat
is strange indeed. (14)

Other examples again convey a mixture of simple incongruity and representative upside-down material – the woman mastering her old husband, a hog butchering a butcher, a fish hooking a man, and a bird shooting a man in a tree.

Heinrich Hoffmann's inclusion of the hunter hunted (12–14), a traditional rhetorical topos of the world turned upside down, among his comic cautionary tales in *Der Struwwelpeter* (1848) illustrates the persistence of the rhetorical tradition, as do Tom Hood's verses written to accompany upside-down sketches by William McConnell, sketches that transform the identity of an image when it is inverted. For instance, the face of a sly man becomes the face of a fox when the book is flipped over, and the picture works together with Hood's added verse:

He means to win –
He'll take you in,
I'll bet you half-a-crown: –
But if you're smart,
Exert your art,
And turn him upside down! (20)

This is the only inversion that suggests correction in Hood's book, as the general drive is to create wonder and amusement out of the doubleness involved with inversion. Interestingly, the child reader's total control of and participation in altering the images by physically turning them over contrasts dramatically with Alice's lack of control of inversions and reversals.

When the topos of the world upside down entered children's literature in the early nineteenth century, then, it most frequently tended to drop comparison as a ground for critique or affirmation of everyday reality, instead emphasizing it as a ground for an amusing distortion. What Frederick J. Harvey Darton says about the momentary triumph of the non-utilitarian and fantastic in the *Butterfly's Ball* is equally true of these books (199 ff.). Although comparatively few in number, such books prove that the world upside down both found its way into and remained in children's literature during the nineteenth century, denying didacticism an absolute hold on children's literature in the early decades of that century.

Another upside-down book that is an analogue of *Alice in Wonderland* is J.J. Grandville's *Un Autre Monde* (1844), an (adult?) work informed by a consistent use of radical inversion to create another world.[9] The introductory illustration of this book, entitled "La Clef des Champs," shows a jester doing a handstand against a background gate, while a large key rests against the fence. The accompanying text reads: "Je veux aller où me conduira ma fantaisie; je prétends moi-même me servir de guide: vive la liberté!" (1169).[10] Compared to the traditional depiction of a man stuck upside down through a globe, this jester, like Carroll's Father William, chooses to alter his position in order to gain a new perspective. (Alice, who is always aware of the contrast between Wonderland and reality, similarly chooses to stay in an altered world and only leaves when the radical inversion attempts quite literally to arrest her.) Altered perspective creates a world in which, among many things, animals and plants talk and new animals are created by combining parts of familiar animals. For example, Grandville presents a spaniel/turtle that has the front legs of a dog, turtle flippers for rear legs, and a spaniel's head sticking out of a turtle's carapace (1256). There is no closer relative to Carroll's Mock Turtle than Grandville's earlier visual portmanteau.

At the outset of his satiric fantasy *Alice's Adventures in Wonderland*, Carroll draws on a very ancient tradition still in use in adult and children's literature in the middle of the nineteenth century. Carroll's development of Wonderland in the singular and unifying context of the topos of the world upside down and antipodes, then, was at the very least potentially familiar to his readers and allowed him to borrow and combine a great range of literary features that includes a structural ground for satiric comparison and contrast, characters and a kind of characterization, themes, and parody.

Alice's fantasy world is composed of a unified string of "impossibilities." Many of these, such as talking animals and man-made objects invested with life, were already familiar parts of children's literature, but they had never been gathered together in such an encyclopaedic way before. Taken together, Carroll's patterned impossibilities create a ground for comparing and contrasting Wonderland with the everyday world of the fantasy frame, a world with which Alice never loses contact. Wonderland is similar to Brome's Antipodes and Swift's Houyhnhnm Land in that it provides a basis for critique, a satiric yardstick for mutual measurement and evaluation; but it differs from both in that it is neither consistently affirmative nor consistently critical. Carroll's fantasy world is closer to the doubleness of Holberg's structure, where Klim's European judgments on Nazar are balanced by Tinnian's Nazurian critique of Europe. But Wonderland is further complicated in that the exchanges and exaggerations developed involve a child's sense of reality, which is necessarily accompanied by irony. Alice's experiences invariably combine the allure of the curious with the pain that results from the associated physical and social awkwardness to create an oxymoronic whole. Carroll's use of this complex structure reconnects the exotic or wonderful elements of the topos with the satiric potential that had been subordinated in earlier world-upside-down children's books and, thereby, restores its satiric possibilities.

The characters who "people" Wonderland are an odd assortment drawn from Alice's natural and artificial everyday world and universally granted the gift of speech. One character, the Gryphon, is especially associated with antipodes. As noted, Mandeville included a report on griffins in his account of his voyages, griffins so enormous that humans used their talons for drinking cups (194). Holberg has an equally large and fierce griffin fly up to attack Klim as he falls into Nazar. Unlike these possible literary antecedents, however, Carroll's Gryphon becomes something of a guide to Alice, informing her, for example, that the threatening Queen of Hearts has never actually beheaded anyone (83). (In this guise he joins another guide, the Caterpillar, and together they suggest an additional literary form at work in Wonderland that provides a ground for contrast and comparison – the dream vision.) The composite nature of the Gryphon – part eagle, part lion – makes him a fit companion for Carroll's invented Mock Turtle (half calf, half turtle), himself a composite figure born out of a recipe for mock-turtle soup that substitutes veal for turtle.

More importantly, Carroll's characterization of Wonderland figures shares the flatness associated with characters in satire, characters shaped by the fact that they are generally mouthpieces for particular ideas or values. In antipodean satire such ideas or values are, in turn, related to traditionally inverted social relationships. The Queen of Hearts and the Duchess, for example, are both one-dimensional exaggerations of the social functions they represent. The first "governs" exclusively through threats of beheading, while the Duchess, seemingly entrusted with nursing a baby, reduces all experience to "morals" and sings a "sort of a lullaby" that substitutes "roughness" for "gentleness" in child care (54–5).

Thematically, Wonderland is dominated by two traditional social inversions: animal/man and youth/age. Both of these inversions function to make Alice feel awkward and inferior. The Mouse, the Lory, the White Rabbit, and other animal inhabitants of Wonderland take offence at Alice's social lapses and frequently, as she puts it, "order her about." Pat, the White Rabbit's servant, is clearly linked to the world upside down. Summoned by his boss, Pat responds: "Sure then I'm here! Digging for apples, yer honour" (34). This response combines a French/English pun (*pomme/*

pomme de terre) with transposed nature and a tricky servant wit that affronts social order. Throughout the book Carroll consistently inverts Alice's everyday social relationships with animals. Instances of "rude" treatment and of being "ordered about" occur with such frequency that Alice is often led to compare and contrast her Wonderland with her everyday experience. When Alice finds herself "going messenger for a rabbit," for example, she imagines a similar situation back home:

'I suppose Dinah'll be sending me on messages next!' and she began fancying the sort of thing that would happen: 'Miss Alice! Come here directly, and get ready for your walk!' 'Coming in a minute, nurse! But I've got to watch this mouse-hole till Dinah comes back, and see that the mouse doesn't get out.' 'Only I don't think,' Alice went on, 'that they'd let Dinah stop in the house if it began ordering people about like that!' (31–2)

Carroll's second major theme of inversion, youth/age, appears first in the argument Alice is reported to have had with the Lory. This argument was to have been resolved in favour of the eldest, but since the Lory had refused to reveal her age, Alice had not conceded (24). Here the youth/age relationship is a source of fun, but it is not inverted. Inversion is first used in "Advice from a Caterpillar," and when it does arrive it is curious indeed, for it inverts a classic inversion. Generally, as in the example from *Carmina Burana* quoted earlier, the youth/age inversion involves a comic exposing of premature claims of adult functions by the young. The child either teaches or disciplines a parent or teacher. Through Alice's recitation of "You are old, Father William" (33–4), performed by order of the Caterpillar, whose very nature suggests transformation and growth, Carroll turns the classic inversion on its head. Alice's Father William remains aggressively youthful into his old age through standing on his head (an exercise he shares with the clumsy White Knight of Looking-Glass Land, who claims to think more productively upside down) and other comic exercises. Carroll parodies the piousness of Robert Southey's "The Old Man's Comforts, and How He Gained Them," a poem that is a moral sermon to the young on how best to prepare for socially "acceptable old age."

The youth/age inversion in Wonderland is more generally developed through Carroll's use of "telescoping," involving rapid changes in physical size. Wonderland proves to be a place where wishing makes it so, as Alice discovers when she wishes to "shut up" like a telescope. But Alice does not foresee (does not use the vision associated with telescopes) the corresponding "opening out" or "closing in" quality of the motion of telescoping and, most importantly, her inability to control either of these motions in any sustained and predictable way. Her unpredictable alterations of size invariably produce awkwardness and sometimes prove to be dangerous. Alice clearly associates size with age when, swollen and trapped in the White Rabbit's house, she develops arguments in favour of the superiority of both staying young and growing older: " 'But then,' thought Alice, 'Shall I *never* get any older than I am now? That'll be a comfort, one way – never to be an old woman – but then – always to have lessons to learn! Oh, I shouldn't like *that*!' " (33). The lessening of lessons is at its satiric best in the Mock Turtle's sad story of a youth misspent studying Mystery, ancient and modern, Derision, Uglification, Fainting in Coils, and the rest of the sob and sigh curriculum forced on "shrimps" under the sea – an underworld within an underworld.

The literary parody in "You are old, Father William" and the parody of educational curriculum in the Mock Turtle's sad story both work to invert didacticism. Carroll undercuts the corrective elements associated with the world upside down by consistently transforming moral and informational didacticism into nonsense through the literary alchemy of parody. It seems, then, that his individual parodies are close to the spirit of earlier children's upside-down books, in which the strangeness resulting from inversion is emphasized to the exclusion of satiric correction. Collectively, however, Carroll's parodies create what Donald Rackin calls a "corrective laughter" that is turned against the harsh moral vision presented in children's books by such writers as Isaac Watts and Mrs Sherwood and, it must be added, against the sterility of informational literature unimaginatively produced.[11]

Carroll's parodies of moral poems and informational literature do not simply use imitative words, style, and tone but invert the attitudes and ideas of the work parodied, and in so doing, they upend what passed for morality and utility in eighteenth- and early-nineteenth-century children's books. Carroll's is a parody that works totally in the spirit of the world upside down. Isaac Watts's *Divine Songs Attempted in Easy Language for the Use of Children* (1715), still memorized by children in the middle of the nineteenth century, provide two major instances of parody. The call to industry and thrift in "How Doth the Little Busy Bee" is reversed to reveal the effortless consuming of fish by a lazily motionless and smiling crocodile (19). The admonition against sloth in "The Sluggard" is altered to a half-baked lobster's rapidly alternating bravado and terror in the absence and presence of a shark (93) and the sorry tale of an owl who chooses the wrong dinner companion and, thereby, becomes dinner (94). A deadly lecture on flattery in Mary Howitt's "The Spider and the Fly" (1834) becomes an invitation to dance in the Mock Turtle's song that accompanies the Lobster-Quadrille (90). And the "sort of a lullabye" sung by the Duchess advises that roughness and severity ought to replace kindness and gentleness in the treatment of children (54). The same kind of overturning is at work when Alice attempts to use geography and math to reassert her identity within the threatening strangeness of Wonderland. Geography is reduced to nonsense when the geographical sets of country and capital of country are confusedly reversed, and the multiplication tables, alas, do not "signify" (19). Carroll attacks the utility of informational books, such as William Pinnock's series of informational "catechisms," with the same logic of parody, conversion to opposites, that he uses on "moral" books. And Alice is stripped of two of the ways people locate themselves honoured in the "real" world.

The topos of the world upside down and its embodiment in antipodes, then, combine to provide a consistently elaborated structural ground for satire, themes, a logic of characterization, and a logic of parody in *Alice's Adventures in Wonderland.* One possible reading based on these features is that the book is a satiric fantasy that presents a child's conception and experience of the adult world exaggerated through adynata to the point of consistent inversion. The everyday problems experienced by children in a world made in every way to adult scale are magnified hyperbolically until Alice is continually at odds with physical and social circumstance. Alice's awkwardness stems from her inability to control either her physical or social growth, and in addition, her realized wish to telescope transfers the problem of scale from the world around her to Alice herself. Alice's physical alterations not only constitute a danger for her, but also make her feel personally to blame for these conditions. At the short end of the scale, Alice shrinks to the height of ten inches and almost disappears (15), while she is comically and pathetically out of touch with herself at the long end and feels she must communicate with her own right foot by post (17). There is little comfort in between, either, for Alice's size forever frightens the smaller animals and causes her unhappiness.

Socially, Alice's fairy tale–like and antipodean ability to talk with animals, far from being an asset as it would be were she in the fairy tale world she imagines herself to be in (33), leads her to commit a variety of solecisms involving the play and eating habits of her cat, Dinah, that have an extraordinarily chilling effect on mice and birds. To Alice's credit, after she receives advice from the Caterpillar, she attempts to alter her size and speech situationally to avoid further offence to others. But the characters and situations she encounters lead to increasingly intolerable oppositions that make her attempts impossible: that is, the curious dual nature of the antipodean world ceases to attract Alice and begins to nightmarishly fulfil the unconscious prophecy in her earlier unintentional pun linking "antipodes" with "antipathies" (11). Carroll unites both meanings of "antipathies": Alice experiences an opposition in feeling, a tension between delight and concern in face of the "curiouser and curiouser" world of Wonderland, and by the end of the framed fantasy, this opposition hardens to an aversion that makes her reject Wonderland. That Alice has learned to move through this simultaneously fetching and threatening world with any degree of control (and is able to reject it entirely when she feels the threatening aspect pull totally away in the adult judgment that sentence precedes verdict in the treatment of children) confirms her potential ability to cope with a seriously flawed everyday world (108).

When the always tenuous balance of delight and threat tips absolutely towards threat in the trial scene, Alice finds herself saying, "I can't help it … I'm growing" (99). Her acceptance of herself as a child moving towards adulthood here is the prelude to her refusal to stand trial and her rejection of the Queen of Hearts' ultimate insane inversion in "Sentence first – verdict afterwards" (108). Alice's rejection of this antipodean logic leads to her defiant refusal to be arrested by the playing cards. Wonderland as a variant of antipodes projects Alice's concerns about being a child who is growing up into an adult world that is at one and the same time attractively curious and threatening. Carroll's upending of the exaggerated everyday world through features of the world upside down and its geographical presentation as antipodes works to alert both the child and adult reader to mutual problems. The fact that Alice wakes to the real world with pleasant memories of Wonderland is at least partially attributable to the fantasy's vision of the childhood she has survived, a vision that recognizes life's oxymoronic mixture of dread and delight and suggests compensatory alterations.

Carroll's textual clue that Wonderland is an antipodean world is neither a random nor a passing allusion. His satiric fantasy is consistently presented in terms of the then ongoing convention of the world upside down. It is not sufficient to say, as Eric Rabkin does, that inversion is "everywhere" in the Alice books (111) or to suggest, as Taylor does, that inversions result from the adult knowledge and concerns Carroll brings to lay at "Alice's feet" (v). The themes, characterization, and parody that Carroll uses to develop his overall satiric structure of inversion are incorporated from antipodean literature. This structural ground creates a double vision, a simultaneous awareness of two worlds, and this dual vision is the basis for the critique of both everyday and antipodean "realities," as well as an argument for compensatory changes in the former.

The Looking-Glass Book

"Why, it's a Looking-glass book, of course."
– Alice

The tradition of the looking-glass book plays an important structural and thematic role in Lewis Carroll's *Through the Looking-Glass and What Alice Found There*.[1] Yet, while a survey of the critical responses to this fantasy reveals that Alice's passage through the physical looking-glass and its attendant reversals have received a great deal of critical attention, her simultaneous passage through the tradition of the looking-glass book has been virtually ignored. This chapter locates the tradition, particularly as it developed in the looking-glass book for children and in Carroll's fantasy, and demonstrates how the fantasy functions to introduce children's literature as a ground for literary reversals that work together with the more obvious physical reversals. Further, this chapter describes how these literary reversals help to create Alice's oxymoronic delight and confusion in Looking-Glass Land, and contrasts these reversals with the literary materials used to produce similar effects in Wonderland. Finally, it suggests the possibility that the fantasy structures of the two Alice books mirror each other.

In "Looking-Glass House," the first chapter of *Through the Looking-Glass and What Alice Found There*, Alice plays a game of "let's pretend" with her uncooperative kitten:

'Let's pretend that you're the Red Queen, Kitty! Do you know, I think if you sat up and folded your arms, you'd look exactly like her. Now do try, there's a dear!' And Alice got the Red Queen off the table, and set it up before the kitten as a *model* for it to *imitate;* however, the thing didn't succeed, principally, Alice said, because the kitten wouldn't fold its arms properly. So, to *punish* it, she *held it up to the Looking-*

glass, that it might see how sulky it was, '– and if you're not good directly,' she added, 'I'll put you through into Looking-Glass House. How would you like *that?*' (127, all but the last, my italics)[2]

Indoors on a snowy November day, Alice plays a didactic game in which she becomes the authoritative and correcting adult in relation to her awkward and mischievous kitten. Imitation is the centre of this game. Imitating adult treatment of her own behaviour, Alice uses a positive model to try to get her kitten to "become" the Red Queen, and when her kitten refuses, Alice attempts to correct its "sulky" behaviour by holding it up to a mirror, in which the kitten's own image is a negative model. In a general way this fantasy-frame play works to establish the logic of the fantasy that follows. For example, it works to set up the important structural chessboard topography and to cast some of the characters that people the fantasy. But, more specifically, Alice's didactic "let's pretend" also introduces the logic of the looking-glass book for children; her words suggest an expansion of the theme of reversal beyond the more obvious physical mirror that has drawn concentrated attention from Carroll's critics.

The looking-glass book for children, born out of the long history of looking-glass books (specifically near the end of the seventeenth century), uses narrative as an exemplary mirror that teaches through either positive models or admonishment. The early history of the looking-glass book in England is thoroughly worked out by Herbert Grabes in *The Mutable Glass: Mirror-Imagery in Titles and Texts of the Middle Ages and English Renaissance.* Grabes lists hundreds of works that employ mirror imagery as "title-metaphor" and develops a typology that includes informational, exemplary, prognostic, and fantasy mirrors (42–66). The looking-glass book for children grew out of the exemplary mirror book at the beginning of the period of sustained and self-conscious production of religious books for children in the middle of the seventeenth century. The first such titled book especially written for children was Abraham Chear's *A Looking Glass for Children* (1673), a book with a clearly religious didactic intention realized through verse narratives and stories that work as positive examples or admonishments. The use of the title formula continued even as specific didactic intentions and attitudes towards the creation of the "good" child altered through the eighteenth and into the nineteenth centuries: that is, the title formula remained a constant through the changes that took place in the "official" or adult-sanctioned literature and its attendant sense of what children ought to be. At the close of the eighteenth century, for example, the work of the French rational/moralist Arnauld Berquin was translated and published in England as *The Looking-Glass for the Mind; or, Intellectual*

Mirror (1792). Although Berquin's original title, *L'Ami des Enfans*, does not suggest the looking-glass metaphor, his English translator sees the collection of stories as "a useful and instructive pocket looking-glass" that "displays the follies and improper pursuits of the youthful breast"(2). So rational/moral children's literature had replaced religious literature, but the looking-glass metaphor remained appropriate.[3] Closer to the dates of publication of the Alice books, the tradition was still alive in *The Laughable Looking Glass for Little Folks* (1857 and 1859), a book with a cover illustration showing a mother holding a baby up to a mirror; this book uses comedy as a moral corrective without surrendering its obvious didactic intention. Regardless of shifts in specific intention through time, the use of narrative as a mirror to alter or reinforce behaviour, then, remained a constant. The connection between Carroll's work and this tradition is supported by Alice's use of the mirror as a modelling and corrective agency in the material quoted above and by the redundancy of "looking-glass" in the titles of both the complete book and its opening chapter. This connection reinforces and widens the reversals that result from the use of the material mirror.

The major critical approach to *Through the Looking-Glass and What Alice Found There* concentrates on the physical reversals that result from Alice's passage through the material mirror. In *The White Knight*, Alexander Taylor develops a number of eighteenth- and nineteenth-century philosophical analogues for Carroll's use of reversals in order to support his sense of the adult intellectual seriousness of Carroll's fantasy (87–97). Wiping his "glosses with what [he] knows," Martin Gardner catalogues and comments on numerous physical reversals in his *The Annotated Alice*; in *Victorian Fantasy*, Stephen Prickett argues that reversal provides the structural and thematic logic of *Through the Looking-Glass* (137 ff.); and Eric Rabkin uses Carroll's structure of reversal as the very model for the genre of fantasy in his *The Fantastic in Literature* (41, 110–11). Consideration here of Carroll's use of the looking-glass book tradition supplements this critical attention to physical reversal by focusing on a second ground of reversal, reversals of a literary order.

Both of the grounds of reversal in *Through the Looking-Glass*, the physical and the literary, depend on Alice's retention of her point of view after she passes through the looking-glass. The physical curiosities of Looking-Glass Land are the direct result of Alice's entering a world of mirror images with her perspective unaltered. Carroll's anecdotal memory of the genesis of his strategy, expressed in a letter some years later, stresses the contribution of Alice Raikes. Carroll had been entertaining several children by posing each of them before a mirror with an orange in one hand and pointing out to them that the mirrored image held the orange in the other hand. Alice

Raikes capped his fun by pointing out that the orange would stay put if the child holding it passed through the mirror (*A Selection of the Letters of Lewis Carroll,* 8). This is equally true concerning the metaphorical or literary mirror. The didactic predisposition that leads Alice to tell her kitten all of its faults (125) and to attempt to correct its sulkiness by threatening to pass it through the looking-glass does not change when she actually pursues her own suggestion (127). Her didactic predisposition is underscored in two scenes. Even after the Red Queen gives Alice a preview of the exciting events she will encounter in each chessboard square of Looking-Glass Land, Alice persists in making what she calls a "grand survey" of the topography and associates her experience with "learning geography" (148). And when Alice meets the imprisoned messenger who has yet to commit the crime for which he is being punished, she argues for a fault/punishment logic based on her sense of exemplary didacticism (175). Conversely, Alice carries her didactic perspective and expectations into a Looking-Glass Land that contains characters, events, and themes born out of an imaginative literature that is the 180-degree reversal of the didactic literature parodied in *Alice in Wonderland.*

In Wonderland Alice frequently elects or is called upon to recite bits and pieces of informational literature and didactic poems that were standard children's literature in the middle of the nineteenth century.[4] She attempts to use this familiar material to restore her everyday sense of self and comfortable order when confronted with the curiosities born out of the logic of inversion, but when she does so, she discovers that the utility of geography and the multiplication tables is undercut by error and that the moral lessons of didactic poems by Isaac Watts, Ann Taylor, Mary Howitt, and others whose work she has dutifully memorized have been turned upside down and transformed to nonsense through parody. Watts's exemplarily industrious and thrifty bee from "How Doth the Little Busy Bee" is changed to a stationary crocodile who effortlessly and smilingly welcomes fish to be its dinner. Ann Taylor's beautiful and useful star "like a diamond" becomes a bat "like a tea tray." And Mary Howitt's cautionary tale about a spider's sinister invitation to a fly to enter its parlour is changed to one about a whiting's invitation to a snail to join a dance. Carroll's consistent parody of the sense-over-sound didacticism advocated by the Duchess in Wonderland overturns the very type of exemplary material traditionally associated with the looking-glass book.

When Alice passes through the tradition of the looking-glass book, she experiences a Looking-Glass Land created to a large degree by imaginative children's literature, a land whose make-up includes nonsense song, nursery rhyme, lullaby, counting rhyme, riddle, and romance. Humpty Dumpty is the major spokesman for this literature at its purest when he recites his own poem "entirely for [Alice's] amusement" (194). At the end of the poem, he substitutes the perfect poetic closure of metre and rhyme patterns for semantic significance:

> *"And when I found the door was shut,*
> *I tried to turn the handle, but – "*

There was a long pause.
  "Is that all?" Alice timidly asked.
  "That's all," said Humpty Dumpty. "Good-bye." (196)

Alice, however "timidly," expects a resolution of the semantic pattern that sense demands based on the coordinating conjunction "but," even after Humpty Dumpty's reading of "Jabberwocky" has displayed a use of language generally at odds with everyday meaning (191–3). Humpty Dumpty speaks the language of his birthplace, the language of nursery rhyme.

Nursery rhymes provide Carroll with at least half of the most prominent *Looking-Glass* characters. Tweedledum and Tweedledee, Humpty Dumpty, and the Lion and the Unicorn all step directly out of the rhymes in which they were born. Their literary heredity totally accounts for their actions and attitudes in Looking-Glass Land from the moment of the announcement of the appearance of Tweedledum and Tweedledee. The links with highly formal sound-over-sense verse are highlighted in Carroll's metrical and rhymed introduction of the twins when the prose conclusion to chapter 3 takes metrical shape and becomes the first line of an absolutely regular seven-syllable, four-beat trochaic couplet completed in the title of chapter 4:

> … feeling sure that they must be –
> "Tweedledum and Tweedledee" (158–9)

Although the nursery rhyme characters step outside of their verses in their relationships with Alice, their attitudes and actions are consistently allied with the spirit of their literary origins.

Unlike the parody-transformed didactic children's literature of Wonderland, then, nursery rhymes and the other forms of imaginative children's literature used to create Looking-Glass Land are unaltered. It is Alice's didactic predisposition, carried over from her looking-glass book preoccupations in the fantasy frame, that is the basis for her inability to accept the fates and attitudes of nursery rhyme characters, fates rooted in their literary origins. This accounts for the duality of Alice's responses to them. She finds these characters and their attitudes and actions fascinating, but at the same time her confusion of literary types leads to her consistently misguided (however admirable) concern for their safety and her perpetually awkward and painful relationships with them. Alice's physical and social awkwardness stems not so much from the curiosities of Looking-Glass Land as from her own unchanged perspective, literary as well as physical.

Lullaby, counting song, and riddle differ from "pure" nonsense in that they suggest purposes. The lullaby is an imaginative song that helps to prepare a child for sleep, while the latter two forms suggest educative and intellectual ends. In all three of Carroll's uses of these forms, imaginative qualities override utility and didacticism as they generally do in the tradition of imaginative children's poetry. Donald Gray suggests that the Red Queen's "Lullabye" is the only parody of a nursery rhyme used in *Through the Looking-Glass* (note 9, 197), but even it is a parody only in the strict sense that it is based on "Hush-a-bye Baby." It does not, as the parodies in *Alice in Wonderland* do, reverse the significance of its model. Rather, in keeping with the sense of reversal suggested by passing through the looking-glass book tradition, it reverses effect. Sung by the adult Red Queen after she and the White Queen complete their testing of Alice, the lullaby puts both her and the White Queen to sleep, each resting comfortably on her particular side of the still awake "Queen Alice" (230). This reversed effect emphasizes Alice's new freedom of movement and other expectations that accompany her "queening."

The shrill song celebrating Alice's formal queening makes reference to both number and the process of multiplication. Having gained some experience of Looking-Glass Land by this time, Alice is alert to the probable irrelevance of both: "Thirty times three makes ninety. I wonder if any one's counting?" (233). Although Carroll's song is a parody of Walter Scott's "Bonny Dundee," his addition of number in the refrain lines adds a strong sense of counting rhymes, such as "Telling Out" from *Gammer Gurton's Garland*, in which number and arithmetical process function as poetic cement rather than as an invitation to calculate. Only Alice, who has brought the informational looking-glass book perspective with her, bothers to complete calculations here.

The "fish" riddle (236) posed by the generally confused and disorderly White Queen at the banquet for Queen Alice also functions more as an occasion for a poem than the putting of an intellectual question. That Alice does not spend the minute offered by the Red Queen to solve the riddle suggests that the playful verse context of the riddle and the apparent lack of utility of the answer ("an oyster") make this game silly from any didactic point of view. The point is not that the riddle is without answer, as is the case with the raven/writing-desk riddle in Wonderland, but that the answer is absolutely subordinate to the playful language used to pose the question.

The remaining type of imaginative children's literature Carroll uses is romance. The plot of "Jabberwocky" and the mediaeval associations of the chessboard characters introduce elements of this form. Romance, however, unlike the totally unaltered nursery rhyme and nonsense song used, is changed by Carroll's language and tone. The typical romance narrative of the young man who meets the test of confronting and destroying a monster is first conveyed by mirror writing and then expressed in the neologisms used to establish a sense of mock antiquity and strangeness. Alice's retention of both her physical and literary perspective works to obscure the romance narrative. Alice responds to "Jabberwocky" by extracting its paraphraseable significance – "Somebody killed something: that's clear, at any rate" (197) – rather than appreciating its narrative tone and linguistic peculiarities.

The romance possibilities of the chess kings and queens are consistently undercut by irony and satire, but the White Knight plays both with and against literary type. He most certainly performs as a romance figure when he does battle with the Red Knight to save Alice and, afterwards, when he promises to be her champion and guide (209–11), but the description of the comic clumsiness of both combatants burlesques chivalric romance and anticipates the zany awkwardness that accompanies the White Knight's merging of features of romance and technology. (This burlesque of romance may have its origins in Samuel Butler's *Huddibras* or in the delightful and didactic *Sir Hornbook; or, Childe Launcelot's Expedition*.)[5] It is, however, precisely the White Knight's awkwardness that most endears him to Alice and creates the telling reversal that sees Alice watch over him at their parting (222). In addition, any potential utility in the White Knight's technological speculations and experiments is totally cancelled out by burlesque and parody.

Carroll's use of the tradition of the exemplary and informational looking-glass books for children combines with his use of the physical looking-glass to create a double ground for reversal in *Through the Looking-Glass*. The imaginative children's literature Alice discovers when she passes through the looking-glass is the logical opposite or reverse of didactic literature. But Alice brings the didactic looking-glass book perspective with her, a fact that shapes her experiences in Looking-Glass Land by complicating her responses to its "indigenous" literature. This combination of looking-glass perspective and imaginative literature functions to make *Through the Looking-Glass* what Grabes calls a fantasy looking-glass book: that is, the process of combining, realized in a series of experiences that unify opposites, reflects Carroll's imagination rather than the facts associated with informational mirrors or the shared sense of acceptable child behaviour reflected in exemplary looking-glasses (63). The fact remains, however, that Carroll uses reversed literary causes (didactic and imaginative children's literature) to produce similar effects in the Alice books, and on this ground the Alice books are united through what amounts to structural mirror imaging. The literary reversals that Carroll uses interplay with a number of instances of other reversals, all working together to suggest that the unity of the Alice books is at least partially the result of mirroring. In Martin Gardner's notes to "Looking-Glass House," he comments on Carroll's characteristic use of "sharp contrast" in the fantasy frames of the Alice books (note 1, 177) and provides a catalogue of "reversals" that result from Carroll's "late addition" of "the looking glass theme" (note 4, 180). The sharp contrasts he cites include the specific date, the season, and the location of the fantasy frames. For instance, Alice is outside in late spring (May 4th) in *Alice in Wonderland* and inside in late fall (November 4th) at the beginning of *Through the Looking-Glass*. These sharp contrasts are, in effect, structural opposites or reversals of each other, and combined with the physical and literary looking-glass, they announce that other reversals will follow.

Other textual evidence supports this suggestion. For example, Alice's entrances into Wonderland and Looking-Glass Land are certainly opposites. In *Alice in Wonderland*, the sleepy Alice fails to discover any pictures or conversations in her sister's book or anything else exciting enough to hold her attention. Finally, she fixes on the passing White Rabbit and is passively plummeted down into Wonderland. In *Through the Looking-Glass*, this passivity is replaced by a very active Alice who works her way into Looking-Glass Land through an elaborate game of didactic "let's pretend." Further, although the reasons for breaking out of the fantasy world are virtually the same in each book, the closing frames can also be seen as reversals. The Wonderland Alice returns to reality, tells her older sister her adventure, and runs off to her tea. It is her sister who relives the adventures in day-dream (locating all the Wonderland creatures and events as simple allegorical extensions of everyday reality) and who envisions Alice, grown into a woman, telling her story to a new generation of children. When Alice leaves Looking-Glass Land, however, she remains the focus of attention and she is hardly carefree. Rather, she is beset by perplexing questions about the fundamental nature of the "reality" she has experienced and invites the reader to share her problem.

Another example of reversal, this time drawn from the fantasy itself, is seen in the turning around of the function of the playing cards in Wonderland and the chess game in Looking-Glass Land. The King, Queen, and Knave of Hearts and the number cards from each of the four suits all originate in a pack of playing cards (and came to Wonderland by way of a mock nursery rhyme that became the real nursery rhyme on which Charles Lamb's fantasy *The King and Queen of Hearts* [1805] was based), but since they do not bring the rules of any specific card game with them, they are only minimally and idiosyncratically associated with rules or order. The heart-suit family gains its prominence from the general monarchical hierarchy of playing cards, and Carroll links the four suits to specific activities suggested by their symbols (the spades are gardeners and the clubs are soldiers, for example). The King and Queen of Hearts exercise their idiosyncratic authority in Wonderland in general and in the trial scene in particular by reducing all order to threat ("Off with her head") and through an arbitrary trial logic that assigns the number 42 to the "oldest rule in the book" (105). The presence of the pack of cards, then, plays no structural role unless it rests in the anti-structure of a game such as "Fifty-two Pickup." (See the scattering of the cards when Alice refuses to be arrested and breaks out of the fantasy.)

The function of the game of chess in *Through the Looking-Glass*, on the other hand, establishes order. The rules controlling the movement of pieces in the game of chess as played on this side of the looking-glass are carried over into Looking-Glass Land and the chess board literally lends the fantasy land its geometrical geography. The chess characters' movements correspond to the game rules: the queens move without directional restriction (which explains the White Queen's sense of living backwards), the knights "wriggle," and Alice as pawn is initially restricted to plodding forward one square at a time. Chess, therefore, not only provides a number of major characters but also lends the fantasy world its structural logic of advance and change. The retention of the rules of the game of chess is the major break with physical reversal in *Through the Looking-Glass* and allies chess with the unaltered imaginative literature found on the other side of the looking-glass, although this literature is indeed the reversal of the didactic literature that preoccupies Alice in the opening frame.

In summary, the tradition of the looking-glass book for children announced in the opening frame of *Through the Looking-Glass* provides an additional ground for reversal that interplays with the physical reversals associated with the material mirror. Carroll's complex manipulation of the tradition that Alice retains even as she passes through it plays an important part both in establishing the nature of the fantasy Alice encounters and in unifying her dual response to it. Further, the opposition evident in the prominence of didactic children's literature in Wonderland and of imaginative children's literature in Looking-Glass Land interacts with a number of other reversals that permeate the Alice books and suggests a basis for their unity, a unity that allows Carroll to complete a circular critique of the child's world and to suggest a wider and richer sense of reality than any achieved in earlier literature for children.

· 6 ·

Dream Vision:
Carroll's Subsuming Form

The last of the three major distorting elements (joining the world upside down and the looking-glass) that contribute to Carroll's fantasy is dream, specifically as developed in the form of the dream vision. To a twentieth-century reader, dream is the most obvious of the elements at work, but it was rarely used in children's literature prior to the Alice books. In the preface to *Sylvie and Bruno* (1889), Carroll emphasizes this fact while noting that the "pattern" he developed in *Alice in Wonderland* some twenty-four years earlier had appeared in "something like a dozen story-books" in the intervening years (241). Two years later, in a diary entry for 11 September 1891, Carroll says that he had purchased a copy of *Mabel in Rhymeland* "as part of the collection I intend making of books of the *Alice* type" (486). At this time he has six books of "the *Alice* type" in his collection.[1] More important than the obvious claim to originality for his work is the suggestion of its formal features reflected in the use of the words "pattern" and "type": Carroll suggests that dream "shapes" *Alice in Wonderland* in addition to providing it with themes and tone. Whether or not Carroll specifically intended to use literary dream vision in the creation of his fantasy, *Alice in Wonderland* and *Through the Looking-Glass and What Alice Found There* are both informed by a number of features common to all dream visions.

The term "dream vision" has been used frequently and with some confusion in criticism of the Alice books. In "Alice's Journey to the End of Night" (1966), for example, Donald Rackin notes "the almost unanimous agreement among modern critics that Alice is a dream-vision," while arguing that this label "turns out to be far more than a matter of technical classification" (392). That Rackin is not using the term to refer specifically to the literary type is clear when he adds, "If it were merely that, one might dismiss the work ... as simply a whimsical excursion into an amusing, childlike world that has little relevance to the central concerns of adult life and little importance in comparison to the obviously 'serious' works that explore these concerns" (392). He is also not using the term as a "technical classification"; rather, he seems to be using it in a catch-all way that defines most of Carroll's imitators, who borrow a form they do not fully understand and who use its components loosely. This is clear when Rackin adds that "if 'dream-vision' is understood as serious thinkers (ranging from mediaeval poets to modern psychologists) have so often understood it, as an avenue to knowledge that is perhaps more meaningful – and frequently more horrifying – than any that the unaided conscious intellect can discover, then it provides an almost perfect description of the very substance of Carroll's masterpiece" (392). Further, it is clearer still in a revised version of his essay (published in *Alice's Adventures in Wonderland and Through the Looking-Glass: Nonsense, Sense, and Meaning*), when Rackin adds "literary" to modify the term in his sentence concerning the views of modern critics cited above (36). But a new confusion arises, since Rackin now seems to be suggesting that "literary dream vision" as a "technical classification" involves works that are "simply ... whimsical, dreamy excursion[s] into an amusing, childlike world" (36). In any event, in both versions of Rackin's generally insightful essay, he takes the path of modern psychology rather than literary form, the path Carroll suggests when he speaks of his pattern and type. It is the pattern or type that is traced in this chapter in order to demonstrate how it may contribute to an understanding of the Alice books.

The argument of this chapter, then, follows Carroll's "formal" suggestion to see where it leads. It differs from prior chapters that simply set Carroll's Alices in the context of earlier children's literature on the basis of textual clues or literary/social history. Although it does present such a context, it also attempts to develop a context that reaches from the form of dream vision used by mediaeval poets to that used in nineteenth-century children's books, including those Carroll saw as imitations of his Alice pattern.

The flaw his imitators introduced into the Carrollian pattern, a pattern they acknowledged borrowing, creates something very close to what Rackin sees as the result of a technical classification – that is, a "whimsical excursion into an amusing, childlike world that has little relevance to the central concerns of adult life" (392). More importantly, this technical classification may miss the central concerns of child life as well as concerns equally relevant to child and adult. Carroll's dream vision is certainly whimsical and amusing, but it is invariably much more, and that "more" results from the use of the distorting elements – the world upside down, the looking-glass book, and the literary form of the dream vision – that Carroll may have picked up out of the "litterature" of the past as it moved from adult into children's books. Also, although it is true, as Rackin suggests, that there is a general agreement that Carroll's fantasies are dream visions, no commentator has concentrated on the Alice books as literary dream visions. William Madden gets close to doing so in "Framing the Alices" (1986), but he only mentions dream vision once, in a very interesting schema about the frame of both books, a frame that begins with and returns to reality through an "outer frame" of lyric verse and prose that wraps around the elements of reality and dream vision, around the waking and sleeping Alice (365). Madden, then, concentrates on the poems that open and close the works, taken together, rather than on the inner structures. Further, he fails to see that the concluding poem returns to a "reality" that is fantastic at its core, and he does not read the sadder possibilities of the line "Life, what is it but a dream?" – a line that may have its source in the round "Row, Row, Row Your Boat" (1851 and 1881). The line seems to verify the suggestion of the "serious question" at the conclusion of the narrative: life may be a general dream that contains everything and dream may not be the property of a particular dreamer.

The features common to the genre of the dream vision include a narrator who falls asleep and experiences in dream the activities of the real people and/or personified abstractions presented in his narrative, a spring setting (May is the common month), and human or animal guides. These are the central features of the description of the genre in both M.H. Abrams's *A Glossary of Literary Terms* (46) and J.A. Cuddon's *A Dictionary of Literary Terms* (204–5). Cuddon also emphasizes the aspect of travel literature that logically makes a guide desirable if not necessary. Both authors use the same examples of the mediaeval dream vision as well as the same examples of the chronological spread that demonstrates the persistence of the form from the seventeenth century (Bunyan's *The Pilgrim's Progress*) through the early nineteenth century (Keats's *The Fall of Hyperion*) and the later part of that century (*Alice in Wonderland*) into the twentieth century (Joyce's *Finnegan's Wake*). Interestingly, *Alice in Wonderland* is only added as an example in late revisions of both books and *Through the Looking-Glass and What Alice Found There* is not mentioned in either. Also, in Abrams's fifth edition of *A Glossary* (1988), he lists but one relevant critical work, *The Allegory of Love* by C.S. Lewis. At about this same time, a great deal of critical attention was paid to the dream vision genre, attention that eventuated in the publication of a number of essays and several books, including *Beginning Well: Framing*

Fictions in Late Middle English Poetry (1988) by Judith Davidoff and *The English Dream Vision: Anatomy of a Form* (1988) by J. Stephen Russell (1988). The following discussion is indebted to insights made by both authors.

The two possible sources for Carroll's expropriation of dream vision for use in fantasy works are the dream visions of the Middle Ages, especially those of Chaucer, and the religious dream vision best illustrated by Bunyan's *The Pilgrim's Progress* but present in lesser works produced in the nineteenth century.

The few examples of dream vision printed for children in the first six decades of the nineteenth century are religious didactic works, perhaps owing to the perennial popularity of *The Pilgrim's Progress*, a facsimile edition of which was part of Carroll's library. Here the anonymous narrator falls asleep and experiences the activities of Christian (and Christiana) Pilgrim and a number of personified abstractions, guided by a number of other personified abstractions across an allegorical landscape setting. Generally, the narrators of dream visions are also the central characters within their dreams, a fact that gives their reports a sense of immediacy and authencity. This is certainly true of Chaucer's narrators in *The Book of the Duchess*, *The House of Fame*, and *The Parliament of Fowls*. Carroll and his imitators all use characters whose actions and thoughts are reported by a narrator who experiences them in dream. Whatever relationships may be suggested concerning the anonymous narrator and Christian and Christiana Pilgrim, the fact remains that he is not a principal player in his own dream, but dreams of a representative pilgrim. Along the way, the moral struggle and landscape parallel elements present in popular folk tales – for example, giants and castles and a long and hazardous journey – elements present in other forms of children's literature. That there are still editions of *The Pilgrim's Progress* published specifically for children is ample evidence of the endurance of Bunyan's work.[2]

In 1820 a religious didactic dream vision entitled *The Child's Dream* presented some of the same issues – the purpose of life, the meaning of death, salvation – from a young child's point of view. The narrative is presented after the fact as the child tells his mother of a dream in which he was led by an angel – "Fair as the queen of May" – beyond the moon, sun, and stars and past mansions in the sky through the pearly gates and into paradise. Here all is changeless:

> No age can tip the head with snow,
>   Nor numbness seize the limbs, mamma
> But vigour doth more vig'rous grow
>   As each up Zion climbs, mamma.

No sickness, death, nor sorrow there,
   To damp their heavenly bliss, mamma
These fruits of sin with sorrow are,
   Deep buried in the abyss, mamma. (7)

Shortly after these generalizations, the religious psychology that motivates the dream vision is given. The child meets his dead sister, Anna, who is now an angel. The burden of loss and the fear of death and its attendant uncertainties that preceded and produced the child's initial unhappiness are replaced by a vision that leads the child to ask to be taught "the happy way / To gain a throne above" (8). This pattern, which moves from an anxiety to the comforting of that anxiety by the use of a core narrative and, as conclusion, to an affirmation of the allaying of anxiety, is the central pattern of dream vision as developed by Davidoff and will be discussed more fully later.

Closer to Carroll's time is the dream vision that his fellow Rugbian, Thomas Hughes, introduces into *Tom Brown's School Days* (1857). Here, Tom's new roommate, George Arthur, falls ill with a fever, an illness that seems to provoke thoughts and fears that are developed in a vision that deals with death and the purpose of life. But predating the surface medical "cause" of George's dream is the death of his father, a minister who died serving his parish during an epidemic. The vision about life's purpose, in which George sees people engaged in significant work on both sides of the river of death separating the transitory present from the eternal future, reassures George that his father's life and death, and in the future his own, have proved and will prove purposeful and worthwhile.

Although Carroll's fantasies have little in common with the tone and theme of religious dream vision (Alice's delayed entrance into the garden may have paradisal suggestiveness), they do share common structural features, such as the dream frame, in which the dreamer's problem is presented, and the dream-core, in which the problem and resolution are worked out. And both Alice books share these features with the dream visions of the Middle Ages, the general form of which Carroll sometimes shares unchanged and sometimes alters by playing it off against formal expectation.

The general nineteenth-century interest in the Middle Ages and the coming of age of literary scholarship that led to the founding of such societies as the Chaucer Society and the Early English Tract Society made such work accessible in editions that seriously attempted to restore the authenticity of the manuscripts. Surely Dodgson, as a professor at Oxford, would have had ample opportunity to know of such work and to read Chaucer's three major dream visions, *The Book of the Duchess, The House of Fame,* and *The Parliament of Fowls.* Whether or not he actually did so is difficult to prove, since works by Chaucer are not gathered in Carroll's library, and Chaucer goes unmentioned in his diaries and letters. Chaucer's works are central as representative dream visions nonetheless, and it is demonstrable that both Alice books share structural and thematic features and, from time to time, the tonality of Chaucer's dream visions.[3] That is to say, Chaucer's uses of the form are generally considered to be representative of it, and Carroll's uses are similar, whether or not he knew Chaucer's works.

The most complete discussion of the overall structure and significance of dream vision available is Judith Davidoff's *Beginning Well: Framing Fictions in Late Middle English Poetry.* Since the following discussion of Carroll's use of dream vision in the Alice books owes a great deal to Davidoff's work, a paraphrase of her description of this form is presented as preface.[4]

Dream vision generally consists of a framing fiction, a prologue, with or without a concluding or "closed" frame, that introduces or wraps around a "core narrative sequence" for which it presents a context. The introductory framing fiction is a brief narrative that presents the physical circumstances leading to sleep and dream in addition to the more important "state of spiritual, psychological, or social distress experienced by the poet-narrator" (61). The dream-core presents a narrative context that facilitates the resolution of this distress by providing a didactic answer to it or otherwise suggesting ways of coming to terms with it. In the closing frame, or "postdream" narrative, the dreamer admits that the dream has provided an alternative method of eliminating distress common to wakeful consciousness. The audience shares in the pattern, since the anxieties that lead to the comforting dream are common to most people (72). There is a great deal of variety in the working out of the form because the dream-core may employ a large number of distinct individual genres or mixed genres, while the unity of "the framing fiction + core structure" may be viewed as "a meta-generic phenomenon," one "that operates on a more basic level, independent of overt literary types" (73). Common to most dream visions, however, there is a "movement from ignorance and need to knowledge and comfort, or else [there is] a parody of it" (72). The reversal through parody, Davidoff says, presupposes that the audience recognizes the pattern.[5]

How do the Alice books work in relation to this pattern, a pattern Carroll acknowledged and found in a number of later fantasies that, he justifiably believed, had borrowed it from him? *Alice in Wonderland* fits both the catalogue of literary handbook features common to dream vision (the narrator or central figure who falls asleep and experiences a "reality" that differs from the everyday, the seasonal setting, the guide) and, more importantly, the more sophisticated description of the features and the pattern of "Dream-Vision Framing Fictions" presented by Davidoff. *Through the Looking-Glass and What Alice Found There* also fits that pattern, but with the proviso that it may parody the essential movement of that form in a powerful and destructive way.

In *Alice in Wonderland,* the opening frame introduces a May setting and a character who falls asleep and in dream follows an animal guide, the White Rabbit, into another world. Immediately preceding this action, Alice is presented as restless and bored, a condition that even adults, who have access to and control of more possible remedies, have trouble controlling. Boredom was a lifelong enemy of Carroll's that he identifies as the source of troubles in key places. Ennui is pictured, together with gloom, spite, and woe, etc., as one of the ill-spirits against which tales, poetry, fun, riddles, and jokes create an umbrella of protection in Carroll's early *The Rectory Umbrella* (1850), and it is noted in the introduction to *Pillow Problems* (1893) as a condition that allows sceptical, blasphemous and unholy thoughts to form (xv). In an attempt to alleviate her boredom, Alice peeps at the book her older sister is reading, only to find it wanting in that it contains no pictures or conversations.

This reference to books is neither random nor without later consequences and matches to a degree Chaucer's use of books in *The Book of the Duchess, The House of Fame,* and *The Parliament of Fowls.* In Chaucer's dream visions, however, the narrators attempt to use books as ways of dealing with their inability to sleep (for causes that begin to become clear as the narratives develop), whereas Alice attempts to use them to gain a focus that will keep her happily awake. The narrator in the frame of *The Book of the Duchess* says he has had insomnia for eight years (1.37) and that he had been reading Ovid's story of Ceyx and Alcione from the *Metamorphosis* as a potential soporific. This story of the final acceptance of the death of a beloved includes the character Morpheus, who is awakened and sent to find and enter the body of drowned King "Seys" to prove his death to his widow Alcione and, thereby, to end her anxiety and to initiate the healing power of grieving. The story is obviously related to the narrator's dream. That dream is dominated by his meeting with the Man in Black, who is locked in grief over the loss of his wife (a reversal of the Ovid story), whom he has lost to Death in a game of chess.

This otherwise "adult" dream parallels Alice's dream in several key ways. The dream-core contains several genres, including the world turned upside down – introduced in the Man in Black's long catalogue of the reversals of his feelings connected with his wife's death (11.558–649) – a form introduced by Alice in her second and final attempt to guess her destination as she falls into Wonderland (10–11). Further, the impact of Ovid's story alters the narrator's state from a flat inability to distinguish sorrow from joy in the introductory frame to a concern that motivates the writing of the verse narrative that is the dream vision just read, demonstrating an acute emotional change. Recent Chaucer criticism (for example, that of J. Stephen Russell in *The English Dream Vision*) argues that the narrator must break through the emotionally retarding use of conventions such as those of dream vision itself in order to reach an authentic sense of the Man in Black's suffering. Russell is certainly right about the original obtuseness of the narrator, evident in his conventional feeling and expression of grief. Both of these must be broken through before he can truly feel for the grief of the Man in Black. This is not accomplished until the end of the story when the grieving man's bald statement of the source of his grief finally ellicites the narrator's recognition: "Is that youre los? Be God, hyt is routhe!" (1310, 279). Chaucer both uses and undercuts the form and expectations of dream vision. The conventional raising and allaying of distress proves to be emotionally facile according to Russell. In *Through the Looking-Glass*, Carroll also uses the form while disallowing the conventional resolution that belies the dark suggestions of Alice's final vision of reality.

When Alice wakes from Wonderland she feels joyful, not bored, and runs off to tea after telling her sister what she has experienced. Her older sister then re-experiences Alice's dream (as a day-dream allegory very like the standard dream vision) and foresees Alice telling many stories, including her own strange dream, to other children. Thus, the original motivating distress – a painful boredom that disallows creativity and growth – is translated to creative energy through the narrative of the dream-core. This transformation seems to belie the "facts" of Alice's dream, a dream that includes pain as well as wonder in an oxymoronic fusion of the antipathies/antipodes experienced in the upside-down vision of child/adult relationships. After all, Alice had only a brief moment earlier exited a dream turned to nightmare, accurately interpreting the Queen of Heart's "Sentence first – verdict afterwards" as "Stuff and nonsense" and challenging the playing cards sent to arrest her (108, 109). And, throughout her dream, the purportedly comforting didactic books she has committed to memory are, when her need for their help is greatest, turned over and stripped of their expected significance and usefulness through parody.

Going even further along the line of development of nightmare, the order suggested by the presence of monarchy (the Heart family) and a governness (the Duchess) in the waking world is totally reversed in Wonderland, in which the Queen's repeated formulaic threat "Off with _____'s head" and the Duchess's constant moral interpretation of Wonderland reality in

"And the moral of that is" are undercut through parody. Even the several guides (all drawn out of nature) who inform Alice provide little or no consistency. The Caterpillar may finally teach her, however momentarily, to control her size lest she unintentionally offend those she meets, but it is while she is with it that she totally reverses Southey's generational message in "You are old, Father William" (43–4). One of the most potentially terrifying brief passages in *Alice in Wonderland* occurs early in "A Mad Tea-Party" when the Dormouse stops an argument Alice had started by positing that "to say what you mean" is the same thing as "to mean what you say" (61). The brief flurry of like-constructed rhetorical chiasma attacking her argument ends with the Dormouse's "You might just as well say ... that 'I breathe when I sleep' is the same thing as 'I sleep when I breathe'!" (61). The Hatter's consider-the-source answer to what the seemingly sleeping Dormouse says (an *ad hominem* argument that attempts to dodge the central issue) takes the potentially universal sting out of his suggestion that life is all dream, a sting developed more fully in *Through the Looking-Glass and What Alice Found There*.

Carroll employs the subsuming pattern of the dream vision, wrapping it around a number of other formal and thematic features to hold them together, while simultaneously attacking any suggestion of the facile use made of it by Alice's sister. The totality created by the opening and concluding framing fictions holds together a dream-core that contains parody, satire, burlesque, the world turned upside down, informational literature, rational/moral literature, game logic, nursery rhyme, and the like, and mixtures of these genres. All of these produce a Wonderland that at once compels attention through the "curious" and repels it through accompanying pain. The pun that introduced antipodes as antipathies, for instance, creates a union of the antipathetic that banishes Alice's boredom. Alice's concluding "joy" is based on her coming to terms with a reality made up of the interlocked wonder and pain of the story she has lived through; it is a merited joy. Her sister misinterprets both Alice's dream and its significance when she reduces it to day-dream.

Alice in Wonderland, then, combines the features of dream vision as fully as Chaucer's *The Book of the Duchess* – the May setting, the guide(s), a narrator (in this case what Henry James calls a centre of consciousness) who falls asleep and experiences a world of personified abstractions, all become the story told, following the pattern of an initial anxiety introduced in the opening frame, the resolution of that anxiety by the potentially various genres used in the narrative(s) of the dream-core, and finally a presentation of that altered physical, psychic, or spiritual state in the closing frame. And just as Chaucer's book both uses and critiques its very form and the conventions it employs to come to an understanding of a more complex and authentic reality, so does *Alice in Wonderland* in a concluding frame that undercuts the conventionality of the allegorical nature of the form as it is developed by Alice's sister.

Carroll's suggestion concerning works that arise allegorically from the half-in/half-out nature of day-dream or that simply borrow the conventions of the dream vision without giving the pattern a sense of particularity and urgency is totally appropriate when the works of the "Alice type" he lists are considered. These works invariably mimic the pattern of dream vision in the Alice books in that they present opening and closing framing fictions that enclose dream-cores, but the physical, spiritual, or psychic anxieties introduced in the frames are unclear or trivial or are not altered through interaction with the narrative(s) of the dream-cores.

In an introductory note to *Elsie's Expedition*, a work published in 1874, only three years after *Through the Looking-Glass*, Frederick Weatherly admits Carroll's influence. Weatherly says his book would not have been written without Carroll's earlier work as model and adds that it imitates "a successful style of Nursery Literature" while hopefully avoiding the charge of plagiarism from "impartial Readers." Weatherly's work opens with Elsie reading a book so large that it covers her legs "like a couple of wee mice in a trap" (1). While the book cages in her attention, she is irritated by the fact that the door of an illustrated train station is closed. Finally, she gets up with great difficulty and, with "pins and needles" in her legs, forces the station door open. Once in the station and on the train, Elsie discovers that the imaginative games she has played with her mother help her along. For example, imaginary money buys her a ticket to "there and back again," and several pieces of fruit pass for her luggage. The characters Elsie meets on her expedition are residents of nursery rhymes, including Little Boy Blue, Little Jack Horner, and the Knave of Hearts, but their nursery rhyme activities and settings are extended. For example, Little Jack Horner is now Mr John Horner, a character grown old and a bit irascible from performing the same plum-pulling act forever. The alterations in the stories of the nursery rhyme figures are related to Elsie's break through the physical barrier of the book the wakeful Elsie was reading, an accomplishment brought about by her active creative participation. Finally, Elsie herself becomes a figure submerged in a magical well, created half of "Ding Dong Bell" ("A Solemn Dirge") and half of Ariel's "Full Fathom Five" from Shakespeare's *The Tempest*. Alas, this wonderful experience is broken when the ding-donging bell becomes the intrusive dinner bell that pulls Elsie slowly and almost begrudgingly back into waking reality.

Although this dream vision cleverly juxtaposes the passive joy of reading a book with the even greater active joy of creating or extending existing narratives, the framing fiction lacks the important element of an accompanying anxiety addressed and alleviated by the comforting dream-core. Further, unlike the effect of joy realized by Alice in the closing frame, Elsie's return to reality is something of a letdown, for the "lesson" that alleviates anxiety in the dream-core does not transcend her dream expedition.

The bookish consciousness of the possibilities of amusement and delight in dream vision among those books listed by Carroll is emphasized most fully in *Our Trip to Blunderland: or, Grand Excursion to Blundertown and Back* by "Jambon" (1890).[6] This book not only acknowledges its debt to Carroll ("Long live Carrollus Le Wis!") but borrows Alice as a character for its opening frame. Here the three young heroes – Norval, Jacques, and Ranulf – have been reading about Alice "and the strange, funny things she saw and did when fast asleep" (2) and pondering how they could arrange a trip to a similar place. Although Norval rightfully points out that Alice only knew that she had been asleep after waking, the boys are not discouraged and actually conjure up Alice in order to ask her how she made her trip. Alice never answers explicitly, but her very presence makes the boys more creative in their own efforts. Soon Norval remembers having accompanied a friend to the Aquarium with passes given to them by his friend's uncle. He hurriedly composes a pass to Wonderland and gets Alice to sign it. Following several more pages about the boys' frustration as they try to will their way into Wonderland, they finally fall asleep, but they find themselves in Blunderland rather than Wonderland owing to Norval's error in printing the pass. This dreamland, created by a combination of past fantasy and mistake, mirrors Wonderland (there is a train ride and the boys find themselves in a world turned upside down, etc.), but it never escapes the simple level of amusement, since it merely mimes dream vision structure and lacks the depth associated with the pattern that ends with the successful alleviation of anxiety.

The most readily accessible and perhaps the best of the imitative books that Carroll lists is Maggie Browne's *Wanted – a King, or How Merle Set the Nursery Rhymes to Rights* (1890). The opening framing fiction certainly follows the pattern, as it presents Merle's physical and psychic anxiety about recovering from a bad tumble taken some two months earlier. Although doctors have reassured Merle that she will regain her total body use, the bed-bound Merle still suffers from pains that she can only alleviate by looking at a screen displaying illustrations of a great number of nursery rhymes. A moment before Merle falls asleep, she stares at the screen illustration of the singularly appropriate tumbling "Jack and Jill" while singing the rhyme. She is then interrupted by a visit from her crotchety old Uncle Grossiter, who would "like to burn all the silly nursery rhyme books" (221). While arguing with Grossiter, Merle chooses "Little Bo-peep" to defend the rhymes, and she repeats and reverses lines from this rhyme while she crosses over into dream.

At the turnstile into Endom (the land of her dream) Merle meets the evil Grunter Grim, who tells her that admission necessitates checking one's body outside (a ruse used to insure that no actual child returns to govern or to help restore the proper governor of Endom, as predicted). Merle, however, with the help of the tree sprite, Topleaf, and the East Wind, flies into Endom intact. Once there she soon finds that things are not quite right and that this is owing to the fact that Grunter Grim has replaced the true king of Endom and forced the nursery rhyme characters into troubled conditions and dire straits: for example, Jack Horner seems to be a conceited lad who judges his own activity with the statement "What a good boy am I," when in fact what he had originally (and quite humbly) said was "To be a good boy I'll try" (231). It is just so with the fates of all the other rhymes: the rhymes were never meant to be uncouth or to contain violence, and their proper development will be regained with the restoration of the true ruler of Endom. Finally, Baby Bunting is made ruler, and the Rhyme Fairy returns to banish Grunter Grim to live in the world, to "live with the people who call Nursery Rhymes nonsense" (305). The allegorical nature of this dream vision is underscored when Uncle Grossiter's voice is confused with that of Grunter Grim at the story's end. Oddly, however, although Endom gets a new ruler and the rhymes are reformed, Merle is still concerned about a character from her dream, Thomas Muriel, who never got his right body back after the confusion resulting from surrendering it under Grunter Grim's regime. Although the land of rhymes is set to rights in the dream-core, this restoration has done little to comfort Merle's anxiety about regaining the use of her body. Further, given the defeat of nonsense in the rhymes and the restoration of events that are quite orderly and straightforward, even old Uncle Grossiter could no longer take offence and call the rhymes silly. Dream vision has failed to allay anxiety and has been used to rationally support reform and to sanitize nursery rhymes.

Carroll's sense that the pattern he worked out in *Alice in Wonderland* was imitated in a number of succeeding fantasies is certainly correct, but it is equally true that none of the imitations uses the form as powerfully and as carefully as he did in his first Alice book. Alice's anxiety concerning her inability to handle boredom is assuaged by the fact that she wins her way through the frequently painful but forever curious world of Wonderland, and when she is returned to waking reality, her happiness not only is restored but has increased.[7] But what of the function of dream vision in *Through the Looking-Glass and What Alice Found There*?

Boredom is also Alice's major problem at the beginning of *Through the Looking-Glass* (she is housebound on a cold and snowy November afternoon six months to the day after her trip to Wonderland), but a slightly older Alice, schooled more fully in moral and informational didacticism, consciously attempts to alleviate her boredom by linking "let's pretend" to her didactic predisposition in order to create a game or two. Unlike the rapid fall into Wonderland following Alice's discovery that her sister's book has no pictures or conversations, Alice slowly feels her way into Looking-Glass Land. The introductory framing fiction shows Alice attempting to use her kitten as a ticket into play. Her first game with the kitten is verbal, as she means to "tell [it] all [its] faults" (125). Following a catalogue of three of the kitten's faults and a threat about future appropriate punishment, Alice's attention turns to the chessboard and, finally, to her sense that her kitten should be able to do a fine imitation of the Red Queen. But Alice soon discovers that Kitty "wouldn't fold its arms properly" and, as punishment, holds it up to the mirror so it can see how sulkily it is behaving, saying " 'And if you're not good directly … I'll put you through into Looking-Glass House. How would you like *that?* " (127).[8] Soon Alice's attention turns totally to the possibility of passing through the looking-glass, of working her way through the altering composition of the glass, as it turns first to a soft gauze and then to a "sort of mist" (127) and, finally, to a "bright silvery mist" that melts away and allows the completion of Alice's passage (128).

The didactic introduction of *Through the Looking-Glass* clashes tellingly with the straightforward use of nursery rhyme, lullaby, romance, and other imaginative forms in the dream-core (compare this with the parodic transformation of didactic work in Wonderland) largely owing to the fact that Alice enters Looking-Glass Land with her this-worldly perspective intact. As argued in chapter 5, which dealt with the function of the tradition of the looking-glass book in Carroll's fantasy, Alice's retention of her didactic perspective makes it impossible for her to react to imaginative literature on its own terms. The consistent use of physical and literary inversion owing to the looking-glass and the looking-glass book lends the dream-core its logic, a logic partially played out on a chessboard topography where a number of movements, including going backward in order to go forward, are possible. The certitude and in some cases smugness of the didacticism that the framing-fiction Alice is imbued with are attacked throughout the dream-core, especially since this didacticism does not answer problems raised by the structure and themes of Looking-Glass Land.

In *Alice in Wonderland*, the meta-generic pattern, moving from anxiety to the cessation of anxiety, is certainly at work, even though there may well be a warning about making this pattern too facile in Alice's sister's attempt at a day-dream duplication of her story. The dream vision structure of *Through the Looking-Glass* is a reversal of *Alice in Wonderland*. The control Alice exercises in the opening framing fiction of *Through the Looking-Glass* results from a combination of play and moral and informational didacticism and continues briefly even after Alice passes through into Looking-Glass House. For example, in her transitional state, the comparatively gigantic and invisible Alice is the player who at first watches and then jokingly intervenes in the movements of the White King and Queen. But after a short stay in Looking-Glass Land and her discovery (and the reader's) that she has retained her original perspective – she must hold the "Looking-glass book" up to the mirror to read it (134) – Alice is rapidly demoted from player to pawn and sets out on an inexorably forward, one plodding move after the other, path until her queening. Compare all this with Alice's entrance and itinerary as she travels through Wonderland. As said above, Alice follows a White Rabbit until she falls into Wonderland; she does not actively participate in working her way in, as she does by passing through the mirror into Looking-Glass House. In *Alice in Wonderland*, there is no logic of advance, no pawn on the chessboard, no specific game of cards, no race with a start and finish line. The "game" engaged in, if it can be called such, has more to do with Alice's increasing commitment to try to maintain an equilibrium, physical as well as social, that will upset neither others nor herself. With the help of the Caterpillar's advice and her own desire for balance, Alice escapes from her unconscious solecisms, which arise from her inexperience and which understandably bother others. It is only at the trial that Alice's renewed growth causes her trouble, and she now defends it when she says, "I can't help it, I'm growing" (99). After this acceptance, Alice is able to reject as irregular the King of Heart's attempt to impose Rule Forty-two as the "oldest rule in the book," and to characterize the Queen of Heart's attempt to reverse sentence and verdict as "stuff and nonsense" (108). Finally, totally in control, she calls the cards sent to arrest her exactly what they are – "Who cares for *you*? ... You're nothing but a pack of cards!" – which turns out to be her exit line from Wonderland (109).

In Looking-Glass Land, Alice's movements are initially confused, as she discovers that she must go backward to go forward; but once she begins her journey across the chessboard, the logic governing the pawn's advance from square to square controls her movements. Owing to her didactic perspective, however, she cannot understand the nature of the compelling imaginative literatures, especially nursery rhyme, at work within the squares. Her pawn status finally disrupts the dreamy communion with the Fawn (note the punning rhyme of names: they are more similar than dissimilar, yet fear enters through the phonetic difference between "f" and "p") in the woods with no name. Although Alice's tutoring by the White and Red Queens is virtually methodical compared with the hit-and-miss bits of aphorism and disconnected "wisdom" she receives in Wonderland and although she is able to survive and, sometimes, thrive on both her "official" tutoring and what she learns from Humpty Dumpty and the other nursery rhyme and romance characters, Alice is finally forced to exit Looking-Glass Land. And this at the very moment of her celebration of mastery, her Queening Banquet, at the end of which she does nothing so orderly as her dismissal of the pack of cards, but screams an agonizing "I ca'n't stand this any longer!" (238) before pulling the tablecloth out from under the chaos created by the artificialism that brings the entire banquet table to squirming, and confused, and aggressive, life (238). So Alice's dream ends with her grasping the shrunken Red Queen and threatening to shake it "into a kitten" (239).

As the awakening Alice shakes the Red Queen back to her kitten, she should be consoled by what appears to be a facile and complete allegorical transformation; but Alice remains adamantly didactic, and instead of retelling the story and running off to tea and play, she insists first on trying to elaborate one-to-one allegorical relationships – so kitten was the Red Queen and Snowdrop the White Queen and Dinah, less surely, Humpty Dumpty (242–3). And, finally and fittingly for the didactic Alice, she wants to take yet a further meta-step outside or away from her painful adventure to discover its source: "Now, Kitty, let's consider who it was that dreamed it all. This is a serious question, my dear … You see, Kitty, it *must* have been either me or the Red King. He was part of my dream, of course – but then I was part of his dream, too!" (244). This pondering on dream obviously links back to Tweedledum's terrifying "If that there King was to wake … you'd go out – bang! – just like a candle!" (168). "A serious question," indeed, and one that widens out to the narrator's incorporation of the reader in "Which do *you* think it was?" (244) before widening still further into the framing poem. Here the narrator/poet momentarily plays the part of Alice's older sister and envisions a situation in which "Children yet, the tale to hear, / Eager eye and willing ear, / Lovingly shall nestle near" (245). But this cosy description of the relationship between hearer and teller fast gives way to an emphasis on dream and a widening possibility bluntly stated in "Life,

what is it but a dream?" – a possibility that displaces significance, the
very stuff of the didactic, with a something else, a possibility that frequently
plagued Carroll himself. There is more than "a shadow of a sigh" that trem-
bles through Looking-Glass Land (see introductory poem, 116).

The meta-generic pattern of *Alice in Wonderland,* a generally conventional shaping whereby the dream-core narrative alleviates the anxiety of
the opening frame and the closing frame recapitulates and affirms that pattern, is reversed in *Through the Looking-Glass.* Alice does not feel anxious at
the outset of this fantasy, for she has learned to combine didacticism and
play to defeat boredom. She is, far from being anxious, rather overly confi-
dent about where she is and what she is doing. The dream-core that grafts
unaltered imaginative literature onto the rules governing the movements of
chess pieces creates a hybrid in which Alice is concerned, caring, and terri-
fied from moment to moment or all at the same time, forcing her to remain
imaginatively alert even though her didacticism generally and ultimately
persists.

From the moment that Alice steps onto the chessboard and becomes a
pawn, she is both tutored and examined by the zanily didactic Red and
White Queens, who, oxymoronically, simultaneously irritate and attract
Alice. The mirror inversions these characters represent and attempt to pass
on to Alice, inversions in which the King's Messenger is jailed, found
guilty, and tried (175) and in which the White Queen bleeds, screams in
pain, and pricks her finger with a pin (176), are very like the "sentence first
– verdict afterwards" logic Alice had rejected before leaving Wonderland.
But in Looking-Glass Land the didactic Alice initially becomes more tolerant of logics that deviate from those of the waking world, so tolerant that
she allows the Queen's characterization of this-worldly memory as inferior,
since it is "a poor sort of memory that only works backwards" (175). Finally, the only three figures Alice warms up to in Looking-Glass Land are
the didactic but comically flawed White and Red Queens and the White
Knight, who cannot sit a horse and whose inventiveness is at its best, as he
himself says, when he is turned unceremoniously on his head (216). It
is these characters Alice comforts and guides as she nears, and after she
achieves, her own queening. This reversal of child/adult roles is especially
poignant in Alice's parting scene with the White Knight and in the lullaby
scene with the Red and White Queens. Here, after the Red Queen teaches
Alice the words to the lullaby, Alice sings it, and each queen falls asleep
leaning against her choice of Alice's shoulders (230). Alice's tolerance of
experiences that deviate from her own in the dream-core helps her deal
with the piecemeal disintegration of the comforting but stultifying didactic
surety of the opening frame.

Oddly, Alice never warms up to the characters from nursery rhymes, characters fated to behave in certain ways because they are generically controlled by their literary contexts and play out, over and over again, narratives that are unavoidable. The rhymes, unlike the didactic poems that dominate Wonderland until Alice upends them through unconscious parody, are presented unaltered. It is, generally, the rhyme characters – Tweedledum and Tweedledee, Humpty Dumpty, and the Lion and the Unicorn – that Alice finds the most unsettling, partially because she can do nothing to alter their fates and partially because they terrify or discomfort her with their theories and pronouncements. Humpty Dumpty totally undercuts didacticism by presenting a theory of language that is idiosyncratic and asocial; Tweedledum makes Alice indignant when he hurtfully suggests that her very identity is contingent on the Red King's dream (168); and the Unicorn interrupts the Lion's weary game of twenty questions ("Are you animal – or vegetable – or mineral?") leading towards the establishment of Alice's identity when he cries out, "It's a fabulous monster!" (206), taking the line straight out of Alice's mouth.

It is interesting that Alice is concerned about dream even within her dream, and that she questions the nature of her experiences in the entire episode with the Anglo-Saxon Messenger and the Lion and the Unicorn, momentarily verifying the experiences as "reality" solely on the ground of the presence of the great dish that had held the problematic plum-cake, and just as rapidly undercutting herself with the possibility that "we're all part of the same dream" (209) (an eighteenth- and nineteenth-century bugaboo in idealist theory), a possibility that upsets her and forces her to reassert the dream as "[her] dream, and not the Red King's!" (209).

The major change in Carroll's use of the dream vision in *Through the Looking-Glass and What Alice Found There* is the reversal of the metageneric pattern employed in *Alice in Wonderland*. The certitude that accompanied Alice's didacticism in the opening frame dissolves throughout the dream-core, allowing her to entertain, however painfully, the possibility of a larger and more complex reality. The closing frame is intimately related to the dream-core, not in the sense that it affirms the defeat of any particular physical, psychological, or spiritual anxieties, but in the sense that it affirms the decrease of didactic certainty and suggests the necessity of continuing to develop even though one is governed by limitation. Finally, the fact that the dream-core is a consistently developed piece of mirror or looking-glass vision, suggests that the conventional pattern has been inverted. When the Alice books are considered side by side, there is a strong suggestion that they are two sides of a complete vision, one that holds oppositions together to create a curious unity. The comprehensive structural nature of the dream vision, with its opening- and closing-frame narratives and a dream-core capable of including any number of genres, helps to balance thousands of elements within a recognizable pattern. Further, it allows Alice to grow by widening her sense of reality.

Appendices

Contents

The appendices contain both complete examples and important parts of representative works from children's literature from the middle of the seventeenth to the end of the nineteenth centuries that provide a context for Carroll's Alice books. Some of this material is available in other publications, but the greater number of works are difficult to find and have never been brought together in relation to Carroll's fantasies. Works readily available, such as "Wanted a King," are not included.

All of the sources and analogues have been used as part of my critical argument in the body of the book. They are arranged here in groups that correspond with individual chapters of the book, providing readers the opportunity to read material cited in the last five chapters, an opportunity seldom provided in studies that consider Carroll's Alice books.

APPENDIX I (CHAPTER 2):
REPRESENTATIVE SPECIFIC SOURCES
AND ANALOGUES

APPENDIX 2 (CHAPTER 3):
REPRESENTATIVE WORKS ILLUSTRATING
THE CLASH BETWEEN DIDACTIC AND
IMAGINATIVE CHILDREN'S LITERATURE

APPENDIX 3 (CHAPTER 4):
REPRESENTATIVE "WORLD UPSIDE DOWN"
BOOKS FROM 1750 TO 1890

APPENDIX 4 (CHAPTER 5):
REPRESENTATIVE LOOKING-GLASS BOOKS
FROM 1673 TO THE 1870s

APPENDIX 5 (CHAPTER 6):
SOME NINETEENTH-CENTURY DREAM VISIONS

Appendix 1
(Chapter 2)
Representative Specific Sources and Analogues

Ann Taylor, excerpt from *The Wedding Among the Flowers*
(London: Darton and Harvey, 1808).

This book, as Ann Taylor confessed in her *Autobiography* (vol. 2, 169), was written in the context of the commercial success of William Roscoe's *The Butterfly's Ball and the Grasshopper's Feast* (1807) and the great rush of imitative books it produced: "[*The Butterfly's Ball* ...] became so popular as to produce numerous imitations much below the original, and my ambition being stirred, I entered the field, pen in hand, with 'A Wedding Among the Flowers.'" Unlike the talking flowers in Tennyson's *Maud*, talking flowers that are psychological projections of the narrator's emotional state, Taylor's flowers have a life of their own, however anthropomorphic. It is finally Carroll who has the gift to make talking flowers that are neither human projections nor humanized, but have a true life of their own, complete with their own reasons for a sense of superiority. The copy of this book at the British Library is a typescript sent there in 1914 by the illustrator's (Isaac Taylor's) son.

> In a grand convocation which Flora enacted,
> Where the bus'ness of all her domain was transacted,
> 'Twas hinted, there yet remained one regulation
> To perfect her glorious administration.
> To some, strength and masculine beauty were given,
> Magestical air and an eye meeting heav'n;

Hidden virtues to many, to others perfume,
Through each variation of sweetness and bloom:
'Twas therefore suggested, with Flora's compliance,
To unite ev'ry charm in some splendid alliance
– The royal assent to the notion was gained,
'Twas passed at three sittings, and duly ordain'd.

'Twas now most amusing to traverse the shade,
And hear the remarks that were privately made:
Such whispers, enquiries, and investigations!
Such balancing merits, and marshalling stations.
The nobles protested they never would yield
To debase their high sap with the weeds of the field;
For, indeed, there was nothing so vulgar and rude,
As to let ev'ry ill-bred young wildflower intrude:
Their daughters should never dishonour their houses,
By taking such rabble as these as their spouses!

At length, my Lord Sunflower, whom public opinion
Confess'd as the pride of the blooming dominion,
Avow'd an affection he'd often betray'd,
For sweet Lady Lily, the queen of the shade,
And said, should her friends or the public withstand,
He would dare to solicit her elegant hand.

A whisper like that which on fine summer eves
Young zephyrs address to the frolicsome leaves,
Immediately ran through the whole congregation,
Expressive of pleasure and high approbation.

No line was degraded, no family pride
Insulted, by either bridegroom or bride;
For in him was all majesty, beauty, and spendor,
In her all was elegant, simple, and tender.

Now nothing remained but to win her consent,
And Miss Iris, her friend, as the messenger went,
The arts of entreaty and argument trying,
Till at length she returned and announc'd her complying.
Complete satisfaction the tidings convey'd,
And whispers and smiles dimpled over the shade.

... There was one city lady, indeed, that the bride
Did not wish to attend, which was Miss London Pride;
And his Lordship declar'd he would rather not meet
So doubtful a person as young Bitter Sweet ...
And though he was sent for, Narcissus declin'd
Out of pique, and preferred to keep sulking behind;
For, having beheld his fine form in the water,
He thought himself equal to any flow'rs daughter;
And would not consent to increase a parade,
The hero of which, he himself should have made.

... My Lady Carnation, excessively dashing
Roug'd highly, and new in the Rotterdam fashion,
Discoursing of rank and pedigree came,
With a beau of distinction, Van Tulip by name.

Isaac Watts, excerpts from *Divine Songs Attempted in Easy Language for the Use of Children* (London, 1715).

Included are the book's preface, the author's introduction to the "Moral Songs," and the poems Carroll parodies: "Against Idleness and Mischief" and "The Sluggard." These poems were never out of print from 1715 throughout the nineteenth century. As Watts makes clear in his introductory comments, they were meant to be memorized and recited or sung for fun as well as to help at moments of spiritual duress. A later literary use demonstrates that the spiritual use was still going on during the education of James Joyce's Stephen Daedalus, whose Aunt Dante recites a very Wattsian poem on page 2 of *Portrait of the Artist as a Young Man* (cf. Watts's "On Obedience to Parents"). Watts's preface is an interesting rationale for memorization.

PREFACE,

EDUCATION OF CHILDREN.

MY FRIENDS,

IT is an awful and important charge that is committed to you. The wisdom and welfare of the succeeding generation are intrusted with you beforehand, and depend much on your conduct. The seeds of misery or happiness in this world, and that to come, are oftentimes sown very early; and therefore whatever may conduce to give the minds of children a relish for virtue and religion, ought, in the first place, to be proposed to you.

Verse was first designed for the service of God, though it has been wretchedly abused since. The ancients, among the Jews and the Heathens, taught their children and disciples the precepts of morality and worship in verse. The children of Israel were commanded to learn the words of the Song of Moses, Deut. xxxi. 19, 20, and we are directed in the New Testament, not only to sing with grace in the heart, but to teach and admonish one another by hymns and songs, Ephes. v. 19. and there are these four advantages in it:

I. There is great delight in the very learning of truths and duties in this way. There is something so amusing and entertaining in rhymes and metre, that will incline children to make this part of their business a diversion. And you may turn their very duty into a reward, by giving them the privilege of learning one of these songs every week, if they fulfil the business of the week well, and promising them the book itself when they have learnt ten or twenty songs out of it.

II. What is learnt in verse is longer retained in memory, and sooner recollected. The like sounds, and the like number of syllables exceedingly assist the remembrance. And it may often happen that the end of a song, running in the mind, may be an effectual means to keep off some temptations, or to incline to some duty when a word of scripture is not upon their thoughts.

III. This will be a constant furniture for the minds of children, that they may have something to think upon when alone, and sing over to themselves. This may sometimes give their thoughts a divine turn, and raise a young meditation. Thus they will not be forced to seek relief for an emptiness of mind, out of the loose and dangerous sonnets of the age.

IV. These Divine Songs may be a pleasant and proper matter for their daily or weekly worship to sing one in the family, at such time as the parents or governors shall appoint, and therefore I have confined the verse to the most usual psalm tunes.

The greatest part of this little book was composed several years ago, at the request of a friend, who had been long engaged in the work of catechising a very great number of children, of all kinds, and with abundant skill and succees. So that you will find here nothing that savours of party; the children of high and low degree, of the church of England dissenters, baptized in infancy or not, may all join together in these songs. And as I have endeavoured to sink the language to the level of a child's understanding, and yet to keep it, if possible, above contempt, so I have designed to profit all, if possible, and offend none. I hope the more general the sense is, these composures may be of the more universal use and service.

I have added, at the end, some attempts of sonnets, on moral subjects, for children, with an air of pleasantry, to provoke some fitter pen to write a little book of them.

May the Almighty God make you faithful in this important work of education: may he succeed your cares with his abundant grace, that the rising generation of the British Empire may be a glory among the nations, a pattern to the christian world, and a blessing to the earth.

SONG XX.

AGAINST IDLENESS AND MISCHIEF.

How doth the little busy bee
Improve each shining hour,
And gather honey all the day
From every opening flower.

How skilfully she builds her cell!
How neat she spreads the wax!
And labours hard to store it well
With the sweet food she makes.

In works of labour or of skill,
I would be busy too;
For Satan finds some mischief still
For idle hands to do.

In books, or works, or healthful play,
Let my first years be past;
That I may give for every day
Some good account at last.

A SLIGHT SPECIMEN OF

MORAL SONGS,

SUCH AS I WISH SOME HAPPY AND CONDESCENDING
GENIUS WOULD UNDERTAKE FOR THE USE OF
CHILDREN, AND PERFORM MUCH BETTER.

THE sense and subjects might be borrowed plentifully from the Proverbs of Solomon, from all the common appearances of nature, from all occurrences in civil life, both in city and country; (which would also afford matter for other Divine Songs.) Here the language and measures should be easy and flowing with cheerfulness, with or without the solemnities of religion, or the sacred names of God and holy things; that children might find delight and profit together.

This would be one effectual way to deliver them from the temptation of loving or learning those idle, wanton, or profane songs, which give so early an ill taint to the fancy and memory; and become the seeds of future vices.

SONG I.

THE SLUGGARD.

'Tis the voice of a sluggard; I hear him
    complain,
"You have wak'd me too soon, I must
    slumber again;"
As the door on its hinges, so he on his bed,
Turns his sides and his shoulders, and his
    heavy head.

" A little more sleep, and a little more slum-
    ber;"
Thus he wastes half his days, and his hours
    without number;
And when he gets up, he sits folding his
    hands,
Or walks about sauntering, or trifling he
    stands;

I pass'd by his garden, and saw the wild brier,
The thorn and the thistle grow broader and
    higher;
The clothes that hang on him are turning to
    rags;
And his money still wastes, till he starves or
    he begs.

I made him a visit still hoping to find
He had took better care for improving his
    mind;
He told me his dreams, talk'd of eating and
    drinking,
But he scarce reads his Bible, and never loves
    thinking.

Said I then to my heart, "Here's a lesson
    for me;
That man's but a picture of what I might be.
But thanks to my friends for their care in my
    breeding,
Who taught me betimes to love working and
    reading."

William Ayton, excerpt from "Advice to an Intending Serialist,"
Blackwood's Magazine 9 (November 1845): 590–605.

This parody of Dickens's "Chirp the First" from "A Cricket on the Hearth"
may or may not have been behind Carroll's "The Looking-Glass House." If
it was, it is not the bits and pieces of domestic materials but the introduction of the idea of didacticism and, especially, responsibility that is important here. Again, Carroll works a kind of magic in *Through the Looking-
Glass* by transforming the adult concepts of altering behaviour by admonishment and example into a game through Alice's transforming "let's pretend."

But your best scene is the opening one, in which you introduce us to the aerial
dwelling of Estrella di Canterini, in Lambeth. I do not want to flatter you, my dear
fellow; but I hold it to be a perfect piece of composition, and I cannot resist the
temptation of transcribing a very few sentences:

"It was the kitten that began it, and not the cat. It isn't no use saying it was the
cat, because I was there, and I saw it and know it; and if I don't know it, how
should anybody else be able to tell about it, if you please? So I say again it was the
kitten that began it, and the way it all happened was this.

"There was a little bit, a small string of blue worsted – no! I am wrong, for when
I think again the string was pink – which was hanging down from a little ball that
lay on the lap of a tall dark girl with lustrous eyes, who was looking into the fire as
intently as if she expected to see a salamander in the middle of it. Huggs, the old
cat, was lying at her feet, coiled up with her tail under her, enjoying, to an appearance, a comfortable snooze: but she wasn't asleep, for all the time she was pretend-
ing to shut her eyes, she was watching the movements of a smart little kitten, just
six weeks old, who was pouncing upon, and then letting go, like an imaginary
mouse, a little roll of paper, which, between ourselves, bore a strong resemblance to
two or three others which occupied a more elevated position, being, in fact, placed
in a festoon or sort of fancy garland round the head of the dark girl who was so
steadfastly gazing into the fire. But this sort of thing didn't last long; for the kitten,
after making a violent pounce, shook its head and sneezed, as if it had been pricked
by a pin, which was the case, and then cried mew, as much as to say, 'You nasty
thing! if I had known that you were going to hurt me, I wouldn't have played with
you so long; so go away, you greasy little rag!' And then the kitten put on a look of
importance, as if its feeling had been injured in the nicest points, and then walked
up demurely to Huggs, and began to pat her wiskers, as if it wanted, which it probably did, to tell her all about it. But Huggs didn't get up, or open her great green
eyes, but lay still upon the rug, purring gently, as if she were dreaming that she had
got into a dairy, and that there was nobody to interfere at all between her and the

bowls of cream. So the smart little kitten gave another pat, and a harder one than the last, which might have roused Huggs, had it not observed at that moment the little string of worsted. Now the end of the little pink string reached down to within a foot of the floor, so that the smart little kitten could easily reach it; so the smart little kitten wagged its tail and stood upon its hind-paws, and caught hold of the little pink string by the end, and gave it such a pull, that the worsted ball rolled off the girl's knee and fell upon the head of Huggs, who made believe to think that it was a rat, and got up and ran after it, and the kitten ran too, and gave another mew, as much as to say that the worsted was its own finding out, and that Huggs shouldn't have it at all. All this wasn't done without noise; so the tall girl looked round, and seeing her worsted ball roll away, and Huggs and the kitten after it, she said in a slightly foreign accent, 'Worrit that Huggs!'

"All this while there was sitting at the other side of the fire, a young girl, a great deal younger than the other; in fact, a little, a very little child, who was sucking a dried damson in her mouth, and looked as if she would have liked to have swallowed it, but didn't do it, for fear of the stone. Now Huggs was a particular pet of the little girl, who wouldn't have her abused on any account, and she said, "'Twor'n't Huggs, aunt Strelly, 'twore the kitten!'

"'Eliza Puddlefoot!' replied the other, in a somewhat raucus and melo-dramatic tone – 'Eliza Puddlefoot! I is perticklarly surprised, I is, that you comes for to offer to contradict me. I knows better what's what than you, and all I says is, that there 'ere Huggs goes packing out of the windor!'

"The child – she was a very little one – burst into a flood of tears."

Jane Taylor, "The Star" and "The Dunce of a Kitten,"
from *Rhymes for the Nursery* (1806).

"The Star" is clearly parodied in the Mad Hatter's "Twinkle, twinkle, little bat!" but the full significance of the parody does not come into play unless the reader knows Taylor's complete poem, two-thirds of which is concerned not with the beauty but with the utility of the star. Carroll completely demolishes utility by locating the bat "like a [useful] tea-tray" in the sky, where its utility disappears. "The Dunce of a Kitten," a poem about the failure of a girl to teach a "sulky" kitten how to read, is very close in spirit to Alice's failure to teach her "sulky" kitten to stand like the Red Queen. Carroll's genius transforms this entire didactic enterprise, "let's pretend" and all, into fantasy.

The Star

Twinkle, twinkle, little star,
How I wonder what you are!
Up above the world so high,
Like a diamond in the sky.

When the blazing sun is gone,
When he nothing shines upon,
Then you show your little light,
Twinkle, twinkle, all the night.

Then the traveller in the dark,
Thanks you for your tiny spark!
He could not see which way to go
If you did not twinkle so.

In the dark blue sky you keep,
And often through my curtains peep,
For you never shut your eye
Till the sun is in the sky.

As your bright and tiny spark
Lights the traveller in the dark,
Though I know not what you are,
Twinkle, twinkle, little star.

The Dunce of a Kitten

Come pussy, will you learn to read?
    I've got a pretty book:
Nay, turn this way you must indeed:
    Fie, there's a sulky look.

Here is a pretty picture, see,
    An apple, and great A:
How stupid you will ever be,
    If you nought but play.

Come A, B, C, an easy task,
    What any fool can do:

I will do anything you ask,
   For dearly I love you.

Now, how I'm vexed, you are so dull,
   You have not learnt it half:
You will grow up a downright fool,
   And make all people laugh.

Mamma told me so, I declare,
   And made me quite asham'd:
So I resolv'd no pains to spare,
   Nor like a dunce be blam'd.

Well get along, you naughty kit,
   And after mice go look:
I'm glad that I have got more wit.
   I love my pretty book.

Anonymous, "The Queen of Hearts," "The King of Spades,"
"The King of Clubs," and "The Diamond King,"
from *The European Magazine*, no. 434 (April 1782): 252.

This single entry from one page of "The Hive" in *The European Magazine* introduces the entire pack of playing cards by presenting a poem for each suit. "The Queen of Hearts" broke free of its adult magazine origins, joined the spoken tradition (it was set to music by 1785), and, twenty-three years later, but slightly altered, was used as the basis for Lamb's *The King and Queen of Hearts*. The potential order suggested by the hierarchy of the pack of cards is drastically undercut by Carroll, who finally describes its complete anarchy in the Queen's reversal of verdict and sentence and Alice's refusal to be arrested.

   The queen of hearts
    She made some tarts,
All on a summer's day,
   The knave of Hearts
   He stole those tarts
  And with them ran away:
   The king of hearts

Call'd for those tarts,
And beat the knave full sore;
The knave of hearts
brought back those tarts,
And said he'll ne'er steal more.

The king of spades
He kiss'd the maids,
Which vexed the queen full sore;
The queen of spades
She beat those maids,
And turn'd them out of door:
The knave of spades
Griev'd for these jades,
And did for them implore;
The queen so gent
She did relent,
And vow'd she ne're strike more.

The king of clubs
He often drubs
His loving queen and wife,
The queen of clubs
returns him snubs:
And all is noise and strife:
The knave of clubs
Gives winks and rubs,
And swears he'll take no part;
For when our kings
Will do such things,
They should be made to smart.

The diamond king,
I fain would sing
And likewise his fair queen,
But that the knave,
A haughty slave,
Must needs step in between.
Good diamond king
With hempen string,
This haughty knave destroy,

Then may your queen,
With mind serene,
Your royal bed enjoy.

Charles Lamb, *The King and Queen of Hearts;*
with the Rogueries of the Knave Who Stole the Queen's Pies
(London: Thomas Hodgkins, 1805).

Lamb uses the original poem (already somewhat altered from *The European Magazine* version) in its entirety at the beginning of his book and runs individual lines from it above William Mulready's illustrations. Lamb's far more elaborate version appears below each illustration and part of the elaboration is, although totally informal, something like a court trial: evidence is given by a servant, the Knave is found guilty and is punished. Carroll's trial scene, in which Alice finds herself replacing the Knave in the dock, may owe something to Lamb.

The Queen of Hearts

High on a Throne of ſtate is seen
She whom all Hearts own for their Queen.
Three Pages are in waiting by:
He with the umbrella is her Spy.
To ſpy out rogueries in the dark,
And smell a rat, as you ſhall mark.

She made ſome Tarts

The Queen here by the King's commands.
Who does not like Cook's dirty hands.
Makes the court-paſtry all herself.
Pambo the knave, that roguiſh elf.
Watches each sugary ſweet ingredient.
And ſlily thinks of an expedient.

All on a Summers day

Now firſt of May does ſummer bring,
How bright and fine is every thing!
After their dam the chickens run,
The green leaves glitter in the sun,
While youths and maids in merry dance
Round ruſtic may poles do advance.

The Knave of Hearts

When King's and Queens a riding go.
Great Lords ride with them for a ſhow
With grooms & courtiers, a great ſtore;
Some ride behind, & ſome before.
Pambo the firſt of theſe does paſs.
And for more ſtate rides on an Aſs.

He stole those Tarts

And took them quite away

Thieves! Thieves!. holla you knavish Jack
Cannot the good Queen turn her back,
But you must be so nimble hasty
To come and steal away her pastry.
You think you're safe. there's one sees all,
And understands, though he's but small

How like a thievish Jack he looks!
I wish for my part all the cooks
Would come and baste him with a ladle
As long as ever they were able,
To keep his fingers ends from itching
After sweet things in the Queen's kitchen.

The King of Hearts

Call'd for those Tarts

Behold the King of Hearts how gruff
The monarch stands, how square how bluff:
When our eighth Harry ruld this land,
Just like this King did Harry stand;
And just so amorous, sweet, and willing,
As this Queen stands stood Anna Bullen.

The meat removed, and dinner done.
The knives are wip'd and cheese put on
The King aloud for Tarts does bawl.
Tarts, tarts, resound through all the Hall.
Pambo with tears denies the Fact,
But Mungo saw him in the act.

And beat the Knave full sore

The Knave of Hearts

Behold the due reward of sin,
See what a plight rogue Pambo's in.
The King lays on his blows so stout,
The Tarts for fear come tumbling out
O King! be merciful as just,
You'll beat poor Pambo into dust

How like he looks to a dog that begs
In abject sort upon two legs!
Good Mr Knave, give me my due.
I like a tart as well as you,
But I would starve on good roast Beef,
Ere I would look so like a thief.

Brought back those Tarts

And vow'd he'd steal no more

The Knave brings back the tarts he stole.
The Queen swears, that is not the whole.
What should poor Pambo do? hard prest
Owns he has eaten up the rest.
The King takes back as lawful debt,
Not all, but all that he can get

Lo! Pambo prostrate on the floor
Vows he will be a thief no more.
O King your heart no longer harden,
You've got the tarts, give him his pardon
The best time to forgive a sinner,
Is always after a good dinner.

'How fay you, Sir? tis all a joke _
Great Kings love tarts like other folk!"
If for a truth you'll not receive it ,
Pray view the picture, and believe it .
Sly Pambo too has got a fhare .
And eats it fnug behind the chair .

Their Majefties fo well have fed ,
The tarts have got up in their head ,
'Or may be 'twas the wine!" hufh, gipfey!
Great Kings & Queens indeed get tipfey!
Now, Pambo, is the time for you :
Beat little Tell-Tale black & blue

Manella Bute Smedley, "The Shepherd of
the Giant Mountains," *Sharpe's London Magazine* I, nos 19 and 20
(7 and 21 March 1846): 298–300, 327–28.

Manella Smedley's story of the shepherd who wins the Duke's daughter and
rises to knighthood by killing a griffin and its young is suggested by Roger
L. Green as a possible source of Carroll's "Jabberwocky." The differences
between the two poems are more striking than the similarities. In Carroll's
compact version of the story of a young hero's successful confrontation with
a monster, there is little or no romance detail, and language itself becomes
the centre of attention. It is interesting that Alice, who has passed through
the looking-glass and retains her this-worldly perspective, needs to hold the
poem to a mirror. Note that Manella Smedley inverted her initials as
author.

Up from his knees he sprang –
There seemed a sudden dawn of deathless light –
Fresh life and hope exultant nerve his limbs;
And as he climbs along his rugged way,
He dares to think upon his priceless prize.
"Hideous and spiteful griffin brook! I see
Your grim looks watching me, I hear your voices
Lift up their shrill and hissing scream. I know ye!
Ye have my bones to grace your ghastly banquet!
Ha! how ye stare upon me! Hans was right;
Ye would devour us all. Your hour is come.

Ay, roll your fiery eyes in wrath, and whet
Your crooked claws, and rear in rage malign
The bright and bristling crests upon your heads!
I care not!
I love to see ye look so terrible,
Else might it pain me thus with fire to burn
Your living forms! Now to the work of death!"
A branch he kindles on a lofty stem,
And lifts it up with toil to touch the nest.
Ha! how the dry bark catches, flames and flares!
The oak itself, so often steeped in blood
That its parched leaves no longer greenly flourish,
And its stiff boughs are hollow, dried, and dead –
It hisses, it rustles, it cracks,
And through the tumult of the rising flames
Pierce the shrill howlings of the tortured brood.
Far on her bloody way
The mother griffin heard,
And measuring a league with every stroke
Of her colossal wings, she rushes upward
Shadowing the mountain with a fearful darkness.
Then Gottschalk thought, "the dream of life is past"
And, heedless of revenge,
The griffin strikes and strives to quench the flame
With her huge wings; strikes with such eager fury,
That Gottschalk marvelled how so fierce a monster
Should yet preserve her children by the risk
Of her own life. In vain! The grisly brood
Lie scorched and stifled in the pangs of death;
And, lo, the flame hath caught the griffin's wings,
As if in thirst for vengeance!
The reeling monster falls upon the grass.
Now, shepherd, now! Where is thy ready staff?
Now, lose no moment! For the wrathful beast,
Frantic with rage and pain, hath reared itself
On its broad feet and stands half tottering,
But dreadful still, and eager for the fight:
Then had the hapless youth been crushed to nothing,
But that he lifted up his heart to God,
And that a vision of inspiring beauty
Rose on his soul, and bade him not despair.

Stroke upon stroke he hurls upon the foe:
He stabs it the fiery eye – the beast
Rears in wild rage, then, quick as thought, the staff
Pierces its undefended breast, and sinks
Sure, deep, and deadly, in the ruthless heart!
It roars as if with the congregated voices
Of a thousand oxen; reels, and strikes its wings
Once more, with impotent fury, on the earth –
And all is over!
The terror of the land lies stiff with death.

All breathless Gottschalk leans
Upon the conquering staff, and looks around
Upon the scene, now steeped in evening coolness:
Soft airs steal up, as if in gratitude,
Fanning his weary brow, and lifting thence
The wavy curls of his abundant hair;
While his young face, all glowing from the battle,
Smiles forth refreshed, in tranquil joyousness.

Anonymous (Thomas Love Peacock), *Sir Hornbook;
or, Childe Launcelot's Expedition. A Grammatico-Allegorical Ballad*,
The Home Treasury edition, edited by Henry Cole
(London: Joseph Cundall, 1843).

Henry Cole presents the totally pedantic grammatical expeditions of
Sir Hornbook (originally published in 1814) as romance allegories. The
knightly aspects of the book are undercut by the grammatical nature of the
expeditions. At a time when the Gothic revival created a fascination with
mediaeval culture, including the exploits of knights, Carroll chose to
present his knight as a physically awkward and pedantic character who is
perpetually preoccupied with zany inventions. Although he functions as
Alice's champion when he first meets her, his idiosyncrasies soon create yet
another reversal, turning Alice into his guardian.

His merrymen all, for conquest born.
With armour glittering to the morn.
Went marching up the hill.

The Home Treasury.

SIR HORNBOOK;

OR,

CHILDE LAUNCELOT'S EXPEDITION.

A

GRAMMATICO-ALLEGORICAL BALLAD.

New Edition.

LONDON:

JOSEPH CUNDALL, 12, OLD BOND STREET.

1843.

VI.

Now steeper grew the rising ground,
And rougher grew the road,
As up the steep ascent they wound
To bold Sir VERB's abode.[18]

Sir VERB was old, and many a year,
All scenes and climates seeing,
Had run a wild and strange career
Through every mode of being.

And every aspect, shape, and change
Of *action*, and of *passion*:
And known to him was all the range
Of feeling, taste, and fashion.

[18] A VERB is a word which signifies to BE, to DO, or to SUFFER: as, "*I am, I love, I am loved.*"

He was an Augur, quite at home
In all things present done[19],
Deeds past, and every act to come
In ages yet to run.

Entrenched in intricacies strong,
Ditch, fort, and palisado,
He marked with scorn the coming throng,
And breathed a bold bravado:

"Ho! who are you that dare invade
My turrets, moats, and fences?
Soon will your vaunting courage fade,
When on the walls, in lines arrayed,
You see me marshal undismay'd
My host of moods and tenses[20]."

[19] The two lines in *Italics* are taken from Chapman's Homer.
[20] Verbs have five moods: The INDICATIVE, IMPERATIVE, POTENTIAL, SUBJUNCTIVE, and INFINITIVE.

"In vain," Childe Launcelot cried in scorn,
"On them is your reliance;"
Sir Hornbook wound his bugle horn,
And twang'd a loud defiance.

They swam the moat, they scaled the wall,
Sir Verb, with rage and shame,
Beheld his valiant general fall,
Infinitive by name 21.

Indicative declar'd the foes 22
Should perish by his hand;
And stout Imperative arose 23
The squadron to command.

21 The INFINITIVE mood expresses a thing in a general and unlimited manner: as, "To love, to walk, to be ruled."
22 The INDICATIVE mood simply indicates or declares a thing, as, "He loves:" "he is loved:" or asks a question: as, "Does he love?"—"Is he loved?"
23 The IMPERATIVE mood commands or entreats: as, "Depart:" "Come hither:"—"Forgive me."

Potential 24 and Subjunctive 25 then
Came forth with doubt 24 and chance 25:
All fell alike, with all their men,
Before Sir Hornbook's lance.

Action and Passion nought could do
To save Sir Verb from fate;
Whose doom poor Participle knew 26,
He must participate.

Then Adverb, who had skulk'd behind 27,
To shun the mighty jar,

24 The POTENTIAL mood implies possibility or obligation: as, "It may rain:"—"They should learn."
25 The SUBJUNCTIVE mood implies contingency: as, "If he were good, he would be happy."
26 The PARTICIPLE is a certain form of the verb, and is so called from participating the nature of a verb and an adjective: as: "he is an ADMIRED character; she is a LOVING child."
27 The adverb is joined to verbs, to adjectives, and to other adverbs, to qualify their signification: as, "that is a REMARKABLY swift horse: it is EXTREMELY WELL done."

Came forward, and himself resign'd
A prisoner of war.

Three children of IMPERATIVE,
Full strong, though somewhat small,
Next forward came, themselves to give
To conquering LAUNCELOT's thrall.

CONJUNCTION press'd to join the crowd[28];
But PREPOSITION swore[29],

[28] A CONJUNCTION is a part of speech chiefly used to connect words: as, "King AND constitution;" or sentences: as, "I went to the theatre, AND saw the new pantomime."

[29] A PREPOSITION is most commonly set before another word to show its relation to some word or sentence preceding: as, "The fisherman went DOWN the river WITH his boat."

Conjunctions and Prepositions are for the most part Imperative moods of obsolete verbs: Thus, AND signifies ADD; "John AND Peter—John add Peter:"—"The fisherman with his boat—The fisherman, join his boat."

Though INTERJECTION sobb'd aloud[30],
That he would go before.

Again his horn Sir HORNBOOK blew,
Full long, and loud, and shrill;
His merrymen all, so stout and true,
Went marching up the hill.

[30] INTERJECTIONS are words thrown in between the parts of a sentence, to express passions or emotions: as, "Oh! Alas!"

Sir HORNBOOK took CHILDE LAUNCELOT'S hand.

And tears at parting fell:

And loudly blew the horn that hung,

Before Sir HORNBOOK'S gate.

Appendix 2

(Chapter 3)

Representative Works Illustrating the Clash between Didactic and Imaginative Children's Literature

Jeremy Bentham, some recollections of Bentham's childhood,
a childhood that was disrupted by imaginative "literature," as quoted
in the introduction to *Bentham's Theory of Fictions* by C.K. Ogden
(London: Kegan Paul, French, Traubner and Company, 1932).

Bentham's witty recollections reveal the kind of childhood shared by many, including the writer of informational books for children, Samuel Griswold Goodrich (see Goodrich, *Recollections*, 320). It was a childhood that was troubled as a result of exposure to both spoken and written imaginative literature. Although one should not minimize Bentham's rational critiques of human social systems and his insistence on happiness as the touchstone of ethics by suggesting any cause and effect relationship between his childhood memories and his adult attacks on superstition, such memories obviously contributed in some small but complex way to his adult preoccupations. His memories certainly lasted a long time and are singularly vivid in their adult telling. Further, Bentham merits a place here, since Henry Cole, who wrote and edited *The Home Treasury* series under the name Felix Summerly, found him to be the central force behind attacks on "fancy."

The subject of ghosts has been among the torments of my life. Even now, when sixty or seventy years have passed over my head since my boyhood received the impression which my grandmother gave it, though my judgement is wholly free, my imagination is not wholly so. (xi)

At Barking, in the almost solitude of which so large a portion of my life was passed, any spot that could be made by any means to assume the purpose was the abode of some spectre or group of spectres. The establishment contained two houses of office ... [and] these shrines of necessary pilgrimage were, by the cruel genius of my tormentors, richly stocked with phantasms. One had for its autocrat no less a personage than "Tom Dark"; the other was the dwelling place of "Rowhead and Bloodybones." I suffered dreadfully in consequence of my fears. I kept away for weeks from the spots I have mentioned; and, when suffering was intolerable, I fled to the field. (xi–xii)

The *Pilgrim's Progress* frightened me still more: I could not read it entirely through. At Westminster school, we used to go to a particular room to wash our feet: there I saw an imperfect copy of the *Pilgrim's Progress:* the devil was everywhere in it, and in me too. I was always afraid of the devil: I had seen him sowing tares, in a picture at Boghurst: how could I know that it was not a good copy from life? (xiii)

Maria and Richard Edgeworth, a brief note extolling informational literature, specifically natural science or "the history of realities," from *Practical Education* (1798).

The Edgeworths were champions of moral didactic literature, especially of the cultivation of the affections as described by J.J. Rousseau. Their argument in favour of the "history of realities," based on age appropriateness and the importance of observation, led them to favour informational literature over "improbable fictions."

There is a class of books which amuse the imagination of children without acting upon their feelings. We do not allude to fairy tales, for we apprehend that these are not now much read, but we mean voyages and travels ... This species of reading should not early be chosen for boys of an enterprising temper, unless they are intended for a sea-faring life, or for the army. The taste for adventure is absolutely incompatable with the sober perseverance necessary to success in any liberal profession. (Vol. 2, 111)

The history of realities written in an entertaining manner appears not only better suited to the purpose of education, but also more agreeable to young people than improbable fictions. Natural history is a study particularly suited to children: it cultivates their taste for observation, applies to objects within their reach ... The histories of the bee, the ant, the caterpiller, the butterfly, the silk worm, are the first things that please the taste of children, and these are the histories of realities. (Vol. 2, 114–15)

Anonymous, excerpts from *The Child's Magazine,
and Sunday Scholar's Companion* (London, June 1834).

This representative religious magazine deliberately intermixed obviously appropriate stories about good and bad children (to be used or shunned as models), much like those printed in 1693 in Chear's *A Looking Glass for Children*, with material concerning natural science, such as "Of the Nature and Formation of Snow" and "View of a Stream of Lava in its Course." These latter topics were at the very least morally and theologically neutral and could be readily linked to religious issues through a concentration on natural design (suggesting a Designer) or the argument that observation of natural phenomenon leads ultimately to looking "through Nature to Nature's God."

CHILD'S MAGAZINE.

SUNDAY SCHOLAR'S COMPANION

JUNE, 1834

WATERING WITH THE FOOT.

A GREAT part of the labour in the cultivation of the land was the water

Vol. XI

AN AWFUL WARNING.

A YOUTH was accustomed to attend the preaching of the Gospel, and was aroused by serious convictions. His mind was affected, from time to time, by what he heard; but the various impressions of the Sunday were effaced by the company and conversation of his profane associates during the week. He yielded to sin; again he was convinced, repented, and struggled; but again he yielded. A serious youth of his acquaintance told me his case. I was deeply pained to hear it, the more so as he possessed several good qualities. I met him just at this period of miserable conflict. "G—," I exclaimed, "why do you not resolve? why will you not cleave to Christ with all your heart? why do you not leave your sinful ways and turn to God?" He answered, with a look of deep distress, "I know I ought; I wish I could; but I am sure I cannot;" and turned away. The next week he was attacked with a sore throat, while he was drinking with his loose companions. He treated it lightly; but it was the commencement of the typhus fever, at that time extremely virulent in the neighbourhood, and in the course of three days he was a corpse!—"To-day if ye will hear his voice, harden not your hearts."

———o———

THE PRAYERLESS FATHER.

A BOY on reading of the earnest prayers of a father for his child, turned to his father, and asked, "Father, why do you never pray for me?" The poor man turned away in a state of anguish, and said, "Child, I never yet prayed for myself." Youthful reader! dost thou pray for thyself? Dost thou implore mercy for others.

———o———

OF THE NATURE AND FORMATION OF SNOW.

WHATEVER is commonly before our eyes is usually regarded by us with less attention than it deserves to be. This is the case with snow. We pass it by, unaware of its wonderful formation, careless of its very great value, and only aware that it is very white and very cold. But an examination of a flake of snow, with the assistance of a microscope, will show to us that in its structure there are great beauty and great skill. It will show to us, in short, that, like all the other works of God, it is exceedingly wonderful.

Where water is frozen, the product is ice; a thick, solid, and transparent substance. A comparison between a piece of ice, however small, and a flake of snow, will speedily convince the reader of the very great difference between the substances of which they consist. Whence is that difference? The grand influence which forms ice is the same as that which forms snow. That influence is intense cold. But in the two cases the cold is exerted upon particles in a different state of cohesion. When aqueous * particles are closely cohered in the form of water, the influence of intense cold upon them produces a solid and ponderous body; that is ice. But when this description of particles is dispersed in vapours and

———————————

* Watery.

greatly rarefied, they are changed by intense cold into frozen particles of a less dense coherence. The difference between the density of those particles which, when acted upon by cold, yield ice, and those which, exposed to the same influence, yield snow, is this; the latter are just twenty-four times lighter, bulk for bulk, than the former. The particles are not only exceedingly rarefied as to their bulk; but the bulk also is exceedingly small. So small indeed is it, that one such particle would present but a very minute object even when viewed with the powerful aid of the microscope.

How, then, the young and curious reader will exclaim, such being the case, can the mere action of intense cold present to our view large flakes of snow? The process by which this is brought about is, indeed, exceedingly curious; and therefore we will give a brief, and, of course, a faint, description of it.

Floating in the upper atmosphere, let the young reader imagine that he can see millions of minute drops, or points of vapour. Acted upon by intense cold, each of these drops or points is converted into a solid substance as fine as one of those little motes which we can sometimes see floating in the radiant sun-beams. As these descend lower and lower in the atmosphere they attract each other, and each flake of snow that we see glistening in virgin whiteness upon the ground, consists of a multitude of those minute atoms of frozen matter, cohering together with the most perfect and beautiful uniformity. Surely, when we perceive that even in a flake of snow so much ingenuity and design are perceivably existent, we ought to keep our attention to surrounding objects perpetually upon the alert. Every thing of God's creation, however minute in itself, or humble in the uses to which it is destined, is calculated to yield great pleasure to the attentive observer.

By an attentive observation of the works of the Almighty, we are led into a pious frame of mind. We cannot pay attention to the innumerable wonders of the natural world without finding ourselves more able and more inclined, with every successive hour, to ;

"Look through Nature up to Nature's God."

This, indeed, is the most valuable end of all studies. All the other uses of knowledge have this one great defect, that they are temporary. But this great end of our studies is eternally useful ; making us better fitted for the eternal world.

The pursuit of natural philosophy is not only useful ; but youth, who indulge themselves in it, are never at a loss for the most refined amusement, which instructs as well as delights ; and, unlike most other amusements, never clogs, and never leaves a sting behind it.

VIEW OF A STREAM OF LAVA IN ITS COURSE.

From a Picture by Signor Tomaso Ruiz.

THE painting from which this subject was copied is a companion to the "View of the Eruption :" the following is a translation of an inscription which the artist had written on the back of the picture :—

"On the 26th of October, 1751, a cleft was perceived below the summit of Vesuvius, and a stream of ignited matter gushing from it like a river of fire. On the following day the appearance was quite tremendous ; the inflamed torrent forcing a channel which impetuously continued its course among the fields, farms, and vineyards which lie between the mountain and the sea. The channel which it made was in one place about five hundred feet in breadth, and the matter cooled to the consistence of stone.

"It extended its course upwards of five miles, and caused incredible damage to the towns, villages, and houses thereabouts : many shocks of an earthquake were felt in the parts adjacent to the mountain. On the 10th of November, the entire summit of the mountain seemed to be all in a flame, accompanied with tremendous explosions : all the wells around for a great distance were dried up, and the Valley of Castagno was filled with volcanic matter to the depth of twenty-seven feet."

MARTHA SYKES.

MARTHA SYKES, whose death took place February 20th, 1833, at the age of fourteen years and a half, was a scholar in the Wesleyan Sabbath-school at Seven Stars, Bowling, near Bradford, Yorkshire. Her attendance was uniformly regular, and she was decent in her demeanour. She was naturally of a pleasant and gentle disposition. At an early period she gave evidence that the instructions of the Teachers, and the exhortations of the Superintendents, were not lost upon her. At thirteen years of age she became concerned about her soul's salvation, and, like other true penitents, she was constantly found at the means of grace ; such as prayer-meetings, band-meetings, and the preaching of the Gospel ; and in her class-meeting she greatly delighted. Being unwell, and a funeral sermon being about to be preached in the neighbourhood, she told her mother she had intended hearing it ; but thought she might be better by the time the sermons were to be preached for the Sunday-schools, at Bradford; and she wished her to go and hear the funeral sermon. When her mother replied, she could not leave her, Martha said, "Do, mother: my sisters can get me anything that I shall want." Her mother then said she would go, and tell her what she could about the sermon; to which she replied, "But, O, you cannot tell me all." Such were her respect for the house of God, and her love to the word of life.

On the Wednesday week following, about two o'clock in the afternoon, a change took place, which indicated that Martha's death was at hand. Soon after this she called her mother, and said, "Mother, I am going to leave you:" her mother replied, she was perhaps sick. But she smiled, and repeated, "I am going to leave you. O bless you, mother: do begin to seek the Lord." Her mother asked her if she were afraid of dying: she gave a heavenly smile, and said, "No!" She added, she had prayed scores of times, and had been made very happy.

Two of her sisters standing by her bed-side, she exhorted them to seek the Lord. Immediately after, she inquired for her father, and said she wanted to see him once more. On his entering the room she fixed her eyes upon him, and said, "Father, father, begin to seek the Lord; begin just now, and do not delay any longer!" Her mother asked her if she were any better: she replied, "No; worse." Referring to the place she was accustomed to retire to for private prayer, she said, the Lord had blessed her there many times.

Shortly after she called for her sister Elizabeth, whom she wished to see once more. Her sister being called, she took her by the hand, and with her dying breath desired her to seek the Lord; and added, "All my brothers and sisters." Her mother said, "O Martha, what must I do?" She replied, with a smile, "I am going to heaven;" and lifting up her arms, she said, "Come, sweet Jesus:" and died.

——0——

William Pinnock, excerpts from *A Catechism of Geography* (1822), *A Catechism of Arithmetic* (1822), and *A Catechism of Optics* (1834); all published in London.

The three Pinnock books presented here are all related to situations and events in Carroll's Alice books; others from among the many informational books published by Pinnock and reprinted for years after his death in edited versions may certainly also reveal connections. The "Catechisms," as the name implies, taught information about the objective world and the fields of study that dealt with aspects of it (for example, in addition to subjects named above were chemistry, history, heraldry, British law, etc.). The process of teaching through conversation was thought to have a special appeal to children and to facilitate memory. Notice how at the beginning of *Alice in Wonderland* Alice checks her sister's book to see if it has pictures and conversations and how she holds conversations with herself.

A CATECHISM OF GEOGRAPHY.

CHAPTER I.

Definitions.

Question. What is GEOGRAPHY ?
Answer. A description of the earth.
Q. What is the earth ?
A. The world, or rather the globe, on which we live.
Q. Of what shape is the earth ?
A. Nearly round, like an orange.
Q.–How large is the earth ?
A. It is more than twenty-four thousand miles round, and eight thousand through.†
Q. How far is it from the sun ?
A. Ninety-five millions of miles.
Q. Does the earth move ?
A. Yes ; it has two motions ; the one round the sun, which it performs yearly ; and the other round its own axis, which it performs daily.‡
Q. What are these motions called ?
A. The first is called its annual motion, and the last its diurnal.
Q. What is caused by the annual motion ?
A. The change and variety of the seasons.
Q. What is caused by the diurnal motion ?
A. The succession of day and night.

* Being flattened at the Poles.
† The circumference of the earth is 24,872 miles, and its diameter is 7,914 miles.
‡ There is, also, a third motion of the earth, called the PRECES-SION OF THE EQUINOXES, which is a slow motion of the two points, where the equator cuts the ecliptic, which are found to move backward and forward fifty seconds every year.

From "The World and its Inhabitants" section

Q. What kind of country is France?
A. France is a very large and populous country, containing about twenty-nine millions of inhabitants, seven hundred and eighty cities, and forty-one towns and villages.
Q. What are its soil, its climate, and its produce?

A. The air is pure and wholesome; and the soil, which is agreeably diversified, produces all the necessities of life ...

Q. What is the character of the French?

A. The French are a polished people, gallant and courageous, but light, inconstant, and excessively vain.

Q. Of what are they particularly fond?

A. Of the arts and sciences, and of games, exhibitions, and dancing.

Q. What is the capital of France?

A. Paris.

Q. How far is Paris from London?

A. Two hundred and ten miles.

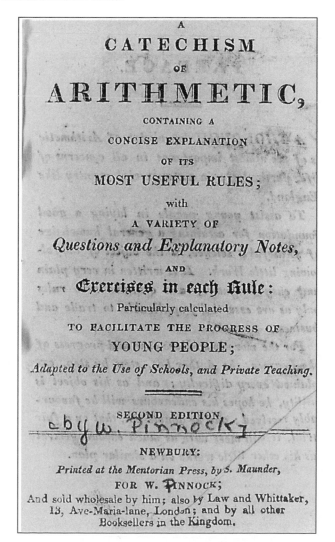

A

CATECHISM

OF

ARITHMETIC,

CONTAINING A

CONCISE EXPLANATION

OF ITS

MOST USEFUL RULES;

with

A VARIETY OF

Questions and Explanatory Notes,

AND

Exercises in each Rule:

Particularly calculated

TO FACILITATE THE PROGRESS OF

YOUNG PEOPLE;

Adapted to the Use of Schools, and Private Teaching.

SECOND EDITION

by w. Pinnock

NEWBURY:

Printed at the Mentorian Press, by S. Maunder,

FOR W. PINNOCK;

And sold wholesale by him; also by Law and Whittaker, 13, Ave-Maria-lane, London; and by all other Booksellers in the Kingdom.

Q. What do you observe in the first case of multiplication ?

A. I observe first, that the multiplier must be so placed under the multiplicand, in such manner, that units stand under units, and tens under tens, &c. and then proceed as the table directs, beginning at units place.

Q. What is the product of 144 multiplied by 5?

A. 720.

Q. How do you know 720 to be the product of 144×5?

A. By working it in the following manner.

$$
\begin{array}{r}
144 \text{ Multiplicand.} \\
5 \text{ *Multiplier.} \\
\hline
720 \text{ Product.}
\end{array}
$$

Q. What do you observe in the 2nd case of multiplication?

A. 1. When the multiplier consists of more figures than one (above the number 12), there must be made as many products as there are figures contained in the multiplier.

2. Let the first figure of every product be placed exactly under its multiplier.

3. Add these products together, and their sum will be the total product.

---

* In working this sum I say, 5 times 4 are 20, in which are no units and 2 tens, I set down 0, and the two tens I carry to the place of tens, then I say 5 times 4 are 20, and the 2 I carried are 22, which are 22 tens, I then put down the 2 tens under the place of tens, and carry the 2 to the place of hundreds, I then say 5 times 1 are 5, and the 2 hundreds I carry are 7, which are 7 hundreds, I set down the 7 and the work is done; and so on with all other operations when the number does not exceed 12.

From A Catechism of Optics

Q. Is the image on the retina inverted?

A. It is; but the position of the image on the retina has nothing to do with that of the object seen, though we turn the head horizontally, or even invert it, fixed objects do not shift, if we know that we are moving.

Q. And if we do not know that we are moving?

A. If we have not some collateral evidence of that, we fancy that all objects move, as anyone must have observed riding a carriage or walking. (47–8)

Q. Has the common looking-glass any other effect than that of representing the images of objects?

A. Yes, it reverses them; – writing which is the right way, is seen backwards in a mirror; and that which is written backwards reads the right way.

Q. What is a multiplying glass?

A. A lens flat on one side, and ground to a number of little flat faces on the other; and when any object is looked at through it, there is an image of the object in every face.

Q. Are there not some instruments that distort the shapes of objects?

A. Yes; mirrors that are portions of cylinders …

Q. Are there not optical instruments that paint the forms of objects?

A. Yes, the camera obscura does so, by a lens in a darkened space; the camera lucida, by a prism in the light; the magic lanterns, by throwing shadows upon a wall or screen; and the phantasmagoria, in which, by moving the instrument, the representations on the screen appear to increase and diminish, or to advance and retreat. (70–1)

Samuel Griswold Goodrich ("Peter Parley"), "Prospectus," cover, and a sample entry from *Parley's Magazine* (Boston: Lilly, Wait, and Company, 1833); sample pages from *The Tales of Peter Parley About America* (Boston, 1828); and a section from *Recollections of a Lifetime, or Men and Things I Have Seen: In a Series of Familiar Letters to a Friend, Historical, Biographical, Anecdotal, And Descriptive*, vol. 2 (New York and Auburn: Miller, Orton & Co., 1857).

Samuel Griswold Goodrich (1793–1860) wrote his most famous works under the pseudonym of Peter Parley. The "Prospectus" to his *Parley's Magazine* presents, in a positive light, the same catalogue of topics that were attacked by Wordsworth, Mrs Sinclair, and Dickens as singularly empty if unaccompanied by imaginative work. Goodrich developed a character and established a particularly friendly voice in Peter Parley, the grandfatherly narrator who took great numbers of nineteenth-century children on informational trips to many of the countries of the world. These books consider the history, geography, economic system, and so on of numerous countries in a narrative form children may readily understand. One result of the journey motif was to introduce exotic material in such a way that the child reader could compare and contrast it with the familiarity of home.

The section from *Recollections of a Lifetime* explains how Goodrich slowly developed the voice and topics of his work and how he intended his informational work as an antidote to what he considered to be the silly and destructive imaginative work that was threatening to make a return in the 1840s. This work at its worst was, he thought (as represented in "Jack the Giant Killer," for example), "calculated to familiarize the mind with things shocking and monstrous … to erase from the young heart tender and gentle feelings and substitute for them fierce and bloody thoughts and sentiments" (vol. 2, note on page 320). This section contains a specific rebuttal to Henry Cole, who, under the name of Felix Summerly, published a number of imaginative works (including "Jack the Giant Killer") under the general title of *The Home Treasury* in the 1840s. Cole had singled out the Parley books as representative of everything wrong with the dominant children's literature. Finally, the section from *Recollections* presented here also contains a sketch Goodrich originally published in his magazine, *Merry's Museum* (1846), in which he attacks the "silliness" of nursery rhymes. The effect of the Peter Parley books on children's literature lasted at least until the boyhood of James Joyce. In *Portrait of the Artist as a Young Man*, Joyce has the young Stephen Daedalus evoke a vision of Peter Parley to represent justice when he is falsely accused of, and punished for, lying about his broken glasses so that he could be excused for not finishing his Latin assignment.

"Propectus" for Parley's Magazine

The design of the publishers, in this magazine, is to offer to the public an entertaining work for children and youth; one that may become with them a favorite; one that will please and instruct them; one that they will regard not as a thing they must read as a task, but which they will love to consult as a companion and friend; one, in short, the reading of which may be permitted to good children as a reward, but that the denial of which may be felt as a punishment by those who are bad. It will consist chiefly of matters of fact, and the editors will endeavor to present truth and knowledge in a guise, as attractive to the youthful mind, as that in which fiction has generally been arrayed …

The contents of the Work will be too various to be enumerated in this place; but in order to convey some idea of the intentions of the conductors, the following may be mentioned as forming a portion of the more prominant subjects;

    I. Geographical descriptions of manners, customs, and countries.

    II. Travels, Voyages, and Adventures, in various parts of the world.

III. Interesting Historical notes and anecdotes of each state, and of the United States, as well as foreign countries.

IV. Biography, particularly of young persons.

V. Natural History, as birds, beasts, fishes, &c.; as well as plants, trees, flowers, &c.

VI. A familiar description of objects that daily surround children in the Parlor, Nursery, Garden, &c.

VII. Original tales consisting of Home Scenes, Stories of Adventure, &c., calculated to stimulate the curiosity, exercise the affections, and improve the judgment.

VIII. An account of various trades and pursuits, and some branches of commerce.

IX. Cheerful and pleasing Rhymes, adapted to the feelings and comprehension of youth.

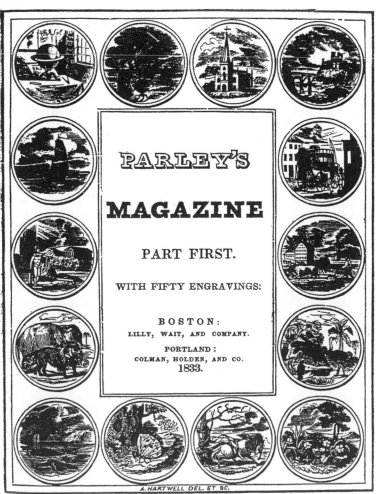

PARLEY'S MAGAZINE

FOR CHILDREN AND YOUTH.

No. 1.   SATURDAY, MARCH 16, 1833.   Vol. I.

TO THE PUBLIC.

If a stranger were to knock at your door, and ask some favor, you would first look him in the face, and then decide whether you would grant it or not. Now I, Parley's Magazine, am a stranger. I come before the reader, and like him who knocks at your door, I ask you to take me in. Like him also, I come with a face, or rather with a cover, which is much the same thing. Pray will you look at it; nay, will you be so kind as to study it? It is, I assure you, unlike some other faces, or covers, only meant to deceive. It is, I hope, an honest index to my real character.

It is said, that men as they grow old, grow deceitful, but youth are supposed to be without guile. Now if I were an old magazine, professing to teach the black arts and misty sciences, you might distrust me. But as I am young, and only hold companionship with the young, I beg you to consider me an ingenuous youth, who means what he says, and says what he means; and who, having nothing to conceal, lets his plans and purposes shine out frankly in his face; one, in short, who has not yet learned the artifices, or adopted the disguises of the world, and whose countenance may therefore be taken as a certificate of his character.

What then does my face or my cover seem to say? It consists of a number of little round pictures, each of which bears a certain meaning. One of them exhibits a church, by which I intend to tell you, that in my pages you will occasionally find something about religion, and those duties and pleasures which spring from it. Not that I mean to preach sermons, for that is not my calling; nor will I weary your patience with long moral lessons, for that would make you dislike me. But I believe that all good people find many sweet thoughts and pleasant feelings in that love, truth and kindness, which religion teaches, and as I only seek the favor of good people, you may expect, sometimes to find these topics in my leaves.

Another feature of my face, exhibits a man gazing at the stars, through a long tube, called a telescope. Seen through this instrument, a star looks as large as a great wheel, and the moon appears like a vast world with mountains, rivers and seas upon it. By this picture I mean to say, that I shall often tell you of Astronomy, which means an account of the sun, moon and stars, and the wonders which are displayed in the heavens.

The next picture exhibits a sort of ball in a frame, which is called a globe, and represents the figure of the earth, which, you know is round. The study of the earth, its mountains, rivers, lakes, seas, cities and inhabitants, is called Geography. It is one of the most pleasing and useful of all studies, and I mean often to discourse of it to n y readers.

Beneath the picture of the globe, is a ship, with its sails spread. It is crossing the deep sea, and by this I mean to tell you that I shall frequently relate tales of mariners and describe their adventures; I shall tell you of the great ocean that occupies nearly two-thirds of the earth's surface; of the gales and tempests that sweep over its bosom, of the tides that agitate its surface, of the plants that grow in its depths, and the fishes of a thousand forms that glide amidst its glassy waters.

The next picture relates to days of antiquity. In ancient times there were nations who executed beautiful buildings, chiseled fine statues in marble, and executed many other charming works of art. These nations, have long since perished, but some of their works remain; as they are interesting and instructive subjects of study, I shall sometimes introduce them to the notice of my older readers.

The next picture, relates to beasts of four feet, called quadrupeds; the next to fishes; the next to insects as bees, butterflies, &c; the next to serpents or reptiles, some of which are large enough to coil about a horse and crush it to death, as if strangled by a strong rope. The next relates to flowers, those beautiful bright things which decorate the face of the earth; and the next to the feathered tribes which fill the air with life and melody.

Of all these things I shall often speak. I shall describe their forms, their colors, their habits, and the places where they dwell. These topics are full of interest; they are worthy of being studied by all, the young as well as the old. The God of nature has displayed wonderful powers in the creation of these his creatures, and we cannot better train our minds to love and reverence, than by considering these his works. In wisdom and in goodness has he made them all, and he who neglects or refuses to study them, passes by untouched and untasted some of the sweetest pleasures, and richest joys that are afforded to the mind and heart.

My next picture represents in the foreground a man ploughing in the field, by which I would have you understand that I shall sometimes speak of tilling the earth, or Agriculture. The large building behind the ploughman, is a Manufactory by which you may suppose that I shall often speak of the arts of making cloths, hats, buttons, and other things. The ship in the distance, means that I shall sometimes discourse of Commerce, that is, the carrying of various articles of use or luxury, from one country to another across the seas.

The next picture displays a man getting into a stage, for the purpose of travelling; you may therefore expect to hear, not only his stories, but many others, relating to various countries. The next and last picture shows an old building in the distance, falling in pieces. The stones which compose its walls are broken and tottering, and seem to speak of days long gone by. And of these "olden times" it is my intention frequently to discourse. It is the business of History to describe what is past, and from history I shall draw many interesting tales. The world has been going on for near 6000 years, and many strange things have happened upon it. These furnish endless themes of interest and instruction, and I hope to amuse my young readers for many hours, with tales of the past.

Such then is my portrait, and such are some of my designs. I propose to use my best efforts to please, and instruct the young Perhaps too, I may occasionally have some thing to say, worthy the attention of older listeners. I humbly ask therefore, for the public favor. I ask for the favor of parents, for I will try to benefit their children. I ask for the favor of children, for if they will admit me into their hearts, and trust me as a friend, I will tell them many pleasing tales, and open to them many new sources of enjoyment. I ask for the favor of all, and if there are any who are too wise or too learned to look into my pages, I will be content if they will drop a yearly dollar into my publishers' pocket.

THE

TALES OF PETER PARLEY,

ABOUT AMERICA.

CHAPTER I.

Parley tells about Himself, about Boston, and about the Indians.

1. HERE I am! My name is Peter Parley! I am an old man. I am very gray and lame. But I have seen a great many things, and had a great many adventures, and I love to talk about them.

2. I love to tell stories to children, and very often they come to my house, and they get around me, and I tell them stories of what I have seen, and of what I have heard.

3. I live in Boston. Boston is a large

cown, full of houses, with a great many streets, and a great many people or inhabitants in it.

4. When you go there, you will see some persons riding about in coaches, and some riding on horseback, some running, and som walking. Here is a picture of Boston.

5. When I was a little boy, Boston was not

What kind of a town is Boston?
What will you see when you go to Boston?

half so large as it is now, and that large building, which stands very high, as you see in the picture, called the new State House, was not built then.

6. And do you know that the very place, where Boston stands, was once covered with woods, and that in those woods lived many Indians? Did you ever see an Indian? Here is a picture of some Indians.

Who once lived in the woods where Boston now stands?

7. The Indians used to go nearly naked, except in winter. Their skin is not white, like ours, but reddish, or the color of copper.

8. When I was a boy, there were a great many Indians, that lived at no great distance from Boston. They lived in little huts or houses called Wigwams. Here is a picture of a Wigwam.

9. The Indians were very ignorant; they

How did the Indians use to go dressed?
What is the color of their skin?
What sort of houses had the Indians?

could not read or write; their houses were very small and inconvenient. They had no such fine rooms in them as our houses have, nor had they any chimneys or fire-places.

10. The Indians had no chairs to sit in, nor tables to eat from. They had no books to read, and had no churches or meeting houses. In winter, they sometimes wore skins of bears and deer, which they shot with bows and arrows, or with guns. Here is a picture of Indians shooting a deer.

Had their houses any chimneys?
Had they chairs or tables?
Had they books? Had they meeting houses or churches?

11. There are no Indians near Boston now; they are nearly all dead, or gone far west over the mountains. But, as I said before, when I was a boy, there were a good many in New England, and they used often to come to Boston to sell the skins of wild beasts, which they had killed.

CHAPTER II.

Parley tells his Adventures.

1. WHEN I was about twelve years old, an Indian, by the name of Wampum, came to my father's house in Boston. He had been a chief, or great man among the Indians once, but he was now poor.

2. He was generally esteemed a good

Are there any Indians near Boston now?
What has become of them?
What had Wampum been once?

Indian, and he loved my father, because he once saved his life, when he was attacked by some sailors in the streets of Boston.

3. He asked my father to let me go home with him. He told me of the excellent sport they had in shooting squirrels and deer where he lived; so I begged my father to let me go, and he at length consented.

4. Wampum lived near Northampton, at the foot of a mountain called Mount Holyoke, just on the bank of Connecticut River. It is about one hundred miles from Boston.

5. There is a good road from Boston to Northampton now, and the stage travels it every day. But the road was bad when I went with Wampum, and there were no stages in America then.

Where did Wampum live?
How far is Mount Holyoke from Boston?
What kind of road is there now from Boston to Northampton?
Was it as good when Parley went with Wampum?

6. So Wampum and I set out on foot. The second day we arrived at Worcester. It was then a very little town, and there were no such fine houses there as now.

7. The fourth day we arrived at Wampum's house, which was a little wigwam at the foot of Mount Holyoke. Here is a picture of it.

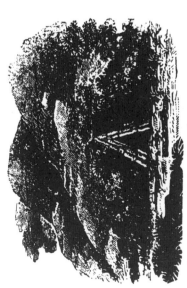

8. In this little house we found Wampum's

What does Parley say about Worcester?

wife and three children; two boys and a girl. They came out to meet us, and were very glad to see Wampum and me.

9. I was very hungry and tired when I arrived. Wampum's wife roasted some bear's meat, and gave us some bread made of pounded corn, which formed our supper.

10. We sat on the floor, and took the meat in our fingers, for the Indians had no knives and forks. I then went to bed on some bear skins, and slept very well.

11. Early in the morning, Wampum called me from my sleep, and told me they were going into the woods a-shooting, and that I must go with them. I was soon ready, and set out with Wampum and his two sons.

What did Parley eat for supper at Wampum's house? How did he sit? How did he take his meat? What did he sleep upon?

From Recollections of a Lifetime

" FLOWERS, PEBBLES, INSECTS, BIRDS ON WINGS—
THESE ARE GOD'S SPELLING BOOK."   Vol. 2, p. 310

LETTER XLIX.

Objections to the Parley Books—My theory as to books for children—Attempt in England to revive the old nursery books—Mr. Felix Summerley—Halliwell's Nursery Rhymes of England—Dialogue between Timothy and his mother—Mother Goose—The Toad's Story—Books of instruction.

My DEAR C******

It is not to be supposed that the annoyances arising from the falsification of the name of Parley, which I have just pointed out, have been the only obstacles which have roughened the current of my literary life. Not only the faults and imperfections of execution in my juvenile works—and no one knows them so well as myself—have been urged against them, but the whole theory on which they are founded has been often and elaborately impugned.

It is quite true that when I wrote the first half-dozen of Parley's Tales, I had formed no philosophy upon the subject. I simply used my experience with children in addressing them. I followed no models, I put on no harness of the schools, I pored over no learned examples. I imagined myself on the floor with a group of boys and girls, and I wrote to them as I would have spoken to them. At a later period I had reflected on the subject, and embodied in a few simple lines the leading principle of what seemed to me the true art of teaching children—and that is, to consider that their first ideas are simple and single, and formed

of images of things palpable to the senses; and hence that these images are to form the staple of lessons to be communicated to them.

THE TEACHER'S LESSON.

I saw a child, some four years old,
   Along a meadow stray;
Alone she went, uncheck'd, untold,
   Her home not far away.

She gazed around on earth and sky,
   Now paused and now proceeded;
Hill, valley, wood, she passed them by
   Unmarked, perchance unheeded.

And now gay groups of roses bright
   In circling thickets bound her—
Yet on she went with footsteps light,
   Still gazing all around her.

And now she paused and now she stooped,
   And plucked a little flower;
A simple daisy 'twas, that drooped
   Within a rosy bower.

The child did kiss the little gem,
   And to her bosom press'd it,
And there she placed the fragile stem,
   And with soft words caressed it.

I love to read a lesson true
   From nature's open book—
And oft I learn a lesson new
   From childhood's careless look.

Children are simple, loving, true—
   'Tis God that made them so;
And would you teach them?—be so, too,
   And stoop to what they know.

Begin with simple lessons, things
On which they love to look;
Flowers, pebbles, insects, birds on wings—
These are God's spelling-book!

And children know his A B C,
As bees where flowers are set:
Wouldst thou a skillful teacher be?
Learn then this alphabet.

From leaf to leaf, from page to page,
Guide thou thy pupil's look;
And when he says, with aspect sage—
"Who made this wondrous book?"

Point thou with reverend gaze to heaven,
And kneel in earnest prayer—
That lessons thou hast humbly given
May lead thy pupil there!

From this initial point I proceeded to others, and came to the conclusion that in feeding the mind of children with facts, with truth, and with objective truth, we follow the evident philosophy of nature and providence, inasmuch as these had created all children to be ardent lovers of things they could see and hear and feel and know. Thus I sought to teach them history and biography and geography, and all in the way in which nature would teach them—that is, by a large use of the senses, and especially by the eye—the master organ of the body as well as the soul. I selected as subjects for my books, things capable of sensible representation, such as familiar animals, birds, trees, and of these I gave pictures, as a

starting point. The first line I wrote was, "Here I am; my name is Peter Parley," and before I went further, gave an engraving representing my hero, as I wished him to be conceived by my pupils. Before I began to talk of a lion, I gave a picture of a lion—my object being, as you will perceive, to have the child start with a distinct image of what I was about to give an account of. Thus I secured his interest in the subject, and thus I was able to lead his understanding forward in the path of knowledge.

These views of course led me in a direction exactly opposite to the old theories in respect to nursery books, in two respects. In the first place, it was thought that education should, at the very threshold, seek to spiritualize the mind, and lift it above sensible ideas, and to teach it to live in the world of imagination. A cow was very well to give milk, but when she got into a book, she must jump over the moon; a little girl going to see her grandmother, was well enough as a matter of fact, but to be suited to the purposes of instruction, she must end her career in being eaten up by a wolf. My plan was, in short, deemed too utilitarian, too materialistic, and hence it was condemned by many persons, and among them the larger portion of those who had formed their tastes upon the old classics, from Homer down to Mother Goose!

This was one objection; another was, that I aimed at making education easy—thus bringing up the child in habits of receiving knowledge only as made into pap, and of course putting it out of his power to relish and digest the stronger meat, even when his constitution demanded it. The use of engravings in books for instruction, was deemed a fatal facility, tending to exercise the child in a mere play of the senses, while the understanding was left to indolence and emaciation.

On these grounds, and still others, my little books met with opposition, sometimes even in grave Quarterlies and often in those sanctified publications, entitled Journals of Education. In England, at the period that the name of Parley was most current—both in the genuine as well as the false editions—the feeling against my juvenile works was so strong among the conservatives, that a formal attempt was made to put them down by reviving the old nursery books. In order to do this, a publisher in London reproduced these works, employing the best artists to illustrate them, and bringing them out in all the captivating luxuries of modern typography. A quaint, quiet, scholarly old gentleman, called Mr. Felix Summerly—a dear lover of children—was invented to preside over the enterprise, to rap the knuckles of Peter Parley, and to woo back the erring generation of children to the good old orthodox rhymes and jingles of England.

I need hardly say that this attempt failed of success: after two bankruptcies, the bookseller who conducted the enterprise finally abandoned it. Yet such

was the reverence at the time for the old favorites of the nursery, that a man by the name of Hallowell* expended a vast amount of patient research and antiquarian lore, in hunting up and setting before the world, the history of these performances, from Hey diddle diddle to

"A farmer went trotting upon his gray mare—
Bumpety, bumpety, bump !"

To all this I made no direct reply; I ventured, however, to suggest my views in the following article inserted in Merry's Museum for August, 1846.

DIALOGUE BETWEEN TIMOTHY AND HIS MOTHER.

Timothy. Mother! mother! do stop a minute, and hear me say my poetry!
Mother. Your poetry, my son? Who told you how to make poetry?
T. Oh, I don't know; but hear what I have made up.
M. Well, go on.
T. Now don't you laugh; it's all mine. I didn't get a bit of it out of a book. Here it is!

"Higglety, pigglety, pop!
The dog has eat the mop;
The pig's in a hurry,
The cat's in a flurry—
Higglety, pigglety—pop!"

M. Well, go on.
T. Why, that's all. Don't you think it pretty good?
M. Really, my son, I don't see much sense in it.
T. Sense? Who ever thought of *sense,* in poetry? Why,

* Nursery Rhymes of England, &c., Collected and Edited by James Orchard Hallowell.

mother, you gave me a book the other day, and it was all poetry, and I don't think there was a bit of sense in the whole of it. Hear me read. [*Reads.*]

"Hub a dub!
Three men in a tub—
And how do you think they got there?
The butcher,
The baker,
The candlestick-maker,
They all jumped out of a rotten potato:
'Twas enough to make a man stare."

And here's another.

"A cat came fiddling out of a barn,
With a pair of bagpipes under her arm;
She could sing nothing but fiddle cum fee—
The mouse has married the humblebee—
Pipe, cat—dance, mouse—
We'll have a wedding at our good house!"

And here's another.

"Hey, diddle, diddle,
The cat and the fiddle,
The cow jumped over the moon—
The little dog laughed
To see the craft,
And the dish ran after the spoon."

Now, mother, the book is full of such things as these, and I don't see any meaning in them.

M. Well, my son, I think as you do: they are really very absurd.

T. Absurd? Why, then, do you give me such things to read?

M. Let me ask you a question. Do you not love to read these rhymes, even though they are silly?

T. Yes, dearly.

M. Well, you have just learned to read, and I thought these jingles, silly as they are, might induce you to study your book, and make you familiar with reading.

T. I don't understand you, mother; but no matter.

"Higglety, pigglety, pop!
The dog has eat the mop;
The pig's in a hurry—"

M. Stop, stop, my son. I choose you should understand me.

T. But, mother, what's the use of understanding you?

"Higglety, pigglety, pop!"

M. Timothy!

T. Ma'am?

M. Listen to me, or you will have cause to repent it. Listen to what I say! I gave you the book to amuse you, and improve you in reading, not to form your taste in poetry.

T. Well, mother, pray forgive me. I did not mean to offend you. But I really do love poetry, because it is so silly!

"Higglety, pigglety, pop!"

M. Don't say that again, Timothy!

T. Well, I won't; but I'll say something out of this pretty book you gave me.

"Doodledy, doodledy, dan!
I'll have a piper to be my good man—
And if I get less meat, I shall get game—
Doodledy, doodledy, dan!"

M. That's enough, my son.

T. But, dear mother, do hear me read another.

"We're all in the dumps,
For diamonds are trumps—
The kittens are gone to St. Paul's—
The babies are bit,
The moon's in a fit—
And the houses are built without walls."

M. I do not wish to hear any more.

T. One more; one more, dear mother!

"Round about—round about—
Maggoty pie—
My father loves good ale,
And so do I."

Don't you like that, mother?

M. No; it is too coarse, and unfit to be read or spoken.

T. But it is here in this pretty book you gave me, and I like it very much, mother. And here is a poem, which I think very fine.

> "One-ery, two-ery,
> Ziccary zan,
> Hollow bone, crack a bone——
> Ninery ten:
> Spittery spat,
> It must be done,
> Twiddledum, tweddledum,
> Twenty-one,
> Hink, spink, the puddings stink——"

M. Stop, stop, my son. Are you not ashamed to say such things?

T. Ashamed? No, mother. Why should I be? It's all printed here as plain as day. Ought I to be ashamed to say any thing that I find in a pretty book you have given me? Just hear the rest of this.

> "Hink, spink, the puddings——"

M. Give me the book, Timothy. I see that I have made a mistake; it is not a proper book for you.

T. Well, you may take the book; but I can say the rhymes, for I have learned them all by heart.

> "Hink, spink, the puddings——"

M. Timothy, how dare you!

T. Well, mother, I won't say it, if you don't wish me to. But mayn't I say——

> "Higglety, pigglety, pop!"

M. I had rather you would not.

T. And "Doodledy, doodledy, dan"—mayn't I say that?

M. No.

T. Nor "Hey, diddle, diddle?"

M. I do not wish you to say any of those silly things.

T. Dear me, what shall I do?

M. I had rather you would learn some good, sensible things.

T. Such as what?

M. Watts's Hymns, and Original Hymns.

T. Do you call them sensible things? I hate 'em.

> "Doodledy, doodledy, dan!"

M. [*Aside.*] Dear, dear, what shall I do? The boy has got his head turned with these silly rhymes. It was really a very unwise thing to put a book into his hands, so full of nonsense and vulgarity. These foolish rhymes stick like burs in his mind, and the coarsest and vilest seem to be best remembered. I must remedy this mistake; but I see it will take all my wit to do it. [*Aloud.*] Timothy, you must give me up this book, and I will get you another.

T. Well, mother, I am sorry to part with it; but I don't care so much about it, as I know all the best of it by heart.

> "Hink, spink, the puddings stink?"——

M. Timothy, you'll have a box on the ear, if you repeat that.

T. Well, I suppose I can say,

> "Round about—round about——
> Maggoty pie—"

M. You go to bed!

T. Well, if I must, I must. Good-night, mother!

> "Higglety, pigglety, pop!
> The dog has eat the mop;
> The cat's in a flurry,
> The cow's in a hurry,
> Higglety, pigglety, pop!"

Good-night, mother!

I trust, my friend, you will not gather from this that I condemn rhymes for children. I know that there is a certain music in them that delights the ear of child-hood. Nor am I insensible to the fact that in Mother Goose's Melodies, there is frequently a sort of humor in the odd jingle of sound and sense. There is, fur-thermore, in many of them, an historical significance, which may please the profound student who puzzles it out; but what I affirm is, that many of these pieces are coarse, vulgar, offensive, and it is precisely these portions that are apt to stick to the minds of children. And besides, if, as is common, such a book is the first that a child becomes acquainted with, it is likely to give him a low idea of the purpose and meaning of books, and to beget a taste for mere jingles.

With these views, I sought to prepare lessons which combined the various elements suited to children—a few of them even including frequent, repetitious rhymes—yet at the same time presenting rational ideas and gentle kindly sentiments. Will you excuse me for giving you one example—my design being to show you how this may be done, and how even a very unpromising subject is capable of being thus made attractive to children.

THE TOAD'S STORY.

Oh, gentle stranger, stop,
And hear poor little Hop
Just sing a simple song,
Which is not very long—
Hip, hip, hop.

I am an honest toad,
Living here by the road;
Beneath a stone I dwell,
In a snug little cell,
Hip, hip, hop.

It may seem a sad lot
To live in such a spot—

But what I say is true—
I have fun as well as you!
Hip, hip, hop.

Just listen to my song—
I sleep all winter long,
But in spring I peep out,
And then I jump about—
Hip, hip, hop.

When the rain patters down,
I let it wash my crown,
And now and then I sip
A drop with my lip:
Hip, hip, hop.

When the bright sun is set,
And the grass with dew is wet,
I sally from my cot,
To see what's to be got,
Hip, hip, hop.

And now I wink my eye,
And now I catch a fly,
And now I take a peep,
And now and then I sleep:
Hip, hip, hop.

And this is all I do—
And yet they say it's true,
That the toady's face is sad,
And his bite is very bad!
Hip, hip, hop.

Oh, naughty folks they be,
That tell such tales of me,
For I'm an honest toad,
Just living by the road:
Hip, hip, hop!

Richard Parker, excerpt from "Conversation IV: The Eye,"
in *Juvenile Philosophy* (1850).

The conversation concerning the function of eyelids and lashes in this excerpt demonstrates the dispassion of informational literature at its purest or worst. In order to made her point about function, the boy's mother relates how the Carthaginians treated a captured Roman general – his lids and lashes were removed in a dark dungeon and he was then tied up facing the sun. Although she labels such treatment "cruel," the narrative is obviously chosen solely on the grounds of its efficacy as a teaching aid. The clinical detachment of the narrative is at least as chilling as any event in "Jack the Giant Killer."

CONVERSATION ON THE EYE.   **49**

CONVERSATION IV.

THE EYE.

CHILD. — MOTHER dear, you told me so many interesting things about rain, and the clouds, and the light, and the beautiful colors, that I am sure I shall never be tired of thinking about them. You also told me all about grandfather's spectacles, and Cousin George's, and about people having eyes too round or too flat, and I believe I shall be looking at everybody's eye, to see whether their eyes are round or flattened.

MOTHER. — That would be a very useless task, my dear, because you could not tell, by looking at them, whether they were too round or too flat. Everybody's eyes look round alike; but the eye is a very beautiful piece of mechanism, consisting of no fewer than ten different parts, each of which has a different name. You are too young to understand all these hard names now, and therefore it will be useless for me to mention them to you. But I will tell you that some of these parts are shaped very much like the glass in your grandfather's spectacles; and it is these parts, in the inside of the eye, that become too round or too flat, and not the·

when looking at a bright object, and then we put up our hand over the eye, to protect it more.

Many years ago, a nation called the Carthaginians took a Roman general prisoner, whose name was Regulus. He was a very good man, but the Carthaginians did not like him, because he had done their nation much harm. When they took him prisoner, they treated him very cruelly, and, among other things which they did, they put him into a dark dungeon and cut off his eye-brows and eye-lashes, and then carried him out and exposed him to the bright sunshine, with his hands tied behind him. Now, do you know how this would affect him?

CHILD.—Oh yes, mother, his eyes would be dazzled by the bright sunshine, and all the dust floating in the air would get into his eyes, and pain him very much.

MOTHER.—Yes, my dear, and he, undoubtedly, suffered very much from this act of cruelty. But I have not told you yet all that God has done to protect your eyes. You know that you can shut your eyes when you please, and open them when you please. You know, also, that when you go to sleep, you always shut your eyes. Now, could you not sleep with your eyes open?

CHILD.—Why, no, mother; everybody shuts the eyes

when going to sleep. Even puss, and the dog, and every other animal.

MOTHER.—Yes, my dear, but when you go to sleep, do you know at what particular moment of time your eyes close?

CHILD.—No, mother; how can I tell? Can anybody?

MOTHER.—No, my dear, no one can tell. The eyes close of themselves, without our shutting them; nor are we conscious of their shutting. But why do you suppose that the eyes close when we go to sleep?

CHILD.—Why, mother, who could sleep with his eyes open?

MOTHER.—A great many people get up when they are asleep, and walk about with their eyes open, without waking up. They are called somnambulists, because they walk in their sleep. But do not your eyes open and shut of themselves, very often, when you are wide awake, without your thinking at all about it?

CHILD.—Why, no, mother; how can my eyes open and shut without my knowing anything about it?

MOTHER.—They do, my dear, very often. Look at my eyes, and see whether I can keep them open long without their moving.

CHILD.—Why, mother, you only *winked* while I looked at you.

Henry Cole ("Felix Summerly"), the "Prospectus" for
The Home Treasury series; prefaces to *Beauty and the Beast* (1843)
and *The Traditional Nursery Songs of England* (1844); and
the introductory poem to *Puck's Reports to Oberon, King of Fairies,
of Some New Exploits of the Pen and Pencil of Fancy* (1844);
all published in London by Joseph Cundall.

Henry Cole and his publisher, Joseph Cundall, launched a series of beautifully illustrated and handsome books for children titled *The Home Treasury*
(1841–49). Although Cole, using the pen-name of Felix Summerly, wrote
some of the works and rewrote others, his major contribution consisted in
selecting the works for inclusion and writing introductions to a number of
the tales, songs, and other imaginative works for children. These included
versions of tales such as "Beauty and the Beast" and "Jack the Giant Killer,"
a collection of verse titled *The Traditional Nursery Songs of England*, an original fairy book titled *Puck's Reports to Oberon, King of Fairies, of Some New
Exploits of the Pen and Pencil of Fancy*, and the restoration of Thomas Love
Peacock's *Sir Hornbook; or, Childe Launcelot's Expedition. A Grammatico-
Allegorical Ballad* (originally published in 1824). In the introductions and
prefaces to his chosen works, Cole's consistent attempt to re-establish the
validity of imaginative literature demonstrates a great deal about the state
of children's literature two decades before Carroll published *Alice in
Wonderland*.

In Cole's prospectus for *The Home Treasury* series, as well as in his prefaces to individual works, he was very alert to the necessity to combat the
dominant children's literature, with its central concern for the cultivation of
"the understanding" at the expense of imagination and play. He echoes the
concerns of Wordsworth, Scott, and Catherine Sinclair and decries the un-
availability of works that address the child's "fancy, imagination, sympathies
[and] affections." Further, he seizes on the popularity of Goodrich's Peter
Parley books and defines his own *Home Treasury* publishing program as providing "a series of works, the character of which may be briefly described as
anti-Peter Parleyism," making Parley serve as a part for the whole.

From the "Prospectus" to The Home Treasury *series*

The character of most children's books published during the last quarter of a century, is fairly typified in the name of Peter Parley, which the writers of some hundreds have assumed. The books themselves have been addressed after a narrow
fashion, almost entirely to the cultivation of the understanding. The many tales

sung or said from time immemorial, which appeal to the other, and certainly not less important elements of a little child's mind, its fancy, imagination, sympathies, affections, are almost all gone out of memory, and are scarcely to be obtained ... As for the creation of a new fairy tale or touching ballad, such a thing is unheard of ... The conductor of this series proposes to produce a series of works, the character of which may be briefly described as anti-Peter Parleyism ...

(Quoted by F.J. Harvey Darton in *English Children's Books: Five Centuries of Social Life*)

Preface to Beauty and the Beast

The modern English versions of "Beauty and the Beast," adopted to the manners of the present period, are filled with moralizings on education, marriage, etc.; futile attempts to grind everything as much as possible into dull logical probability; and the main incidents of the tale are buried among tedious details of Beauty's sisters and their husbands. I have thought it no sin to get rid of all this, without regard for Mrs. Affable, and to attempt to re-write the legend more as a fairy tale than a lecture.

Preface to The Traditional Nursery Songs of England

So my dear Madame, you think Nursery Songs are mere trash, not worth utterance or remembrance, and beneath the dignity of the "march of mind" of our days! I would bow to your judgement, but you always talk too loud in the midst of a song; look grave at a joke – and the leaves of that copy of Wordsworth's Poems ... still remain uncut.

The Home Treasury.

Puck's Reports to Oberon,

KING OF FAIRIES, OF SOME

NEW EXPLOITS OF

THE PEN AND PENCIL OF

Fancy.

PRESENTED TO MORTALS BY COMMAND OF THE KING OF
FAIRIES, AND ORDERED TO BE PUBLISHED IN FELIX
SUMMERLY'S HOME TREASURY, BY JOSEPH
CUNDALL, 12, OLD BOND STREET,
LONDON.

1844.

INTRODUCTION.

LATE one fine bright moonshiny
    night,
      About the time—when twelve was
      going to chime,
And ev'ry little boy or girl should have his or
    her head—in bed ;
The King (MIGHTY OBERON) of the fairies,
    In full state and glee,
Was stretching his dainty little limbs
      On gossamer floating from the fans of a chest-
      nut tree.
Far and near, the sky was soft and clear,
And not a sound above the ground, could you
    hear I trow,
Save a watch-dog's very loud bow-wow,

The King was unattended by his court ;
His Queen had gone to a village sport.
For she always delighted to put her head in
    at a rustic wedding.
    By the King's side, stood his tried
    And trusty PUCK, messenger of good or
      evil luck,
    His master's pleasure to abide.
The drollest, queerest, gleesome wight washe,
In height not quite inches three :
All head and legs, like cribbage pegs ;
With a pair of long delicate gossamer wings,
Such elegant fanciful things as you and I never
    see.
May be you've heard a word or two about
    him before.
For his tricks and gambols
In his nightly rambles
Would fill indeed more books than you could
    ever read.

There's one has talk'd about him some hun-
    dred years ago or so,
Who has drawn his portrait to the letter,
And I think I can't do better
Than quote him here.
" That shrewd and knavish sprite
Called Robin Goodfellow : are you not he
That fright the maidens of the villagery ;
Skim milk ; and sometimes labour in the quern
And bootless make the breathless housewif
    churn ;
And sometime make the drink to bear no barm
Mislead night wanderers—laughing at thei
    harm ?"

The King was in a chatty mood, and so begai
    to seek,
From his premier PUCK, what his subjects hac
    been doing
(Good or evil brewing)

During the last week.
And when they had disposed of each affair,
And had closed each why and where:
    Puck whisper'd his Majesty that the fairy
        Fancy
    Had again express'd her desire
    To leave the place of her birth
    To retire from the court
And make a short stay among the dwellers of
      earth.
Says Puck,
    " Sire, you know for years and years,
    In spite of her struggles and tears,
    Mortals, in their scorn, drove her forlorn,
    To seek her airy home again:
Once they would have all things plain
Before their eyes, nothing indefinite, nothing
      to surprise;
    Faith and hope should be bound with a rope,
    The imagination was a useless, foolish thing;

" Poetry mere push-pin."
There was one Jeremy Bentham;
(Would they had sent him here, for us to
      make his brains a little clear,)
A long headed prosy fellow, who did nothing
      but bellow,
And rail at Fancy all day long,
In country or in town
He hunted her down,
Till her small voice was heard no more, and
      her reign seem'd o'er.
And now a most strange change
    Has come about,
    For folks with a shout,
In the north, south, east, and west,
    Strive their hardest and best,
    To extend her rule and region;
      Scarce a soul but agrees
      To join her legion of devotees,
        And unite to invite her back:

So this very night
Should it please your Majesty to listen,
It may requite your attention
If I take the liberty to mention,
Or lay before you
A tale or two
I borrow'd from a store of a score
Which she wishes to send or lend to a heap
Of little children just now fast asleep,
Who never her best wishes lack."

Appendix 3

(Chapter 4)

Representative "World Upside Down" Books from 1750 to 1890

Anonymous, cover, "Introductory Poem" and "The Reward of Roguery, or the Roasted Cook," from *The World Turned Upside Down; or the Folly of Man Exemplified in Twelve Comical Relations Upon Uncommon Subjects* (London: Alderman Church Yard, 1750).

This adult chapbook is the first world-upside-down book that is demonstrably linked to children's literature, since it is mentioned by the Taylor sisters as a book they read as children and one that was a strong influence in their writing of *Signor Topsy-Turvy's Wonderful Magic Lantern; or, The World turned upside down* (1810).

Introductory Poem

Philosophers of old will tell us,
As Tycho, and such merry fellows,
That round this habitable ball
The beamy sun did yearly fall;
No wonder then the world is found
By change of place Turn'd Upside Down:
If revolutions strange appear
Within the compass of the sphere;
If men and things succession know,
And no dependance reigns below;

THE

WORLD

TURNED

UPSIDE DOWN

OR THE

FOLLY OF MAN

EXEMPLIFIED

IN TWELVE COMICAL RELATIONS

UPON

UNCOMMON SUBJECTS

Illustrated with Twelve curious Cuts
Truly adapted to each Story

PRINTED AND SOLD IN LONDON

Since tis allow'd the world we dwell in,
Is always round the sun a sailing;
Experience to our knowledge brings;
That times may change as well as things,
And art than nature wiser grown,
Turns every object upside down,
Whim's epidemic takes her rise,
And constancy's become a vice.

He that to do is fortunate,
The darling minions of his fate!
To morrow feels his fate's displeasure,
Spoil'd his hoarded idol treasure!
And like this man, his emblem shows,
A sudden revolution knows.
His fortune grows profoundly scurvy
Turns the poor earthworms topsy turvy,
Becomes the tennis ball of fools,
Things quite form'd out of nature's rules.
Such as you see Atlas bear
Upon their backs this mighty sphere.
The young, the old, the middle aged,
Are all in this great task engaged;
And strive with wondrous eagerness
Which all the greatest part possess.
Since folly then has got the ascendant,
He's most a fool that han't a hand in't;
And as the mad brain'd world runs round
Still keeps towards the rising ground.

The Reward of Roguery, or the Roasted Cook

Once on a time, some while ago,
Perhaps a thousand years or so,
A cook there dae't, of greasy hue,
As ever was offered to our view,

In Pudding Street, near Mutton Lane,
Who was a very knave in grain;
He every Sunday after service,
With his 'prentice, honest Jervis,
Would take a walk for conscience sake,
And drink a mug, and eat a cake;
And when was darkish, walking home
From Totten'am Court to Marybone,
As passing by some farmer's yard,
With Tray the Spaniel for his Guard,
Set the officious Cur to bring
A fowl, or duck, or some such thing ...

[This goes on for years and makes him rich, until he forgets to bring Tray with him and is caught stealing by farm animals who capture him and take revenge.]

Accordingly the Turkey makes
A roasting fire of rotten stakes;
The Rabbit reaches down the spit
For rump of beef at Christmas fit,
And now like prey of mighty size,
Our honest cook a roasting lies ...

Anonymous, excerpts from *The World Upside Down*
(London: n.p., c. 1807).

The five excerpts reproduced here illustrate the mixture of the generally in-congruous with specific topoi of the world turned upside down. The abso-lute lack of didacticism in these energetic and zany combinations of illustration and verse is remarkable but fits the brief production of such work in the first decade of the nineteenth century, a production that in-cluded *The Butterfly's Ball and the Grasshopper's Feast* and its host of imita-tions.

Here's a jolly old boar,

With his pipe and full pot,

And the sow that is riding,

The goat in full trot.

Here a Magpie is feeding.
A child with a fork.
And an Elephant teaching.
A Captain to walk,

Here's a horse and a mare.
In a chaise drawn by me
And schoolmaster bruin.
Is mending a pen.

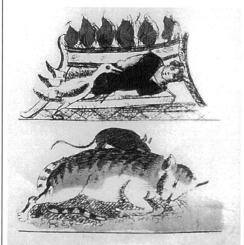

Here a goose roasts a cook
And bastes her with fat.
And here a small mouse kills.
And eats a great cat,

Here's a fish has a man.
Dangling safe at his hook,
Here's the cock and the hen.
Both swims in the brook.

Ann and Jane Taylor, title page, "Advertisement," "Introduction,"
"The Cook Cooked," and "The Boy Turned Giant," from
*Signor Topsy-Turvy's Wonderful Magic Lantern; or,
The World turned upside down.*

This book establishes a printed connection to the world-upside-down tradition in adult literature. The connection has been commented on by Percy
Muir in *English Children's Books, 1600–1900* and Alexander Taylor in *The
White Knight.* The strong reversed connection between a boy's wish to be a
giant so that he can perform a task and his then becoming too large to enter
his house and Alice's wish and her entrapment inside the White Rabbit's
house when she uncontrollably swells seems more than coincidental.

SIGNOR TOPSY-TURVY'S

WONDERFUL

MAGIC LANTERN;

OR,

The World turned upside down.

BY THE AUTHOR OF "MY MOTHER," AND OTHER POEMS.

ILLUSTRATED WITH TWENTY-FOUR ENGRAVINGS.

LONDON:

PRINTED FOR TABART & Co. AT THE JUVENILE AND SCHOOL
LIBRARY, NO. 157, NEW BOND-STREET; AND TO BE HAD
OF ALL BOOKSELLERS:

By B. McMillan, Bow Street, Covent Garden.

1810.

[*Price 3s. 6d. Bound.*]

ADVERTISEMENT.

———

THOSE grandmammas and aunts who afe versed in the nursery learning of fifty years ago, may perhaps recollect a little volume entitled, " The World turned upside down:" The Biographers of Signor Topsy-Turvy, and his Magic Lantern, beg leave to apologize for having stolen a few ideas from that learned original, which they had been recommended to revise for the amusement of modern nurseries ; and if they appear to have done but little good by the undertaking, they hope it may be allowed that they have not done any harm.

INTRODUCTION.

———

I Can't tell the story for truth, but 'tis said,
That the first *Magic Lantern* that ever was made,
   Perplex'd the inventor extremely ;
For houses, and people, and all that he shew'd,
In spite of his efforts, could only be view'd
   Upside down, which was very unseemly !

At length out of patience, and quite in despair,
He thought the best way to pass off the affair,
   Was to bring it at once to a sequel ;
He therefore gave out he'd invented a shew,
So wonderful, magical, comic, and new,
   As nothing in nature could equal.

The nobility, gentry, and public at large,
With alacrity paid the philosopher's charge,
   And throng'd to his rare exhibition ;
And nought could exceed the huzzas and encores,
As houses, and horses, and people, and doors,
With their feet in the air, and their heads on the floor,
   Past by,—'twas so droll a position !

They said it was such an original thought,
That people of rank and intelligence, ought
   To give it their full approbation ;
So ladies and lords to the scholar repair'd,
And as the procession proceeded, declar'd,
   It really surpass'd expectation !

At length a shrewd fellow from college that came,
Who envied, 'twas said, the philosopher's fame,
   (As cross and conceited as could be),
Stole up to the sliders, and *turning them round*,
To the company's grief and dismay it was found,
   That now, they were seen as they *should be !*

The tumult was dreadful,—the gentlemen rose,
And said they *would* see *upside down*, if they chose,
   They came with no other intention ;
And begg'd that, upon a philosopher's word,
He would not let any one be so absurd
   Again, as to spoil his invention.

Now lest there may still be some pedant in town,
To laugh at this turning the world upside down,
   With argument witty and weighty,
We've taken the trouble, at wonderful cost,
To copy the sliders (long thought to be lost),
   And appeal to the whole literati.

         B 4   A.

THE COOK COOKED.

A hare, who long had hung for dead,
  But *really* brew'd sedition,
Once set a scheme on foot, and said,
She could not take it in her head,
  That *hares* should be nutrition :

A turkey next began to speak,
  But said her task was harder,
Because the cook had tucked her beak
Behind her wing, for half a week
  That she'd been in the larder.

At length, with some ado she said,
  That as for her opinion,
If any prudent plan were laid,
Her latest drop of blood should aid,
  To rescue the dominion.

A murmur more than usual grave,
  Then issued from an oyster,
Who moaning through a broken stave,
Full many a doleful reason gave,
  Against his wooden cloister.

Eels, sliding on a marble shelf,
  The growing treason aided ;
And e'en a turtle 'woke itself,
To reprobate the cruel pelf,
  In callepash that traded.

So hand and foot, and fin and paw,
   In mutual faith were shaken ;
And all the patriots made a law,
To murder every cook they saw,
   The moment he was taken.

Ere long a wretched wight was found,
   And carried to the kitchen ;
The traitor of a jack went round ;
The turkey dredg'd, the cook was brown'd,
And chanticleer the banquet crown'd,
   With songs the most betwitching.

                            A.

THE BOY TURNED GIANT.

A paper kite who'd been to try,
Her pinions in a windy sky,
Became unluckily entangled
Upon a tree, from which she dangled :
" O ! now for wings," her owner cried,
" And then this knot could be untied ;
" Or as, till I'm a little older,
" They'd very likely hurt my shoulder,
" O ! how I wish that I could be
" Myself, as lofty as the tree."

   The fable then proceeds to show,
That instantly he seem'd to grow ;

THE BOY turned GIANT.

His head increasing as it rose,
Shot thirty feet above his clothes ;
His arms and legs, with sudden vigour,
Became proportionably bigger ;
And in the twinkling of an eye,
He seem'd a tenant of the sky.

Alas ! that moment he began
To wish himself a common man.
Through trees, at foot of which he'd gambol'd,
With difficulty now he scrambled,
At every turn the branches bare,
Tearing off handfuls of his hair ;
And winds that only brush'd the plain,
Blew round his head a hurricane.

Return'd,—it was in vain he tried
Beneath his native roof to hide ;
His knee was at the second floor !
His foot alone block'd up the door !
At length, while in this wretched plight,
He mourn'd his solitary height,
With sudden pleasure and surprize,
He dwindl'd to his native size.

One simple moral caught his eye,
While on his visit to the sky,
With all the pains he underwent ;
" Whate'er thy station, be content,
" Nor wish to change a good in hand,
" For things you do not understand."

                                             A.

Anonymous, excerpts from *Il Mondo Rovesciato; or The World Turned Upside Down* (Cornhill: John and Arthur Arch, 1822).

This book presents twenty-three standard visual representations of the world upside down done by the seventeenth-century artist Giuseppe Salviati (Porta), followed by his summary illustration in which Europe and Africa have changed hemispheres and are spelled backwards to suggest a general 180-degree reversal. Included here are animal/man and youth/age reversals accompanied by verses, as well as the summary illustration.

How the tables turn'd! – the Man, alas!
Stoops with grave loads, subservient to his Ass.

The son, imperious o'er the Sire forlorn,
Inflicts the beating he so oft has borne.

All lands have changed their latitudes; each breeze
Has veer'd; and ships, reverted, plow the seas:
O'er all things Magic seems to spread her robe,
And powerful Laughter lords it o'er the globe.

Anonymous, excerpts from *The World Turned Upside Down;
or, No News, and Strange News* (York: J. Kendrew, 1828 and 1830).

The introductory antipodean illustration and verse and representative pages
that emphasize the disparity between the commonplace and the impossible
are presented here. Again, this book has no didactic drive except when
didacticism is the butt of the joke.

FRONTISPIECE.

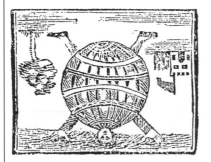

Here you may see what's very rare,
    The world turn'd upside down:
A tree and castle in the air,
    A man walk on his crown.

THE

WORLD
TURNED UPSIDE DOWN;
OR,
No News, and Strange News.

TAILOR RIDING A GOOSE.

York :
Printed and Sold by J. Kendrew, Colliergate.

To see a good boy read his book,
    is no news;
But to see a goose roasting a cook,
    is strange indeed!

To see a boy swim in a brook,
    is no news;
But to see a fish catch a man with a
        hook,
    is strange indeed!

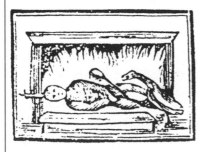

I'll roast ye, and baste ye,
But who will may taste ye.

Spare me, Mr. Fish,
    I didn't molest you.
I'll spare you no longer
    Than till I dress you.

To see an eagle spread her wings,
    is no news;
But to see an old man in leading
      strings,
    is strange indeed!

Take care, grandpapa, lest
    You should fall,
And if you want your
    Chair – pray call.

To see a gardener gather a salad,
    is no news;
But to see an ass singing a ballad,
    is strange indeed!

My voice is so fine,
    And so charming the tune,
I expect for to sing at
    The opera soon.

J.J. Grandville (J.I. Gerard), excerpts from *Un Autre Monde*
(Paris: H. Fournier, 1844).

The cover illustration, frontispiece, title page, and two illustrated pages that are closely linked to the work of Carroll and Tenniel are presented here. The tennis rackets in the cover illustration suggest a relationship with the image of the world as a "tennis ball for fools" used in *The World Turned Upside Down* (1750), while the frontispiece of the world broken into two parts and the title-page juggler doing a handstand both suggest reversal (compare with Carroll's Father William). Marguerite Mespoulet suggests a strong connection between Tenniel and Grandville in *The Creators of Wonderland*. The two illustrators most certainly knew each other's work, since Tenniel illustrated for *Punch*, while Grandville's work frequently appeared in *Chivari*, magazines that had a following on each side of the Channel. The connection between *Alice in Wonderland* and *Un Autre Monde*, both of which use reversals generally and the world turned upside down specifically, has not been made previously. Carroll certainly shared with Grandville an interest in the idea of the portmanteau, with its roots in the composite animals presented in the margins of mediaeval psalters.

Frontispiece

Title Page Illustration
La Clef des Champs

Je veux aller où me conduira ma fantaisie;
je prétends moi-même me servir de guide: vive la liberté!

La poursuite

Les héraldiques

Heinrich Hoffmann, excerpts from *The English Struwwelpeter;*
or Pretty Stories and Funny Pictures for Little Children
(Leipsic: Friedrich Volcxmar, 1848).

Hoffmann's collection of hilarious, although never "pretty," stories are the kind Alice shows a knowledge of when she refuses the invitation to "Drink me." Alice is obviously a wide reader, being familiar with cautionary tales as well as nursery rhymes, fairy tales, lullabies, riddles, informational books, etc. Her knowledge of the cautionary tale is acted upon here, demonstrating that she has been alert to intended adult content when experiencing it. Hoffmann's parodies include a classic topos from the world upside down – "The Story of the Man that went out Shooting" becomes the story of the man who is shot by a rabbit who has stolen his rifle.

The Story of the Man that went out Shooting

This is the man that shoots the hares;
This is the coat he always wears:
With game-bag, powder-horn, and gun
He's going out to have some fun.

He finds it hard, without
    a pair
Of spectacles, to shoot the
    hare.

The hare sits snug in leaves and grass,
And laughs to see the green man pass.

Now, as the sun grew very hot,
And he a heavy gun had got,
He lay down underneath a tree
And went to sleep, as you may see.
And, while he slept like any top,
The little hare came, hop, hop, hop,
Took gun and spectacles, and then
On her hind legs went off again.

The green man wakes and sees her place
The spectacles upon her face;
And now she's trying all she can
To shoot the sleepy, green-coat man.
He cries and screams and runs away;
The hare runs after him all day
And hears him call out everywhere:
'' Help! Fire! Help! The Hare! The Hare!''

At last he stumbled at the well,
Head over ears, and in he fell.
The hare stopped short, took aim and, hark!
Bang went the gun—she missed her mark!

The poor man's wife was drinking up
Her coffee in her coffee-cup;
The gun shot cup and saucer through;
" Oh dear!" cried she; " what shall I do?"
There lived close by the cottage there
The hare's own child, the little hare;
And while she stood upon her toes,
The coffee fell and burned her nose.
" Oh dear!" she cried, with spoon in hand,
" Such fun I do not understand."

Tom Hood, excerpts from *Upside Down; or, Turnover Traits*
(London: Griffith and Farran, 1868).

This book, with accompanying upside-down sketches by William Mc-
Connell, is a delightful attack on perception, establishing that perspective
has a transforming power.

UPSIDE DOWN;

OR.

Turnover Traits.

FROM ORIGINAL SKETCHES, BY THE LATE

WILLIAM McCONNELL,

WITH ILLUSTRATIVE VERSES BY

TOM HOOD.

LONDON:

GRIFFITH AND FARRAN,
(SUCCESSORS TO NEWBERY AND HARRIS),
CORNER OF ST. PAUL'S CHURCHYARD.
MDCCCLXVIII.

[*Entered at Stationers' Hall.*]

AS GREEDY AS A PIG.

His face is flat
And very fat—
    His body's round and big—
He eats all day,
And people say,
    "He's greedy as a pig!"

His legs are short,
A funny sort
    To run or dance a jig,—
He looks like this
Because he is
    "As greedy as a pig!"

His name is Jack,
But folks, alack,
    All call him "Tiggy Tig!"
Because, you see,
This urchin, he
    "Is greedy as a pig!"

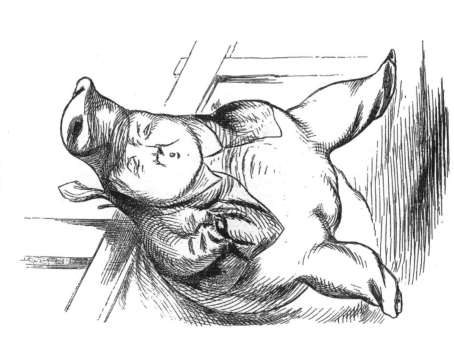

A PIG.

AS GREEDY AS

AS MARKED AS A ZEBRA.

DARK hair,
Fine eyes,
Graceful air,
Middle size,
Neat figure,
Small hand—
Foot no bigger,
Manners grand,
Stately walk,
Dress in stripes,
Pleasant talk,—
These are types
Proving plainly as Algebra,
She's as marked as any Zebra!

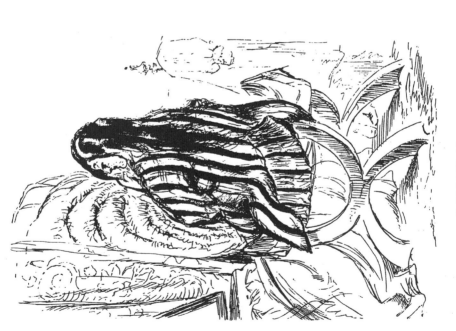

A ZEBRA.

Jean Jambon (pseudonym), *Our Trip to Blunderland;
or, Grand Excursion to Blundertown and Back*
(Edinburgh and London: William Blackwood and Sons, 1877).

This book was listed among several others in Carroll's diary note for 11 September 1891 as a book of "the Alice type." When the three young travellers arrive in "Blunderland," the first things they see are a man riding a horse backwards and a boy in a man's clothing observing an old man dressed as a schoolboy.

When the noise was at its height, Norval said to the chairman, "It seems to get greater nonsense at every verse."

"To she bure it does," said he; "you are etting ginto Blunderland, and hings don't thappen there as dey tho in pother laces."

"Yes, indeed," said an old gentleman; "look out at the floor and you will hear with your own toes what cruel of a place this is."

Neither he nor the chairman could help speaking thus, being in Blunderland; but Norval guessed that the old gentleman meant he was to look and see what kind of a place the train had got into, so turned and gazed out at the window. The first thing he saw was a man riding with his face to the horse's tail, holding the reins like the tiller-ropes of a boat, which was rather difficult, as he had top-boots on his hands. A little further on came an old man who had a string tied to his leg, the other end of which was held by a pig in a poke-bonnet and a stylish shawl. Next he saw a very old man with short trousers and a pinafore, a satchel over his shoulders, and a slate hanging at his side, at whom a boy not older than himself, in a green coat with brass buttons, and a white hat, carrying a gold-headed cane, was looking through an eye-glass.

Jaques had joined Norval, and suddenly called out, "What are they doing in that field?"

"Oh," said the chairman, "they are tigging the durnips."

What they were really doing was emptying carts of large stones on the field.

Appendix 4
(Chapter 5)
Representative Looking-Glass Books
from 1673 to the 1870s

Abraham Chear, excerpts from *A Looking Glass for Children;*
Being a Narrative of God's Gracious Dealings with some Little Children;
recollected by Henry Jessey in his Life-Time. Together with sundry seasonable
Lessons and Instructions to Youth, Calling them early to remember
their Creator: Written by Abraham Chear late of Plymouth, 2d ed.
(London: Robert Boulter, 1673).

This is the first children's book that associates itself with the tradition of the looking-glass book and its long, generally satiric history. Children's books as conceived by the religious writers of the seventeenth century fit snugly into the exemplary form of the looking-glass book. As Chear put it in a verse on page 24 of his book, "Those worthy Mirrors of their Age, / obtain'd a precious Name; / Their living Pattern should engage / your souls to do the same." Chear uses the lives of spiritually "worthy" children as positive models, and the lives of "fallen" children as admonitions to do otherwise. Included are a few "puritan elegies" that find the qualities and the significance of people present in the very letters of their names. One's life, so to speak, is mirrored in the letters of one's name and is worked out through anagrams.

To the Reader:

The motive provoking me thus to recollect this little book, is chiefly from consideration of my daily observation of Youth's great need of all endeavors to prompt them to that which is good, they being naturally addicted to be drawn away through their own inclinations, and the powerful prevalency of Satan to sin and disobedience.

First, of Mary Warren, Born in May 1651, Aged ten years in May 1661

When this child was about five or six years old, she had a new plain Tommy coat; and when she was made ready, was to be carried with other children into May-fields. But having looked upon her coat, how fine she was, she presently went to her chair, sate down, her tears running down her eyes, she wept seriously by herself; Her mother, seeing it, said to her, How now? Are you not well? What's the matter that you weep? The child answered, Yes, I am well, but I would I had not been made ready, for I am afraid my fine clothes will cast me down to hell. Her mother said, It's not our clothes, but wicked hearts that hurt us. She anewred, Aye mother, fine clothes make our hearts proud. (7)

The story of Mary Warren is interesting in that it is obviously a story to be used by children as a positive model and, thereby, immediately clashes with Chear's assumptions in "To the Reader." Such exemplary children, Chear emphasizes, should be copied by the reader:

> Those worthy Mirrors of their Age
>   obtain'd a precious Name;
> Their living Pattern should engage
>   your souls to do the same. (24)

Written to a Young Virgin, Anno 1663

… When by spectators I am told
What Beauty doth adorn me:
Or in a glass when I behold
How sweetly God did form me.

Hath God such comeliness display'd
And on me made to dwell?
'Tis pity, such a pretty maid
As I, should go to hell. (27)

These two verses have the looking-glass literally included in them. The first emphasizes the child as pattern, while the second presents a particular pattern in a verse narrative.

To My Cousin Sam

Dear Cousin Sam, my pretty Lam,
     this song to you I send;
Whatever play, aside you lay,
     learn this from end to end.
With God begin, take heed of sin,
     know Jesus out of hand.
Betimes you must, flee youthful lust,
     its first assaults withstand.

Spend not your days, in wanton plays,
     though naughty boyes entice:
They first begin, in little sin,
     but end in deadly vice.

If naughty Boyes, allure with toyes,
     to sin, or lies to tell;
Then tell them plain, you tempt in vain,
     such wayes go down to Hell. (40)

Anonymous, *Proverbs in Verse, or Moral Instruction Conveyed in Pictures,
for the Use of Schools* (London, 1790).

The title page of this book uses a traditional illustration in which a mirror
is being held in place to allow or force someone to come to terms with self.
Here it is Truth who holds the mirror to Folly, who "shrinks back" from his
own image.

Proverbs in Verse,

OR

MORAL INSTRUCTION

CONVEYED IN

PICTURES,

FOR THE USE OF SCHOOLS:

On the Plan of Hogarth moralized,

BY THE SAME AUTHOR.

WITH FIFTY SIX CUTS:

TO WHICH ARE PREFIXED

RULES FOR READING VERSE.

Know thyself's the great axiom in life,
Truth to Folly here shows its grimace;
It shrinks back; with itself, as in strife,
On seeing its face in the Glass.

LONDON:
SOLD BY SOUTER, 1 PATERNOSTER ROW.

Arnault Berquin, excerpts from *The Looking-glass for the Mind;
or, Intellectual Mirror. Being an Elegant Collection of the Most Delightful
Little Stories, and Interesting Tales, Chiefly translated from that much
admired Work, L'Ami Des Enfans* (London: E. Newbery, 1792).

It was not Berquin, but his English translator, who gave his book the
looking-glass title. The title and preface make totally clear that this is a

rational/moral looking-glass book in which reason replaces religious belief as the basis for proper behaviour.

The stories here collected are of the most interesting kind, since Virtue is constantly represented as the Fountain of Happiness, and Vice as the Source of every Evil. Nothing extravagant or romantic will be found in these Tales, neither enchanted Castles, nor supernatural Agents, but such Sciences are exhibited as are in the Reach of the Observations of Young People in Common Life, the Whole being made familiar by an innocent Turn of Thought and Expression, and applied to describe their Amusements, their Pursuits, and their Necessities.

As a useful and instructive pocket Looking-glass, we recommend it to the instruction of every Youth, whether Miss or Master; it is a mirror that will not flatter them, nor lead them into error, it destroys the follie and improper pursuit of the Youthful Breast, points out the dangerous paths they sometimes tread, and clears the way to the Temple of Honour and Fame.

A Lady attended by Virtue and Prudence presenting her Children to Minerva from whom they are receiving the Looking Glass

THE
LOOKING-GLASS

FOR THE
M I N D;

OR,

INTELLECTUAL MIRROR.

BEING

AN ELEGANT COLLECTION OF THE MOST
DELIGHTFUL LITTLE STORIES,
AND INTERESTING TALES,

Chiefly translated from that much admired Work,

L'AMI DES ENFANS.

A NEW EDITION,
WITH SEVENTY-FOUR CUTS, DESIGNED AND
ENGRAVED ON WOOD
BY BEWICK.

LONDON:
PRINTED BY J.CROWDER,
FOR E. NEWBERY, THE CORNER OF
ST. PAUL'S CHURCH-YARD.

M,DCC,XCII.

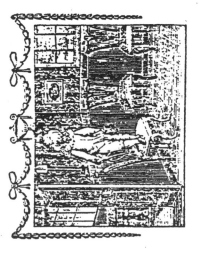

LITTLE ANTHONY.

ON one of those fine mornings, which the month of June frequently affords us, little Anthony was busily employed in preparing to set out with his father on a party of pleasure, which, for several days before, had engrossed all his attention. Though, in general, he found it very difficult to rise early, yet this morning he got up soon, without being called, so much was his mind fixed on the intended jaunt.

It often happens, with young people in particular, that, all on a sudden, they lose the object they flattered themselves they were almost in possession of. So it fared with little Anthony; for just as they were ready to set out, the sky darkened all at once, the clouds grew thick, and a tempestuous wind bent down the trees, and raised a cloud of dust.

Little Anthony was running down the garden every minute to see how the sky looked, and then jumped up stairs to examine the barometer; but neither the sky nor the barometer seemed to forebode any thing in his favour. Notwithstanding all this, he gave his father the most flattering hopes that it would still be a fair day, and that these unfavourable appearances would soon disperse. He doubted not but that it would be one of the finest days in the world; and he therefore thought, that the sooner they set out the better, as it would be a pity to lose a moment of their time.

His father, however, did not choose to be too hasty in giving credit to his son's predictions, and thought it more adviseable to wait a little. While Anthony and his father were reasoning on this matter, the clouds burst, and down came a very heavy

heavy ſhower of rain. Poor Anthony was now doubly diſappointed, and vented his grief in tears, refuſing to liſten to the voice of conſolation.

The rain continued without intermiſſion, till three o'clock in the afternoon, when the clouds began to diſperſe, the ſun reſumed its ſplendour, the element its clearneſs, and all nature breathed the odours of the ſpring. As the weather brightened, ſo did the countenance of little Anthony, and by degrees he recovered his good humour.

His father now thought it neceſſary to indulge him with a little walk, and off they ſet. The calmneſs of the air, the muſic of the feathered ſongſters, the lively and enchanting verdure of the fields, and the ſweet perfumes that breathed all round them, completely quieted and compoſed the troubled heart of the diſappointed Anthony.

" Do not you obſerve (ſaid his father to him) how agreeable is the change of every thing before you? You cannot have yet forgotten how dull every thing appeared to us yeſterday; the ground was parched up for want of rain; the flowers had loſt their colour, and hung their heads in languor; and, in ſhort, all nature ſeemed to be in a ſtate of inaction. What can be the reaſon, that nature has ſo ſuddenly put on ſuch a different aſpect?"

aſpect?"—" That is eaſily accounted for, Sir, (ſaid Anthony) it undoubtedly is occaſioned by the rain that has fallen to-day."

Anthony had no ſooner pronounced theſe words, than he ſaw his father's motive for aſking him the queſtion. He now plainly perceived the impropriety of his late conduct, in being ſo unhappy about what was evidently ſo univerſally ſerviceable. He bluſhed, but his father took no notice of it, judging that his own ſenſe would ſufficiently teach him another time, without reluctance, to ſacrifice ſelfiſh pleaſure to the general good of the community at large.

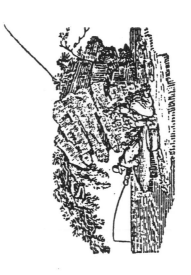

Anonymous, excerpt from *A Looking-Glass for Youth and Age;*
or, A Sure Guide to Life and Glory, set forth in a heavenly Dialogue
between a Godly Gentleman and his only Daughter, a Child of ten years of age
(London: n.p., c. 1800).

This book is an example of the use of the looking-glass book in evangelical religious didacticism. It echoes the religious origins of the form as developed in seventeenth-century children's literature. It is obvious that the looking-glass form, together with the informational work presented next, was thought to be serviceable by writers with a wide range of attitudes towards proper children. Carroll's parodic range includes rational/moral and informational books and some few works that present acceptable religious morality, but there is no identifiable book of religious didacticism parodied at length in the Alice books. See Humphrey Carpenter's chapter on Carroll in his *Secret Gardens*, in which he interprets *Alice in Wonderland* as an "unconscious" attack on transubstantiation.

Father. Child, wilt thou place thy affections on the follies and vanities of this life, as worldlings do?
Daughter. No Sir, but pass a short time of my sojourning here as Pilgrims do: and long to be with Christ, and be dissolved.
Father. Dear Child, in the next place, if God should bless you with children, don't set thy heart upon them too much, lest thou provoke a jealous God to remove those blessed objects from you for looking more on the gift than the giver; for they are certain cares but uncertain comforts. (6–7)

William Pinnock, excerpt from *A Catechism of Optics*
(London: William Pinnock, 1820).

Pinnock's numerous "Catechisms" of information, on such subjects as arithmetic, geography, perspective, history, and heraldry, were extraordinarily popular. As the formula title suggests, children were meant to learn the information present through dialogue or conversation. The material was meant to be memorized, just as Watts asked children to memorize his religious songs. Presented here are a few simple questions and answers that touch on reversibility, running in place, and other issues important in *Through the Looking-Glass*. Pinnock's publications, together with those of Samuel Griswold Goodrich, were very important in the first half of the nineteenth century.

Q. Is the image on the retina inverted?

A. It is; but the position of the image on the retina has nothing to do with that of the object seen, though we turn the head horizontally, or even invert it, fixed objects do not shift, if we know that we are moving.

Q. And if we do not know that we are moving?

A. If we have not some collateral evidence of that, we fancy that all objects move, as any one must have observed when riding a carriage or walking. (47–8)

Q. Why is [the astronomical telescope] limited … ?

A. It inverts objects, or turns them upside down; therefore it doesn't answer so well for objects upon the earth. (66)

Q. Has the common looking-glass any other effect than that of representing the images of objects?

A. Yes, it reverses them; writing which is the right way, is seen backwards in a mirror; and that which is written backwards reads the right way. (70)

Newman (One of the Writers in Punch) and Hain Friswell,
excerpts from *The Laughable Looking Glass for Little Folks*
(London: Dean & Son, 1857 and 1859).

Here the looking-glass form is turned into a lighter-hearted form of comedy, but it is still comedy intended to teach by presenting proper and improper models of behaviour. The W. McConnell illustration of a woman holding up a child to a mirror has roots in the earlier illustrations by Bewick and others, and could serve for either exemplary or admonitory didacticism. More importantly, the image is very close to Alice's didactic posture when she takes her kitten to the looking-glass to show it how "sulky" it is, which leads to her suggestion of passing through the looking-glass, an action suggested initially as a punishment for her kitten.

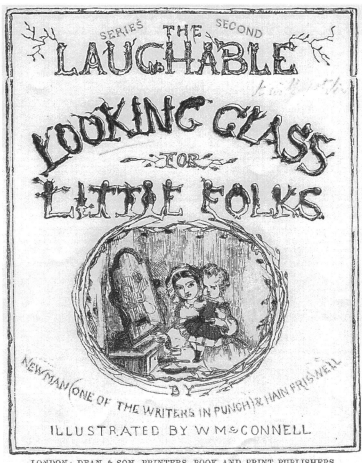

SERIES THE SECOND
LAUGHABLE
LOOKING GLASS
FOR
LITTLE FOLKS
BY
NEWMAN (ONE OF THE WRITERS IN PUNCH) & HAIN FRISWELL
ILLUSTRATED BY W MᶜCONNELL
LONDON: DEAN & SON, PRINTERS, BOOK AND PRINT PUBLISHERS,
11, LUDGATE HILL.

THE ILL-NATURED, OR SELFISH BOY.

THERE lived a boy, who always cross
And selfish was ; who'd keep his horse,
 His battledore, or kite
All to *himself* ; and he would say,
You " *shant.*" If some one wished to play—
 Rather than play he'd fight.

On the first day he went to school,
His father, the first grief to cool,

A kite bought, with great wings
That would up mount into the sky,
Just like a skylark when, quite high
IIe flies, and flying sings.

The boys around him gathered then,
And hoped that he would play with
them.
But no, he would not do it,
Alone he'd fly his kite; so he
Did try, but it hung in a tree—
So torn you could see through it.

Loud laughed the boys to see him
stand
Quite rueful, with the string in hand.
Let this a lesson be,

Said one; I would have shown you how
To fly your kite—'tis useless now,
Both unto you and me.

One day his Aunt bought him a drum;
And said—"Here, Tommy, hither come,
        And be a dear, good boy;
Let others play with this, with theirs
They'll let you play, and you'll go shares
        In many a pretty toy."

But when the drum was tied around
His neck, Tom pouted, puff'd, and frowned;
        And, as his drum he beat,
He thought the boys will envy me
When, with this drum, they look and see
        Me marching down the street.

Just at that time his Grandpa came,
Who cried out, " Tommy, what a game!
        " Pray, let me see that toy."
Tom cried, "I shan't," and ran
        away,
Nor would he for his Grandpa
        stay,
        The foolish, selfish boy!

But see what selfish boys be-
        fall:
He thought not, if he thought at
        all,
        The punishment would come

So soon.   He slipped, and down the stairs
He fell, 'midst shrieks, and cries, and tears.
Right headlong through his drum.
Not only did he spoil his toy,
But also—serve him right, bad boy—
He cut his face and nose;
He scratched his chin, and bruised his head;
His lip was also cut, and bled
All down his birthday clothes.

THE QUARRELSOME CHILDREN.

MANY roses on one tree
Blossom together, and agree ;
Cherries, on one stalk combined,
Never quarrelling, I find ;
Lambs, that o'er the meadows bound,
Friendly live the summer round.
Yet these have nor sense, nor soul,
Envious passions to control.
Then should dearest children be
Found less wise than brute or tree?

John and Mary, Fred and Kate,
Meet Dick's birth to celebrate.

Toys and games, in heaps, they bring—
All looks cheerful as the spring.
Like the spring—alas! how soon
Angry clouds obscure the sun!
Mary's doll is twice the size
Of cousin Kate's, and moves its eyes.
Mary boasts, and Kate is cross.
John has got the biggest horse.

RED, offended, will not play:
Dick has hid his ark away.
Sullen looks and answers short
Soon succeed, and end their sport.
Angry words (I'm shocked to say)
Often end in cruel fray.
They who lately playmates were,
Fight and pull each other's hair.
Sometimes blood to flow is seen;—
Let me close the hateful scene!

See yon building, vast and high,
Tow'ring up from earth to sky;
Brick, and stone, and lead, and wood,
In well ordered lines bestowed.
For an instant, let's suppose
Brick and stone should fall to blows,
Wall and buttress, roof and base,
Squabbling for each other's place;

Soon the whole to earth would fall
In a shapeless ruin all.
From this fable, children, learn
Ne'er to let ill passions burn.
Envious tempers peace destroy,
Friendship doubles every joy;
While harsh words and wrangling raise
Keen regrets for future days.

Appendix 5
(Chapter 6)
Some Nineteenth-Century Dream Visions

Anonymous, *The Child's Dream*
(London: printed by J. Catnach, c. 1820).

This is a representative religious dream vision (in the tradition of Bunyan's *The Pilgrim's Progress*) specially produced for children during the religious revival of the first part of the nineteenth century. For all of the book's apparent simplicity, it is a rather complex presentation of a child's coming to terms with both the death of a loved one and his own personal mortality. This complexity is established by the rearrangement of the formal sections of the dream vision. The reader learns that the speaker's own anxiety and fear in the face of death have been introduced by the death of his sister, but this is not stated in the opening frame. Rather, it is introduced after the reassuring and conventional depiction of an afterlife, of heaven, that the boy is guided to and through by an angelic figure, part heavenly maid and part the Queen of May. This journey takes place in the dream-core that follows the opening frame. This central discovery buffers the child dreamer and the child reader from death, wrapping death round with a narrative about its ultimate defeat; the narrative allays anxiety and allows the child a concluding vision of the reunion of his family in heaven. Of immediate importance here is the fact that the three-part structure of the mediaeval dream vision — the presentation of anxiety, the narrative that helps allay anxiety, and the conclusion that confirms that anxiety has been allayed — is still alive in the nineteenth century and is used in a children's book. A well-known dream vision that is incorporated into a longer narrative is George Arthur's dream in *Tom Brown's School Days*, a mid-century book that had a large readership.

THE
CHILD'S
DREAM.

O, you know whom I saw last night,
    When sleeping in my bed, mamma?
A shining creature all in white,
    She   seem'd   a   heavenly   maid,
    mamma.

I saw her tripping o'er the dew,
    Fair as the queen of May, mamma,

2 THE CHILD'S DREAM.

She look'd, she smil'd, and to me flew,
    And bade me come away, mamma.
She gently drew my curtains wide,
    And whisper'd sweetly mild, mamma,
While graceful kneeling at my side,
    That I should be her child, mamma.

And then she beckon'd me on high,
    In purest joys to dwell, mamma,
Where, in bright mansions of the sky,
    Are joys no tongue can tell, mamma.
I look'd, I lov'd, I blush'd awhile,
    O! how could I say no, mamma;
She spoke so sweet, so sweet did smile,
    I was oblig'd to go, mamma.

For love my infant heart beguil'd,
    I hail'd the rapt'rous theme, mamma,
My infant fancy turn'd as wild,
    As you may think my dream, mamma.
Methought we wander'd in a grove,
    And then thro' pleasant fields, mamma,
In joyful converse we did move,
    As music rapture yields, mamma.

And as the beauteous flow'rs we press'd
    And as their odours flew, mamma,
A fervent wish rose in my breast,
    To share those sweets with you, mamma.
I was, I was, I know not how,
    O! had you been with me, mamma,
Such wonders open'd to my view,
    As none but angels see, mamma

THE CHILD'S DREAM. 3

She took me in her snow-white hand,
   And led me through the air, mamma,
We soon lost sight of sea and land,
   And rang'd I know not where, mamma.

Yet to the verdant fields of earth,
   I cast a look of care, mamma,
To think that you who gave me birth,
   And all my friends were there, mamma

The heavenly maid my sorrow saw,
   And sweetly chas'd all gloom mamma,
Me to her breast did gently draw
   And whisper'd you should come, mamma.

Swift as our thoughts in youthful day
   We glanc'd beyond the spheres, mamma,
There music sounding by the way,
   Heaven rush'd upon our ears, mamma.

Far through the realms of boundless space
   We pass'd in rapid flight, mamma;
I saw the angels anxious gaze,
   And hail us with delight, mamma.

Sun, moon, and stars we knew before,
   Were lost unto our view, mamma,
The former things were now no more,
   But all things now were new, mamma

For we had gain'd the arch of heaven,
   Where glory full appears, mamma,
And saw the source whence motion given
   Impels the distant spheres, mamma.

And music's most seraphic tone
   Swell'd in angelic strains, mamma,

6   THE CHILD'S DREAM.

As we approach'd the radiant throne
   Where God supremely reigns, mamma.

One universal blaze of light,
   Shone thro' the wide expanse, mamma,
And not one shade of cheerless night
   Could cloud the raptur'd sense, mamma.

The pearly gates were open'd wide,
   Soon as we knocked there, mamma—
But oh! but oh! on every side,
   What heavenly glories were, mamma.

The happy spirits flocked around
   To welcome me above, mamma,
And loud the golden harps did sound,
   In praise of Him they love, mamma.

I heard a heavenly hymning host,
   A holy happy train, mamma,
Praise Him whose form in glory lost
   Is by reflection seen, mamma.

They clad me in a shining vest,
   And crown'd my head with light, mam ma,

THE CHILD'S DREAM.   7

Clasp'd round my shoulders and my breast,
  The robe of glory bright, mamma.

As o'er the heavenly plains we pass'd,
  Our heavenly joy increas'd, mamma,
I wish'd! I wish'd! it long might last,
  So charming was the feast, mamma.

No age can tip the head with snow,
  Nor numbness seize the limbs, mamma
But vigour doth more vig'rous grow
  As each up Zion climbs, mamma.

No sickness, death, nor sorrow there,
  To damp their heavenly bliss, mamma
These fruits of sin with sorrow are,
  Deep buried in the abyss, mamma.

The rushing tears which do arise
  When we are sick, you know, mamma,
Are wip'd by Jesus from all eyes,
  Such love he then doth show, mamma.

All who his precepts shall obey,
  And virtue's paths do tread, mamma,

8   THE CHILD'S DREAM.

Shall rise to realms of endless day,
   And children be of God, mamma.

With wintry storms the ground ne'er pines,
   The fields are ever green, mamma
For there the sun of glory shines
   In skies the most serene mamma.

I saw my sister Anna there,
   A virgin in full blow, mamma,
Such things to me she did declare
   As only angels know, mamma.

Her robes were all a flowing stream,
   Of silver dipp'd in light, mamma,
But ah! it wak'd me from my dream,
   It shone so clear and bright, mamma.

Now I will walk with Anna's God,
   And be an angel too, mamma;
For in yon high and bright abode,
   They constant pleasure know, mamma.

Then teach me now the happy way
   To gain a throne above, mamma,
That I with them in endless day,
   May praise the God of love, mamma.

Then you and I, and father dear,
   Will join our Anna there, mamma,
In presence of the Lamb appear,
   And dwell for evermore, mamma.

London.---Printed by *J. CATNACH*, 2 & 3,
Monmouth-court, 7 Dials.

Frederick E. Weatherly, *Elsie's Expedition*
(London: Frederick Warne and Company, 1874).

This is one of a small group of works published after Carroll's Alice books
that Carroll identified as attempts to work with the same "pattern" or
"type" that he had used in his two fantasies. These works certainly do attempt to reproduce the pattern of the dream vision, but they generally fall
short in establishing that pattern. Further, they present trivial thematic material. In *Elsie's Expedition*, Elsie's particular anxiety is that she feels trapped
by the nature of the book as intermediary, literally trapped by the outsize
book she is reading and figuratively trapped in that the book refuses her entry into its world. Dream opens the book's closed door to a train station
and allows Elsie to participate in, rather than simply to observe, the imaginative world behind it. Full participation comes in the final chapter, in
which Elsie is the heroine of what Carroll would have called a poetic portmanteau combining elements of "A Solemn Dirge" or "Ding Dong Bell"
with Ariel's song from *The Tempest*. The obvious weakness here is the closing frame, which attempts to affirm the positive dream-core simply by having Elsie's readjustment to "reality" occur very slowly. A greater weakness is
that Weatherly fails to come to terms with some of the more threatening
suggestions of the composite rhyme in which he puts Elsie.

ELSIE'S EXPEDITION.

BY

FREDERICK E. WEATHERLY, M.A.

AUTHOR OF

"MURIEL, AND OTHER POEMS."

THE ILLUSTRATIONS BY H. CROSS.

LONDON:

FREDERICK WARNE AND CO.,

BEDFORD STREET, STRAND.

NEW YORK: SCRIBNER, WELFORD, AND ARMSTRONG.

NOTE BY THE AUTHOR.

I admit that this book would in all probability
never have been written, had I not seen "Alice's
Adventures in Wonderland." That it is an *imitation*
of a successful style of Nursery Literature I also
admit; but of the charge of *plagiarism* I appeal
to impartial Readers to acquit me.

Oxford, 1874.

ELSIE'S EXPEDITION.

CHAPTER I.

NDERNEATH a shady oak tree, at the corner of a pleasant garden, if you had looked carefully, you might have seen a straw hat trimmed with pink ribbons; and if you had ventured to lift up the straw hat, as I did, you would have found under it a little face very intently poring over a large picture-book—indeed, so large was the book, that the little legs of the reader were completely covered, like a couple of wee mice in a trap.

ELSIE.

Of course you don't know who the little girl is. How should you? Even if you looked at her, you would not know. So I will tell you. Her name is Elsie.

That's all. I suppose she has another name —but that's neither here nor there.

Where? I don't know. Do you?

Little Elsie has been reading her large book all the morning, and, as it is very interesting and not very difficult, the words being rarely of more than one syllable, she has managed to keep awake, in spite of the warm summer wind and the buzzing gnats.

Perhaps what pleases her most is looking at the pictures—one in particular, a railway station. It is a fine building of red brick, built in that elegant and popular style known as "Carpenter's Gothic," with a great many coloured and fantastic bricks floating vaguely about all over the walls, and straggling up under the gables, playing bo-peep with the caps and shoots of the roof.

Strangely enough, to Elsie's thinking and to her exceeding annoyance, the door is shut; and though there are several porters standing placidly about the place, not one of them is polite enough to open the door to her.

"Why won't you open the door?" said Elsie, giving the stupidest of the porters a poke in the face with a little dimpled finger. But the man vouchsafes no answer, and is apparently perfectly oblivious to her pokes or her presence.

"You stupid man, you! I want to go inside, like the little girl in the book," she said.

Still the porters neither moved nor spoke.

Little Elsie was tired, for the book was heavy; so she laid it on the grass, still open at the picture of the tantalizing station. She got up with great difficulty, for she had "pins and needles" in both her little legs. She looked at the station from various distances—now stooping—now holding back; and at last lay down on her knees and chest, supporting her chin in her hands, and burrowing with her elbows into the deep cool grass.

"Now, if you were a church, I shouldn't wonder, you know," she went on, apostrophizing the obstinate station, "because they always keep the churches shut except on Sundays; but being a station, you ought to be open.—And as for you, you stupid men," —and once more she poked the placid porters in their faces.

"I wonder, now," she mused—"I wonder if I could open the door myself? The little girl in the book did; and she didn't dress herself, and I do: I'm much older than she was!"

As she spoke, Elsie put her little hand to the station door, and to her great delight and surprise, it opened, and in she walked.

CHAPTER II.

THE inside of the station was very unlike the outside; and Elsie could not help wondering how those porters outside managed to preserve such dignified indifference to the noise and confusion going on within.

However, as she kept her wonder to herself, it didn't much matter. Seeing everybody rushing to the ticket-office, Elsie thought she would rush also, and accordingly edged her way into the crowd. Behind her was a chimney-sweeper, and in front a little old man dressed in a blue coat and brass buttons, with trousers and waistcoat to match. The chimney-sweeper kept coming very close to Elsie, much to her dismay, and would persist in asking her to brush off "some o' this nasty dirty flour" that was on his jacket. Elsie, not at all caring to blacken her fingers or her clothes, followed very close on the heels of the little old man —so close, in fact, that she stepped on one of his shoes, which was very much down at heel. Whereupon, the little old man turned round, and said savagely,

"Where yer pushing to?"

"I'm not pushing two," answered Elsie, indignantly, and ignorant of her offence.

"Yes, yer are!"

"You aren't two, are you?" said Elsie.

"What d'yer mean?" snarled the little old man.

"You said pushing two, and I'm only pushing you; and you're one, not two—so there!"

"Pooh!" said the little old man, "pooh! who are you?"

"If it comes to that, sir!" answered Elsie, "who are you?"

"Pooh!" again said the little old man, with a snort, "pooh!"

"Ah! I know who you are," exclaimed Elsie. "But you aren't like yourself a bit: you are so cross. You got out of bed the wrong side this morning, I'm sure. Where's your horn, eh?"

"What d'yer mean?" again growled the little old man.

"Your horn—don't you know? I've seen you before—lots of times—only you were younger then. I used to sing a little song to you. I'll sing it now if you like,"—and, without waiting for his consent, she sang:

"'Little Boy Blue, blow me your horn,
Or I'll tread on your coat-tails, and crash on your corn.'"

There was a general laugh, in which the little old man did *not* join; and he was still more enraged when he heard the rhyme taken up and repeated around him in various keys and voices:

"'Little Boy Blue, blow me your horn,
Or I'll tread on your coat-tails, and crash on your corn.'"

At last Elsie reached the aperture of the ticket-office, and, by standing on tiptoe, just managed to see the face of the clerk.

"If you please, I want a ticket," she said.

"Where for?" asked the clerk.

"There and back again, of course," answered Elsie, pertly, for she was astonished that the clerk should ask her such a question.

"Where?" he roared.

"There," repeated Elsie. "There and back again. T, H, E, R, E,—*there*. Don't you know how to spell?"

"Spell? No," said the clerk. "Can you? Well, here's your ticket," he went on. "I suppose it's all right," he said, in a shuffling sort of voice, as though afraid to confess his ignorance of the locality. "Besides, there are so many accidents to arrange that I really can't be bothered."

"Thank you, sir; much obliged," said Elsie, mollified, as she pocketed her ticket and was moving off.

"Here! Hi! Stop! You haven't paid," shouted the clerk.

"Oh! I forgot," said Elsie. "Hold out your hand."

The clerk, half angry, half amused, held out his hand.

Elsie put her hand in his, and said, "There! There's the money."

"There's no money that I can see," responded the clerk.

"Oh, but you must pretend it's money," explained Elsie; "that's what mamma does to me."

"Oh, come, that won't do," replied the clerk, testily; "you must pay your money, or you can't go by train."

"But I haven't got any money," pleaded Elsie—"not any *real* money, you know; and you're so stupid, you won't pretend it's money. Mamma always does."

A gentleman standing behind Elsie, seeing her dilemma, paid for her ticket, and set her mind at rest. She imagined ever afterwards that he was the typical individual

> "With a pocket full of money,
> And a cellar full of beer."

Whether he was blessed or cursed with these possessions, Elsie never succeeded in discovering.

Intent on her journey, she darted off to take her seat in the train.

"Now, ma'am," said a porter, very civilly, "where's your luggage?"

"Dear me," said Elsie, "how very odd! Mamma always said the porters never would do anything for one unless they were tipped. Are you quite sure you're not making a mistake, my good man?" she added, turning to the owner of those creaking corduroys.

The man looked at her in blank astonishment, executed a profound salaam, and repeated,

"Where's your luggage, ma'am?"

"Oh, here's my luggage," replied Elsie, pro-

ducing from her pocket an apple and three biscuits. "That does for luggage when I go out with my train on the dining-room table."

The porter said nothing: received the articles—labelled them, put them in the luggage-van, and came and informed Elsie of the fact.

"I've got no money," said Elsie, still fancying the man expected a tip.

"Madam," said the porter, in a deep voice quivering with emotion, "we gets our wages, and we is content."

And having so delivered himself, he withdrew,

CHAPTER XIV.

WITH a faith and charity that did Elsie infinite credit, she took off her boots and stockings, and laid them carefully at the side of the well.

The summer sun shone so gaily through the leaves, and the winds sprang up just enough to rustle them, so that they sang to her, as she put one little bare foot after another into the cool clear water,

"Ding, dong, bell!
Elsie's in the well!"

Slowly, slowly, down she glided, while everything above grew farther and fainter. All round her the water was flickering bright and opal, changing from tint to tint in the softened sheen that rained from above.

As her two little bare feet lighted on the silver sand at the bottom of the well, and as she looked round to see Pussy, but in vain—she heard this little song sung by lips unseen above. Very softly and sweetly the sound came falling through the water.

"Full fathom five
In Woodside well,
Little Elsie
Sinks to dwell!

Her blue eyes to those below
Reflex of the heavens will show;
Her sweet laugh shall speak the love
And music of the world above.
Ding-dong! ding-dong! ding, dong, bell!
Elsie lives in Woodside well!"

And the water ran and rippled over the silver gravel, whispering joyfully,

"Ding, dong, bell!
Elsie lives in Woodside well."

*   *   *   *   *

Ding-dong! ding-dong!
Dingle-dingle! ding, DING, DONG!

What loud bell was that ringing in Elsie's ears, disturbing the peacefulness of Woodside Well?

"Miss Elsie! Miss Elsie!"
What familiar voice was that calling her?

She rubbed her eyes to make sure that she really was where she thought she was—down in the bottom of Woodside Well. But as she rubbed them, all the bright water, and the cool green mosses and ferns, and the glancing silver gravel seemed to fade away!

She looked up, and there was Mary standing over her where she lay on the grass—her picture-book in front of her.

"Well, Miss Elsie!" cried Mary, "you *were* sound asleep to be sure! Didn't you find your picture-book rather a hard pillow?"

144   *ELSIE'S EXPEDITION.*

But little Elsie was thinking of the happy
Woodside Well, and the pretty song she had
heard. And very, very slowly did the little
maiden cross the bright green lawn at Mary's
injunction to "come to dinner."

Edward Holland, *Mabel in Rhymeland, or Little Mabel's Journey
to Norwich and Her Wonderful Adventures with the Man in the Moon
and Other Heroes and Heroines of Nursery Rhyme*
(London: Griffith, Farrow, Kender and Welsh, 1885).

This fantasy uses a dream vision structure and dream vision elements to introduce some very interesting issues, but there is no consistent development
of them throughout the book. Mabel's original anxiety is that, as a girl who
has just learned to read, she cannot accept certain spellings, preferring the
phonetic "laft" to the conventional "laughed." The issues associated with
the clash between the aural and the conventional are not used in the dream-
core or in the closing frame. Holland does, however, raise issues concerning
the clash of "reality" and "rhyme" in the dream-core that are worthy of further development. These include the Man-in-the-Moon's doubt of Mabel's
existence because of his failure to locate Mabel in a nursery rhyme (he tries
Mabel in "Little Jack Horner" and "Little Miss Muffet"): " 'But if you are
not in the book, you can't be real, you know' " (15). Further, they include
the trial of one of the Wise Men of Gotham who is accused of "wilfully, feloniously, and with malice aforethought [constructing] and [contriving]
verses in imitation of the rhymes on which [the rhyme populations'] very
existence depended" (122–3). They also include the possibility that the
Man-in-the-South has altered a rhyme by inserting "He" in place of himself
in order to avoid looking like the fool who "burnt his mouth / With eating
cold plum-porridge" (126). King Arthur considers such tampering a "very
serious case" because "a man who is capable of such an offence would
whitewash a cathedral, or paint a statue" (126). Finally, they also include

Merlin's prediction "that if a human child found its way amongst us, we
should all of us fade away, and be as though we had never been" (127). The
fact that Mabel has indeed found her way into Rhymeland does make it
fade away, but this fading is facilely explained by the "So it *was* only a
dream after all" last line. In a similar way, unfortunately, Holland employs
the empty form of the dream vision – both the central pattern of anxiety
comforted and the confirmation of that comforting go missing.

> *Mabel with the sparkling face,*
>   *For whose eyes this tale was written,*
> *When first we might your features trace,*
>   *When first a mother's eyes, love-litten,*
> *Gazed upon your infant form,*
>   *And wove a web of hopes around you;*
> *And when your father's heart was warm*
>   *With joys first felt when first he found you; –*
> *'Twas then he thought to use some art*
>   *To knit the ties of Nature stronger,*
> *That he within your loving heart*
>   *Perchance might live a little longer;*
> *So should he by Death's cruel knife*
>   *Be severed from your young affection,*
> *He yet might, in your riper life,*
>   *Live in your earliest recollections.*

CHAPTER I.

THE MAN IN THE MOON.

ITTLE MABEL was lolling on a sofa, and looking out through the window, dreamily watching the shadows as they seemed to chase each other across the fields. She had been reading her book of nursery rhymes until she felt quite sleepy, for, being but a very little girl, she had not long learnt to read; and though she knew most of the rhymes by heart, which was a great help, yet still it was hard work sometimes conscientiously to wade through such words as 'laughed,' which she found in the rhyme about

B

the little dog that saw the cow jump over the moon. For
though, perhaps, there was nothing more wonderful in the
little dog's behaviour than in that of the cow, yet that consideration did not at all help little Mabel to understand how
l–a–u–g–h–e–d could spell 'laughed.' Her theory was that
l–a–f–t would have been a much simpler way of getting over
the difficulty, and unless the usual mode of spelling such
words were invented on purpose to puzzle little girls who were
learning to read, it was really very difficult to account for it.

It was an afternoon in April, and clouds and sunshine had
been succeeding each other all day. All at once little Mabel
saw a rainbow. *Such* a beauty. Not a little bit of one, you
know, but a large distinct rainbow, and it seemed to be only
one field from the house where she was. Now she had often
been told that whoever could get to the foot of a rainbow
would find a bag of gold there (which is very probably true),
and this one seemed so near that she thought it a pity not to
try—not that she was greedy for money, but she thought what
a splendid doll she might buy if she could only get the bag
of gold. Somehow or other, while she was only thinking of
going, she found herself running across the fields, the rainbow
growing bigger and brighter, and looking more solid as she
got nearer to it, till at last she really was at its foot, and
would probably have begun to look for the bag of gold had
she not seen that somebody, whom she did not know, was
there before her.

This was a quaintly-dressed little old man who was making
grimaces, and was rubbing himself as though he were very

THE MAN IN THE MOON. 11

much hurt. He took no notice of Mabel, but continued to rub himself and make exclamations of pain.

'Well, I did come down too soon after all,' said he; 'that is, if coming down too soon means coming down too quickly ; and how I ever am to get up again I'm sure I don't know,'

he went on, looking up at the rainbow in a disconsolate manner.

'Get up again where ?' asked Mabel.

'Why, to the moon, to be sure,' he replied in a sulky voice. 'Where else do you suppose ?'

'You don't mean to say that you have come down from the moon?' said Mabel, astonished. 'Why, perhaps you are the Man-in-the-Moon himself!' she added delightedly.

'Of course I am,' said he, 'and that is the reason I came down too soon, I suppose.'

'Oh! do tell me all about it,' said Mabel. 'I've seen you often, ever so often, when you were up there. But however did you manage to get down?'

The Man-in-the-Moon sat down on a fallen tree, and after one or two fretful ejaculations, as though he had not quite got over his hurt, replied as follows:—

'You see I was standing up there so long that I began to find the time pass away very slowly; so to amuse myself I thought about things I had read, and among others of that stupid rhyme:

> ' " The Man-in-the-Moon
> Came down too soon
> To ask his way to Norwich ;
> The Man-in-the-South
> Burnt his mouth
> With eating cold plum-porridge."

Now, said I to myself, of all the nonsensical things that ever were said about me, that is the most nonsensical, and I have a great mind to go down to the earth just to show them that I don't go down too soon to ask my way to Norwich or to any other place. Well, just at that moment I saw this fine rainbow, and thought what a good opportunity it would be. So I put one leg over it,—like sliding down the bannisters, you know,—and off I started. At first I rather liked it, but gradually it got steeper and steeper, and I slid down faster and faster, until I came,—bump!—down on the ground. And it hurt me ever so much, I can tell you, besides nearly spoiling my clothes. And I really don't know,' continued the little man in a tone of anguish,—'I really don't know how I ever am to get up again.'

A short silence now ensued, broken only by the sighs of the Man-in-the-Moon.

'As to jumping up again, I don't believe it's possible,' he at length went on. 'That story about the cow jumping over the moon is all nonsense, you know, because I was there all the time, and must have known all about it if it had ever happened. Whatever shall I do?'

'Why,' said Mabel, 'you know that you ought to ask your way to Norwich. That is what the book says, and I should think that that would be your best plan.'

'Very good,' said the little man; 'but what is your name?'

'Mabel,' she replied.

'Very well, then; Miss Mabel, please to tell me the way to Norwich.'

'But I don't know the way to Norwich myself,' pleaded Mabel. 'You must ask some one else.'

'Oh no! It does not say that I must ask some one else; it only says that I must ask my way, and if you do not tell me, you must take the consequences.'

This was such a poser that poor little Mabel was quite confounded, and did not know what to do. At last she thought that she saw a way out of the dilemma. So she answered, 'But it says that you came down too soon to ask the way. Now you said yourself that you came down too soon, so you have no right to ask the way.'

There was no answering this, of course; so the little old man looked more disconsolate than ever.

After a long pause, he looked up suddenly and asked, 'Didn't you say that your name was Mabel?'

'Yes,' she replied.

'Mabel? Mabel?' he repeated to himself. 'I don't remember any Mabel. Let me try to recollect.' Then he went on:

> ' " Little Miss Mabel
> Sat eating at table
> All on a Christmas day,
> She put in her thumb
> And pulled out a plum,
> And said, " What a big one,—Hooray!"'

No; that does not sound right at all. Why, of course not. That was little Jack Horner. Let me think again:

> ' " Little Miss Mabel
> Sat in the stable
> Eating of curds and whey."

No; that was Miss Muffet, who sat on a tuffet, whatever that may be. And who you *can* be, I'm sure I don't know,' said he, looking at Mabel suspiciously.

'Why, I told you before that I'm little Mabel,' said she, 'and I live quite close to this place; and if you would only come up to the house with me, they would be so surprised to see you. Oh, *do* come!'

THE MAN IN THE MOON. 15

'But if you are not in the book, you can't be real, you know,' said he.

'Why!' said Mabel astonished, 'there are ever so many people who are not in my rhyme book. There are papa, and mamma, and nurse, and ever so many.'

'But they can't be real,' said the Man-in-the-Moon, shaking his head; 'you may think so, but they can't be real if they are not in the book. However, it's no use sitting here talking, and I have thought of a plan. *I* came down too soon to ask my way to Norwich, but you did not; so you must come with me, and ask the way for me.'

CHAPTER XII.

KING ARTHUR.

CRY was now raised that the king was coming, and little Mabel, all eagerness, yet half frightened, took hold of the hand of the Priest - all - Shaven - and - Shorn and turned to see the sight. And of all the sights she saw at Norwich this one struck her the most. In front of a cavalcade of noble-looking knights, clad all in armour, but with their visors up, rode the king on a very powerful horse, which, although quiet, champed the bit and arched his neck as though proud of his

119

rider. The king himself rode without armour, and was clad
in some sad-coloured but rich material, and Mabel did not at
first observe that he was a very tall and powerful man,
because he was so well-proportioned that that was seldom
noticed until he was compared with others near him. But
what attracted her attention most was the expression of his
face—so noble and so calm, as though no emotion might
ruffle it, while his eyes seemed to be looking through or past
everything there, as though he saw a world that was invisible
to the others. His face wore a rather saddened expression,
but so much love and kindliness for all things beamed from
his eyes, that though Mabel felt a deep reverence for him,
she could not feel afraid. The people did not cheer as he
passed by, but all uncovered their heads in profound respect;
and many a muttered blessing might be heard, called down
on the head of good King Arthur.

'The king is going to the Hall of Justice,' said the Priest-
all-Shaven-and-Shorn, 'and we must go there too, to pay our
respects to him.' Mabel, nothing loath, took the Priest's
hand to go with him, but had not gone far when Mistress
Mary came up and asked Mabel to walk with her, as she
had something to tell her. 'My little darling,' whispered
Mistress Mary, putting her arm round Mabel's waist, 'I am
very happy, and I do *so* want to tell somebody all about it,
and there is no one here that I can tell except you. I am—
that is—the Man-in-the-South has asked me to marry him,
and—and' (here she turned her head away) 'I have said
yes.' She then stooped down and kissed Mabel in such an

earnest manner that the latter was not sorry that the
approach of the Man-in-the-South saved her from having to
say anything about the match, for she did not much like

him, and could scarcely congratulate Mistress Mary on her
choice. But the latter was so full of her new-found
happiness that she did not notice Mabel's silence, and the

Man-in-the-South was so polite and obliging that little Mabel began to think that she had judged him harshly, and that perhaps he was a very nice man after all.

Thus they went along till they came to a great gateway, through which they entered a lofty hall whose roof, soaring far above, was framed of massive but beautifully carved timbers. The king sat on a dais at the farther end. His knights stood near the throne, and behind them was a great Gothic window of stained glass through which the sunlight came streaming, flooding all the place with gorgeous hues of crimson and blue and purple. Hanging along the walls were the banners of the knights, while in front of the king stood gaily apparelled heralds with richly embroidered tabards and silver trumpets. Mabel was a little awed by the sight, and wondering whether she would have to go and introduce herself as at King Cole's palace, was much relieved to hear that the king would first try the criminals brought before him.

The heralds having sounded their trumpets to enforce silence, a prisoner was brought before the king. You may imagine Mabel's surprise when she saw that it was one of the Wise Men of Gotham whom she had seen in the market-place but a short time before, and she wondered what he could have been doing to be placed in such a position. The king having asked of what crime he was accused, was told by the public prosecutor that it was one of the most serious that could be imagined in a community such as theirs, viz. that he had wilfully, feloniously, and with malice aforethought made, constructed, invented, and contrived verses in imitation of the rhymes on which their very existence depended; and that he had moreover altered and mutilated other the aforesaid rhymes, to the manifest danger and detriment of the commonwealth and the peace of our sovereign lord the king, his crown and dignity.

The Wise Man having pleaded not guilty, the first witness was called. This proved to be Little Boy Blue, who said that the prisoner had tried to make him learn a rhyme different from any he had ever heard before. On being asked if he had learnt it, he said 'No;' and being asked why, he replied that it was because he had an objection to learning anything unless he was obliged, and that in common with most other boys of his acquaintance, he thought that schools were all nonsense and ought to be done away with. Being asked what he knew further about the matter, he produced a paper, which he said had been given to him by the prisoner. This was read aloud by the clerk of the court, and contained the following :—

> ' Is this the way ? '
> Asked Mr. Kay
> From each, both great and small.
> And some said ' Hey ? '
> And some said ' Nay,'
> And some said nothing at all.

> I walked out in a high-crowned hat,
> Somebody passed me and knocked it flat.
> ' Why did you do so, sir, I pray ? '
> ' Oh, just for a joke,' and he walked away.

I went after and tweaked his nose,
Which rather annoyed him, as I suppose.
' Why did you so,' he said, ' I pray ? '
'Oh, just for a joke,' and I walked away.

He came after and kicked me sore,—
Kicked me behind, and kicked me before ;
And I can't sit down, at least with ease,
So no more jokes for me if you please !

THE TRIUMPHANT CONTROVERSIALIST.

' Fiddle-de-dee ! '
Said he to me,
And I retorted ' Pah ! '
When he said ' Pooh ! '
I answered ' Shoo ! '
And finished him off with ' Bah ! '

The next witness was Little Tom Tucker, who said that he was present when the paper was given to Little Boy Blue by the prisoner. In the course of his examination he admitted that he had not read the rhymes, and added (without being asked) that he was of the same opinion as the previous witness, with respect to going to school and learning anything.

The next witness was the Little-Man-who-had-a-Little-Gun, who said that the prisoner after having in the course of conversation propounded some revolutionary sentiments with regard to the rhymes which were their common property, suggested the following alteration, viz. that in the rhyme,

' Hey, diddle, diddle,
The cat and the fiddle,'

the latter part should be altered to

> The little dog laughed
> To see such *craft*

(instead of sport as in the original), for the sake of the
rhyme ; and that when he, the witness, objected on the
ground that the word 'craft' was scarcely applicable to a
cow's jumping over the moon, and that in fact the rhyme
would be obtained at the expense of reason, he, the prisoner,
got quite angry and told him that the rhyme should be so
altered, even if King Arthur and all his knights objected to it.

The proceedings were here interrupted by the Man-in-the-
Moon, who rushed into the hall, and forcing his way up to the
king, called out 'Justice!—my lord the king, justice!' He
was so breathless and excited that it was some time before he
became calm enough to tell his story. At length, on the
king asking him who had done him an injury, he pointed to
the prisoner and said, 'He—he—that is the man! Your
Majesty, learned in all the wisdom of Rhymeland, knows the
rhyme that concerns myself. Well, that—that man—out of
sheer malice has written and published a version which runs
thus :—

> ' " The Man in the Moon
> Came down too soon
> To ask his way to Norwich." '

' That is quite correct,' interrupted the king.

' Yes, your Majesty,' replied the Man-in-the-Moon ; ' but
hear what comes next :—

'*He* went by the South
And burnt his mouth
With eating cold plum-porridge.

That is that I — I — the Man-in-the-Moon, burnt *my* mouth with cold plum-porridge,' said he, overflowing with indignation as he went on, 'when everybody knows that it was the Man-in-the-South who did so. Justice on the miscreant! my lord the king, justice!'

'This is a very serious case,' said the king calmly. 'I think nothing of the imitative rhymes made by the prisoner, their artificialness and the want of that simplicity of idea and diction which characterizes the real rhymes, would at once proclaim their spurious origin. But to tamper with the rhymes that our ancestors have handed down to us is a more serious matter. A man who is capable of such an offence would whitewash a cathedral, or paint a statue. I consider the evidence to be conclusive of the prisoner's guilt, and I sentence him to be kept in close confinement, and to be compelled to read every new novel that is published.'

A movement of horror and pity ran through the vast audience that thronged the hall at the severity of this sentence, and the unfortunate Wise Man of Gotham gave vent to lugubrious howls as he was led away to undergo his dreadful punishment.

All this time Mistress Mary had had her arm round little Mabel's waist, and a pause occurring, Mabel turned to speak to her, and was surprised to see what a change had

taken place within the last few days. Her face, which used
to wear a rather sour expression, was beaming with happy
smiles, and she seemed to take no note of what was going on
around, as she listened to the Man-in-the-South who was
whispering in her ear.

All at once there was a slight commotion among the
throng of knights on the dais, and an old man with a very
long snow-white beard, wearing a very tall pointed hat and
clad in a long gown covered with curious figures, came
through them and advanced to the front of the dais. He
fixed his piercing black eyes on Mabel, and it seemed to her
that as he did so a shudder ran through the crowd. The
sunlight faded from the window, and a dark gloom filled the
vast hall that had been so bright before. Turning to the
king, he said in deep impressive tones that reverberated
through the sudden silence that had fallen on those assembled,
' Your Majesty knows that I—Merlin—have always fore-
told that if a human child found its way amongst us, we
should all of us fade away, and be as though we had never
been. THAT HUMAN CHILD IS HERE — AND THE END HAS
COME.'

Little Mabel in her fear and anxiety did but catch a
glimpse of a wild, despairing, reproachful glance from Mistress
Mary, and of an expression of wondering bewilderment on the
faces of her other friends, when she perceived that their shapes
and features were becoming blurred and indistinct, and that
the whole scene with all the figures in it was fading away.
In desperation she fixed her eyes on King Arthur, who sat

mute and impassive on his throne. ' I *will* keep him in sight,' she thought to herself, and she was delighted to find that he did not seem to be fading away like the others. He appeared to become smaller and smaller, it is true, but even more and more distinct—till,—she rubbed her eyes, —yes—he was only a china shepherd on the mantelpiece in the old room at home !

So it *was* only a dream after all.

MORRISON AND GIBB, EDINBURGH,
PRINTERS TO HER MAJESTY'S STATIONERY OFFICE.

Jean Jambon (pseudonym), *Our Trip to Blunderland;
or, Grand Excursion to Blundertown and Back*
(Edinburgh and London: William Blackwood and Sons, 1877).

An excerpt from this book functions to show representative upside-down
figures in Appendix 3 (169–70) and another appears here as an example of a
derivative and totally whimsical dream vision (see discussion on page 71).

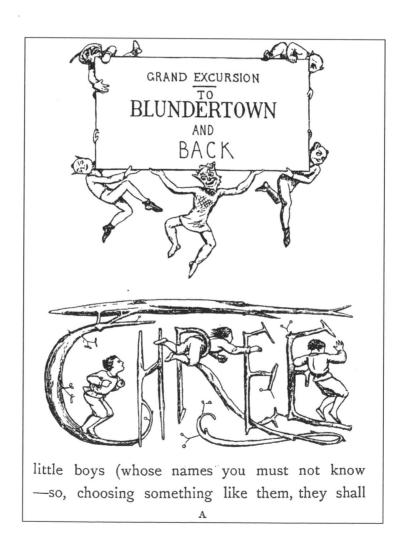

little boys (whose names you must not know
—so, choosing something like them, they shall

A

2   IF WE COULD.

be called Norval, Jaques, and Ranulf) had been reading all about Alice, and the strange, funny things she saw and did when fast asleep.

"I wonder," said Jaques, "if I could ever get to sleep like her, so as to walk through looking-glasses, and that sort of thing, without breaking them or coming up against the wall!"

"Oh," said Ranulf, "wouldn't it be nice if we could! only the funniest thing is how she got through the wall. I don't see how being asleep would help her to do that."

Norval, the eldest, broke in—"Oh, you big stupid! she didn't go through it; she only thought she did."

"Well, then," said Jaques, "I want to think it too. Last night when I was in bed I tried to go to sleep, and to get through the wall; but when I fell asleep I forgot all about it, and dreamed that I was sick, and that the doctor gave me a big glass of something horrid."

"Ah, but," said Norval, "that was because you tried. Alice didn't try, you know. She

HOW TO DO IT.   3

knew nothing about being asleep till she woke up."

"Well, I didn't know I was asleep till I woke up, either," answered Jaques.

Ranulf looked very wise, although he was the smallest, and said, "Perhaps if Alice was here, she would tell us how to do it."

"Of course I would," said a sweet voice behind them; and, turning round, who should they see but little Alice herself, looking exactly as she does on page 35, where she is getting her thimble from the Dodo?

"Oh, how awfully jolly!" cried Norval; "will you help us?" He was very much surprised, not at seeing Alice, but at not being surprised.

"Indeed I will," said she, "although I don't know, you know, whether boys can manage it."

Ranulf was just going to say, saucily, "A great deal better than girls, I should think," when Norval, who was older, and knew better how to behave, checked him, and said—

4

BY ORDER.

"But, Alice, dear, surely if it's done by going to sleep, boys can do that as well as girls."

"Well, so they can," said she; "but then, you see, everybody who goes to sleep doesn't get to Wonderland."

"Oh, but perhaps," said Jaques, "if you will go to sleep too, you will come with us, and show us the way."

"Ah! I can't do that to-day," said Alice, looking very grave; "for, you see, when I came to you I was just going to give Dollys their dinner —such a nice dinner! cake and currants; and it would be cruel to leave them looking at it till I came back."

Now Norval suddenly remembered that he knew some boys whose uncle was a Director at the Aquarium, and who, when he could not go with them and pass them in himself, gave them a written order; so, turning to Alice, he said—

"Oh, but if you would give us a pass, it might help us." And sitting down at the writing-table, he wrote in stiff letters, imitating the papers he

SHUT UP.   5

had seen, and laying the pass before her, said, "Now, write 'Alice' there ever so big, and put a grand whirly stroke under it."

Alice obeyed, and the pass was ready.

"Now then," said she, "you had better go to sleep."

Norval threw himself down on a sofa; Jaques and Ranulf coiled themselves up on the rug.

Norval could not resist the temptation to keep one eye half open, that he might see what Alice did. But she, noticing this, held up her little forefinger, and said, "Come, come, that won't

6 PLAGUEY BOYS.

do." Thus rebuked, Norval shut his other eye.

"Now, all go to sleep at once," said Alice.

"I'm nearly asleep already," said Jaques.

"Oh!" said Norval.

"No!" said Ranulf.

"That's talking, not going to sleep," said Alice. All was still for a little, then Jaques half uncoiled himself and looked at Ranulf.

Ranulf uncoiled himself and looked at Norval. Norval raised his head, and looked at Jaques. On finding that they were all awake, the three burst out laughing.

"That's laughing, not going to sleep," said Alice.

Down they all flopped again, and then Alice, to help them, said, "Hushaby baby, on the tree-top!"

"I'm not a baby," said Ranulf, much offended, as he was nearly six.

"I'm not on a tree-top," said Jaques.

"You've waked me up," said Norval.

WE'LL BE GOOD. 7

"That's chattering, not going to sleep," said Alice.

"I'm sure I must be asleep now," said Norval.

"So am I," said Jaques.

"And me too," said Ranulf.

"That's talking nonsense, not going to sleep," said she. "I see it's no use; Alice's way won't do with wild rogues like you, and I really must go back to Dollys."

"What *are* we to do?" said Norval; "we can't fall asleep. Don't you think we could get to the funny places you went to without going to sleep?"

"Will you do what I tell you?" asked Alice, holding up her little forefinger in a dignified kind of way.

Jaques had some misgivings about compromising his position as a small lord of the creation by agreeing to do what a little girl told him'; but his anxiety to see some wonders prevailed, and they all said that they would obey.

"Shut your eyes, then, and don't open them till I tell you, and perhaps something will happen."

OVER THE SLEEPERS.

9

only they were rather different from other bycycles, as, in place of the small hind-wheels, there were funny little fellows, made up of a head and three legs; and as they stood on one foot, with the other two in the air, and their noses thrust

AN EYE-OPENER.

8

Norval rolled down from the sofa to the side of his brothers. Then all squeezed up their eyes quite tight, and although they heard a curious rumbling noise, did not open them.

"That's right," said Alice; "you would have spoiled everything if you had peeped. Boys who don't do what they are told spoil everything, and themselves besides. Now you may look!"

They had squeezed their eyes so tight that it took ever so long to get them unfastened. Jaques got his open first, and saw that little Alice was gone.

"Oh, Alice, where are you?" he cried.

A distant voice replied, "Off to Dollys!"

Just as he was going to say, "What a shame, when I squeezed so hard!" Norval and Ranulf got their eyes open, and before Jaques could speak, they gave a wild shout, "Hurrah! hurrah! hurrah!" Jaques' head had been looking the wrong way, but when he turned round he saw what the others had seen—

THREE BYCYCLES,

through the end of the bar, they looked very comical. Still more funny was it when the boys went forward to look closer, and the little three-legged men made them a bow, which they did by touching their caps with one leg, bobbing forward on another, and back again. The wheels and treddles were made of gold, the seats were lined with crimson velvet, and the little men had blue tights and silver caps and shoes; so everything looked very smart. The boys could not understand how the bycycles stood upright without anything to hold the wheels, and began talking about them, wondering whether they could move of themselves. They had scarcely spoken of this, when, as if to show off their powers, the little men began to turn round on their three legs, and move slowly about the room. They steered their way among the furniture most cleverly, and at last as each stopped beside one of the boys they all touched their caps, and bobbed from one leg to another, as before.

"Are we to get up?" said Jaques, timidly.

Bob went all the little men.

"Does that mean yes?" said Norval. Bob.

"But where are we going?" said Ranulf.

"To Wonderland, of course," said Jaques.

"All right," said the other two, and they all scrambled up on the bycycles.

The moment they were seated, the three little men gave a shrill whistle, as a railway engine does before it starts, and off they went at a tremendous pace. The boys had barely time to think how hard the drawing-room wall would be, when the whole party went straight through it as if it had been, like circus hoops, filled in with paper. Norval went across the library and out at the window, but papa did not seem to notice him; he only got up and closed the sash, as if he had felt a draught. Jaques passed through the butler's pantry, but the butler only scratched his ear, as if something had tickled him. Ranulf shot at a slant through the nursery, clutching a penny trumpet off the table as he passed, but nurse

12   DISTANCE LENDS.

only gave a shiver, and said, "Deary me, I do feel so queasy queer!"

They were going so fast, that Norval, looking round the moment they were outside the house, saw papa's head, not bigger than a black pin's, looking out of a window, that seemed smaller than a halfpenny stamp; and Jaques caught sight of Oscar, the house dog, who looked like a comma with its tail wagging. Besides, they kept mounting up in the air as well as going on, so that the fields looked no bigger than the squares of a chess-board, and the trees between them, in their autumn tints, like rows of brass nails on a green-baize door. Before they could count fifty, the world itself, when they looked back, was like one of those funny worsted balls that show a number of different colours. The little men were spinning so fast that their silver caps, blue hose, and bright shoes ran into circles, till they looked like silver wheels with a blue enamel ring on them.

"Isn't it funny that we aren't frightened?" said Jaques.

FAST IDEAS.   13

"I think we would be if we had time," said Norval (who was the thinking one of the three), "only we are going so fast that there's no time to be frightened."

"Perhaps it's because we're asleep like Alice, after all," said Ranulf, looking very wise.

"Oh no; because you see when people are asleep they are still, and we are going so fast that it would be sure to wake us," replied Jaques.

"But we can be still and go fast all the same, can't we?" said Ranulf.

"Oh no, you silly!" said Jaques.

"Oh yes," said Ranulf; "because we can go still faster; and if we can go still faster, why can't we go still fast?"

"Oh yes, to be sure," said Jaques; "and besides, of course, a man can be fast and still at the same time, for if he is made fast with rope he must be still."

"And we *are* going fast still," said Norval, as the bycycles flew on; "but I don't see yet how we can be still and fast both."

The three seemed likely to get into a regular muddle about this, when their attention was suddenly called off by Jaques catching sight of something that looked first like a new threepenny-piece, and in another second like a big shining tin plate.

"What's that?" said Jaques. While he was saying this, it had grown as big as a drum.

"Perhaps it's a giant's dish," said Ranulf. It was now as big as a circus.

"It's getting too big for that," said Jaques. By this time it was as large as a race-course, and in another second it was too great to be like anything.

Norval, who had been thinking, was just going to say, "Perhaps it's the moon," when the Man in the Moon put his head out at one side, and looking as grumpy as possible, called out—"Hi, you rascals! what do you want here?" He had evidently been wakened out of a nap by the whirr of the bycycles, for he wore a big red

nightcap, and had got only one eye open.

"We aren't rascals," said Jaques; "if you say that, we'll tell papa."

"Oh," said Norval, "are you the fellow that came down too soon?"

Notes

1 This oversight is especially odd in light of the descriptions of children's literature prior to Carroll's work presented in such books as Percy Muir's *English
Children's Books, 1600–1900* and F.J. Harvey Darton's *Children's Books in
England: Five Centuries of Social Life*. Sarah Trimmer published a history of children's literature in the *Guardian of Education* as early as 1803, and Carroll's library contained *The Child and His Book, some account of the History and Progress
of Children's Literature in England*, by Louise Francis Field (1895), as well as
Horace Scudder's *The Child in Art and Literature* (1894). Further, Carroll's
library included a great number of religious, moral, informational, and imaginative books for children.

2 John Docherty states that the Carroll/MacDonald relationship is most suc-
cinctly characterized by Blake's "Opposition is true friendship," but more often
than not he argues that the thematic and structural features of the Alices exclusively "derive from" MacDonald's work.

3 From *The Theatre* (1887) (reprinted in Gray's Norton Critical Edition of the
Alice books, p. 281). See *The Lewis Carroll Picture Book* (1899) by Stuart
Dodgson Collingwood. The language and argument Carroll develops here
are similar to those employed in his description of the genesis of *Sylvie and
Bruno* (1890).

4 "Portmanteau" is most fully described by Carroll in the preface to *The Hunting
of the Snark* (1876). It is the name of the product of a process that fuses two or
more words into one. Carroll gives the example of "fuming" and "furious"

blending into "frumious." The process extends readily into illustrations, such as the compression of a young cow (veal) and a turtle into an animal sharing parts of each. The Mock Turtle's friend, the Gryphon, is a classical composite monster that lived on in bestiary books and heraldry.

5 This meets the elements listed by M.H. Abrams in *A Glossary of Literary Terms* (1985).

CHAPTER TWO

1 See the description of the sources of nursery rhymes prior to 1800 given by Iona and Peter Opie in *The Oxford Dictionary of Nursery Rhymes*, 3–4. Among other adult sources, the Opies list "rude jests," street songs, songs "out of taverns," satires of religious practices, and "romantic lyrics."

2 Green originally thought very little of Tillotson's suggestion of the Dickens parody as the source of the "Looking-Glass House" chapter. Compare his enthusiasm in his edition with his earlier comment: "… of this rather trifling similarity readers may form their own opinion" (note concerning Carroll's diary entry for 12 January 1869, in *The Diaries of Lewis Carroll*, vol. 2) (London: Cassell and Company 1953), 279.

3 See William A. Madden, "Framing the Alices," *Publications of the Modern Language Association* 101, no. 1 (May 1986): 362–73. Madden focuses on the nature and functions of the poems accompanying the Alice books, discussing them in terms of Romantic and Victorian poetics.

4 See Roger Lax and Frederick Smith, *The Great Song Thesaurus*, 16. The brief poem was written by Eliphalet Lyte and set to music originally entitled "Beautiful Bells." Lax and Smith believe the round was sung before the 1881 date, however.

CHAPTER THREE

1 See F.J. Harvey Darton's chapters on the moral tales "The Dawn of Levity" and "Two New Englands: 'Peter Parley' and 'Felix Summerly,' " in *Children's Books in England: Five Centuries of Social Life*, and his "Peter Parley and the Battle of the Children's Books" (1932) for a background discussion of this period.

2 When Dickens was a boy, his grandmother and his governess told him exceptionally terrifying stories, such as "Captain Murderer." These tales both attracted and repulsed him, and fed his creativity. Contrast Dickens's use of such stories with the way Jeremy Bentham processed the memory of horror stories told to him by family servants when he was a child; the stories told to Bentham caused him major anxieties and inconveniences and most likely contributed to his establishing reason, utility, and happiness as yardsticks to measure all

social institutions and values. Interestingly, this champion of rationality willed that his body be put on perpetual exhibition at the University of London, where one can view it still. According to his will, his body, it seems, was meant to serve as a relic of rationality as opposed to the showing of relics of superstition in churches. Oddly, Bentham, who developed a "moral arithmetic" to evaluate all human institutions, goes unmentioned in *The Annotated Dickens*.

3 In *Children's Books in England*, F.J. Harvey Darton dates the "day of less interesting catechisms" as beginning in 1800 with *Historical and Miscellaneous Questions* by Richmal Mangnall, a book that begat Pinnock's self-styled "improvements" on the questions, which begat a number of other "improvements" (48).

4 Both Cole and Goodrich champion the use of illustration in books for children, but differ in their reasons. Consistent with Goodrich's entire program, illustrations are important because they help to establish and to maintain concentration on the factual, on the acquisition of new knowledge of the world. Cole is even more interested in illustration, choosing, for example, to use copies of acknowledged masters in his books. He also believes that illustration may serve text in a functional way. For example, in *Bible Events* (2nd series) he uses Raphael's *Loggi* and comments on "Moses in the Bulrushes": "Would you not like to know who that pretty baby is, and how he comes to be lying so near the water's edge? And what that crowd of women are doing, who surround him with looks of admiration and pity?" (28). Above all, however, Cole is interested in the creation of a sense of wonder at great artistic vision: "The more you know of Raffaell's [*sic*] pictures, the more you will love them, they will always bring to your mind images of beauty and grandeur. I am sure you will learn to respect Raffaell's memory, and teach others to do so likewise" (iv).

5 *The Rectory Umbrella* and other family publications, considered together with the inventive games played by the Dodgson children, attest to the general imaginative tenor of family life attributed to their encouraging mother by Derek Hudson (59). Their sterner father, meanwhile, was capable of writing joyful nonsense such as that included in a letter to Charles (6 January 1840) about the purchase, from an ironmonger's in Leeds, of a file, a screwdriver, and a ring as gifts for his son. The letter reads in part: "At last the Mayor of Leeds will be found in a soup plate covered up with custard, and stuck full of almonds to make him look like a sponge cake that he may escape the dreadful destruction of the Town. Oh! Where is his wife? She is safe in her own pincushion with a bit of sticking plaster on the top to hide the hump in her back, and all her dear little children, seventy-eight poor little helpless infants crammed into her mouth, and hiding themselves behind her double teeth. Then comes a man hid in a teapot crying and roaring, 'Oh, I have dropped my donkey. I put it up my nostril, and it has fallen out of the spout of the teapot into an old woman's thimble and she will squeeze it to death when she puts her thimble on' " (from

Belle-Lettres: A Journal of Letters, vol. 1 [Vancouver: Vancouver Society of Letters and Correspondence, July–August 1980], 10). For the interesting theory that Carroll's portrayal of his mother and father was stock Victorian family patterning and that his fictional presentation of the irrational, dominating mother (the Queen of Hearts, the Duchess, the chess queens) and the withdrawn father (the King of Hearts, the chess kings, and the missing father of Sylvie and Bruno) was a more psychologically accurate paradigm, see "Papa and Mama" (171–86) in *Lewis Carroll: Fragments of a Looking-Glass* by Jean Cattégno.

6 It does not take a trained eye to see that the bad spirits portrayed are boys, while the good spirits flying under the umbrella are girls, but this is another story.

7 In his *The White Knight*, Taylor argues that Carroll draws a self-portrait in the character of the White Knight. Taylor suggests that Carroll gently satirizes his own interest in all sorts of invention and speculation as well as his own awkwardness. The White Knight even turns his inability to sit a horse as well as might be expected into a virtue, when he says he does his best thinking when thrown "upside down."

CHAPTER FOUR

1 The arguments establishing Carroll's introduction of the world upside down through the figure of antipodes in *Alice's Adventures in Wonderland* were originally developed in my note in *The Explicator* 43, no. 2 (1985): 21–2.

2 Taylor need not have looked to adult works for discussions of such phenomena, since they were considered at length in informational books for children such as Pinnock's *A Catechism of Optics* (1820).

3 Textual citations are from Roger L. Green's Oxford World's Classics edition.

4 See W.S. Ramsom, ed., *The Australian National Dictionary; A Dictionary of Australianisms on Historical Principles* (Melbourne: Oxford University Press, 1988). One of the earliest cited uses here is from the *Sydney Herald* (12 December 1833): "[Australia and New Zealand] are the Antipodes! The world is turned upside down!" William Pinnock's *Geography Made Simple* (London: William Pinnock, 1847) may be the earliest children's informational book to comment in some detail on the "British Antipodes."

5 That the Mad Hatter's watch, which reads the day of the month but not the time of day, displays the 6th of May has caused a great deal of comment. In *The White Knight*, Taylor uses this temporal discrepancy to verify that Wonderland is located at the centre of the earth. Since there was an exact two-day difference between lunar and calendar time on the day the story was originally told, 4 May 1862, Taylor argues for lunar dating on the grounds that the sun has no effect at the centre of the earth (57). Irene Meloni adds a nice touch to this argument in *La logica del nonsenso* when she says, "… il sostantivo 'bat' …

adatta perfettamente la versione del Cappellaino al mondo sotterraneo di Wonderland dove non esistono stelle ma, tutt'al piu, pipistreeli" (51). (The substan-
tive "bat" … fits perfectly the version of the little mysterious place at the centre
of the subterranean world of Wonderland where there are no stars but where
there are many bats. [Note the *stelle/pipistreeli* rhyme in Italian.]) All this adds
up to a very clever argument, but it overlooks both the alternative location
of the other side of the earth as well as the Hatter's admission that his clock is
wrong owing to the March Hare's substitution of the "best butter" for oil when
last he cleaned it (62). In his *The Annotated Alice*, Martin Gardner says that "it
is hard to believe that Carroll had all this in mind" (note 4, 96). For the sake of
symmetry, the date should be the 4th of May, since *Through the Looking-Glass*
opens on 4 November, exactly six months later.

6 See David Kunzle's "World Upside Down," in *The Reversible World*. Kunzle lists
  seven types of inversion.

7 Kunzle distinguishes between the proverb and the world upside down on the
  basis of social class and function. The proverb is reactionary, accepting the
  world "as it is" while preaching guile and cynicism: the world upside down
  "recognizes social contradiction and conflict" and suggests confrontation (74).

8 See Helen Grant's chapter in *Studies in Spanish Literature of the Golden Age*,
  where she argues that the apparent subversive surface of the topos may be used
  as a conservative force that exposes the terror of upheaval and fully endorses
  the status quo.

9 See Marguerite Mespoulet's *The Creators of Wonderland* and Mario Praz's "Two
  Masters of the Absurd: Grandville and Carroll" for discussions of Grandville's
  work in relation to the Alice books.

10 I want to go where my fantasy takes me; I'll be my own guide: long live liberty!

11 Rackin presents a diverse picture of pre-Carrollian children's literature and
   suggests connections with early Romantic works for children while briefly
   describing the narrowly didactic literature of Carroll's immediate evangelical
   predecessors.

CHAPTER FIVE

1 Carroll originally titled his second Alice fantasy *Behind the Looking-Glass and
  What Alice Found There* (my underlining) and did so from the completion of
  the manuscript in 1869 through his diary entry for 25 June 1870. Green claims
  that Carroll's new title was suggested by his acquaintance Harry Parry Liddon
  (yes, "Harry Parry," oh, rare!) (288). That the Liddon suggestion was made
  is undeniable, but the quoted text this note accompanies most certainly suggests
  the title – "I'll put you *through* [my italics] into Looking-Glass House. How
  would you like *that*?" (127).

2 A comic aside on the beginning of the shift towards imagination in the contest between didactic and imaginative literature is presented in the alteration of Berquin's book by a thirteen-year-old girl in 1848: *The Looking-glass for the Mind; or unintellectual mirror, being an inelegant collection of the most disagreeable silly stories … With twenty-four ugly cuts*, cited in *The Osborne Collection of Children's Books*, vol. 1 (Toronto: Toronto Public Library, 1958), 233.

3 The looking-glass title formula reappeared in children's literature in the late eighteenth century and was used frequently in the nineteenth century. *The Looking Glass: containing select fables of La Fontaine, imitated in English* (London 1784) and *A Looking-Glass for Youth and Age; or, A Sure Guide to Life and Glory* (1800) demonstrate the co-presence of rational and evangelical looking-glass books at the beginning of the nineteenth century. William Godwin used the formula in his biography of William Mulready, the illustrator of many children's books; he titled the biography *The Looking Glass: A True History of the Early Years of an Artist* (1805). Further, "E.B. Elliott" (Mary Belson), a popular writer of children's books, was known as the "looking glass maker." *The Children's Mirror; or, which is my likeness?* (1859) is another close contemporary of Carroll's book.

4 Informational books, perhaps the most frequently published form of children's literature in the first four decades of the nineteenth century, play an important role in the Alice books that has gone unmentioned in all of the three critical editions available. "Peter Parley" (Samuel Griswold Goodrich) and William Pinnock produced a great number of such books, which remained popular throughout the century. Pinnock's informational "Catechisms" of geography and arithmetic, which were meant to be memorized by child readers, may well be specifically at work in both books.

5 *Sir Hornbook* (1822), an "anonymous" work attributed to Thomas Love Peacock, was republished (1846) in the celebrated series of children's books collectively titled *The Home Treasury* put together by "Felix Summerly" (Henry Cole) in the 1840s. It is noteworthy that Carroll never used the increasingly popular material borrowed from mediaeval romance in a consistently serious way.

CHAPTER SIX

1 In addition, Carroll lists *From Nowhere to the North Pole* by Tom Hood; *Elsie's Expedition* by F.E. Weatherly; *A Trip to Blunderland* by Jambon; *Wanted – A King* by Maggie Browne; and *The Story of a Nursery Rhyme*.

2 When Huckleberry Finn lives with the Shepherdsons, *The Pilgrim's Progress* is one of several books on his night table, but Huck makes short work of it when he says it is "about a man that left his family; it didn't say why" (83).

3 Shakespeare, Carroll's favourite writer, also uses the form in *The Taming of the Shrew*, a play that omits the return to the frame; Davidoff says this omission was very common in the early dream visions.

4 Dream vision is but one of the forms Davidoff discusses. Further, she deals with issues that are not germane to the concerns of this chapter, such as differences between French and English dream vision. The reader is urged to read her book to gain many additional insights concerning framing fictions.

5 In Carroll's case, the pattern as used in *Through the Looking-Glass* could be recognized as a reversal of the pattern first met in *Alice in Wonderland* by any reader of Carroll's first fantasy.

6 This book is entitled *A Trip to Blunderland* in Carroll's diary entry for 11 September 1891 (486).

7 Probably the twentieth-century children's fantasy closest to Carroll's dream vision spirit in the Alice books is Norton Juster's *The Phantom Tollbooth*, a book that presents boredom as a terrifying condition. A passing bird, upon hearing Milo's wail of boredom, flies home to its children as fast as it can go. When Milo returns to the formerly boring reality, he finds it so attractive he has no time for another trip through the tollbooth.

8 The mirror or looking-glass genre was frequently employed in the dream-core of dream vision – see Davidoff (73).

Works Cited

Abrams, M.H. *A Glossary of Literary Terms.* 5th ed. Fort Worth, Chicago, etc.: Holt, Rinehart and Winston, 1985.

Anon. *The Child's Dream.* London: printed by J. Catnach, c. 1820.

Anon. *The Child's Magazine, and Sunday Scholar's Companion* 4 (1830).

Anon. *The Laughable Looking Glass for Little Folks.* London: Dean and Son, 1857 and 1859.

Anon. *Il Mondo Rovesciato; or, The World Turned Upside Down.* Cornhill: John and Arthur Arch, 1822.

Anon. *Proverbs in Verse, or Moral Instruction Conveyed in Pictures, for the Use of Schools.* London, 1790.

Anon. "The Queen of Hearts," "The King of Spades," "The King of Clubs," and "The Diamond King." *The European Magazine,* April 1782, 252.

Anon. *The World Turned Upside Down; or the Folly of Man Exemplified in Twelve Comical Relations Upon Uncommon Subjects.* London: n.p., 1750 and 1780.

Anon. *The World Turned Upside Down; or, No News, and Strange News.* York: J. Kendrew, 1828 and 1830.

Anon. *The World Upside Down.* London: n.p., c. 1807.

Bakhtin, Mikhail. *Rabelais and His World.* Translated by Helene Isolsky. Lincoln: University of Nebraska Press, 1984.

Bentham, Jeremy. Some statements about his childhood, quoted in C.K. Ogden, *Bentham's Theory of Fictions.* London: Kegan Paul, French, Traubner and Company, 1932.

Berquin, Arnauld. *The Looking-Glass for the Mind; or, Intellectual Mirror. Being an Elegant Collection of the Most Delightful Little Stories, and Interesting Tales,*

Chiefly translated from that much admired Work, L'Ami des Enfans. London: E. Newbery, 1792.

Brome, Richard. *The Antipodes.* 1640. Reprint, edited by Ann Haaker. Lincoln: University of Nebraska Press, 1966.

Browne, Maggie. *Wanted – a King, or How Merle Set the Nursery Rhymes to Rights.* 1890. In *Beyond the Looking Glass.* Edited by Jonathan Cott. New York: Stonehill Press, 1973.

Bullein, William. *Dialogue Against the Fever Pestilence.* 1594. Reprint, edited by Mark W. Bullen. London: Early English Tract Society, 1888.

Bunyan, John. *The Pilgrim's Progress.* New York: Holt, Rinehart and Winston, 1963.

Butturff, Douglas Rolla, ed. *The Monsters and the Scholar: An Edition and a Critical Study of Liber Monstrorum.* Dissertation, University of Illinois, 1969.

Carpenter, Humphrey. *Secret Gardens: A Study of the Golden Age of Children's Literature.* London: George Allen & Unwin, 1985.

Carroll, Lewis. *Alice's Adventures in Wonderland.* Edited by Donald J. Gray. New York: W.W. Norton, 1971.

– "Alice on Stage." From *The Theatre.* Reprinted in *The Lewis Carroll Picture Book.* Edited by Stuart Dodgson Collingwood. London, 1899.

– *Alice's Adventures in Wonderland and Through the Looking-Glass.* World's Classics series. Edited by Roger L. Green. Oxford: Oxford University Press, 1982.

– *Alice's Adventures under Ground; A Facsimile of the 1864 Manuscript with Notes by Martin Gardner.* New York: Dover, 1965.

– *The Diaries of Lewis Carroll.* Edited by Roger L. Green. New York: Oxford University Press, 1954.

– *The Nursery "Alice."* London: Macmillan and Company, 1890.

– *Pillow Problems.* 1895. Reprint, New York: Dover Publications, 1958.

– *The Rectory Magazine.* A facsimile edition with an introduction by Jerome Bump. Austin and London: University of Texas, 1975.

– *The Rectory Umbrella and Mischmasch.* 1850. Reprint, London: Cassell & Company, 1932.

– *A Selection of the Letters of Lewis Carroll to His Child Friends.* Edited by Evelyn Hatch. London: Macmillan and Company, 1933.

– *Sylvie and Bruno.* 1889. In *The Complete Illustrated Works of Lewis Carroll.* London: Chancelor Press, 1982.

– *Useful and Instructive Poetry.* London: Geoffrey Bles, 1954.

Cattegno, Jean. *Lewis Carroll: Fragments of a Looking Glass.* New York: Thomas Y. Crowell Company, 1974.

Chaucer, Geoffrey. *The Works of Geoffrey Chaucer.* Edited by F.N. Robinson. Boston: Houghton Mifflin Company, 1957.

Chear, Abraham. *A Looking Glass for Children.* 1673.

Clayton, E.C. *The World Turned Upside Down.* London: Dean and Son, 1876.

– *Topsy Turvy; or, Strange Sights to See.* London: Dean and Son, 1878.

Cocchiara, Giuseppe. *Il Mondo Alla Rovescia*. Torino: Editori Boringhieri, 1981.

Cole, Henry. "Prospectus" for *The Home Treasury* series, as quoted by F.J. Harvey Darton in *Children's Books in England*.

– ("Felix Summerley"). *Puck's Reports to Oberon, King of Fairies, of Some New Exploits of the Pen and Pencil of Fancy*. London: Joseph Cundall, 1844.

–, ed. *Sir Hornbook; or, Childe Launcelot's Expedition. A Grammatico-Allegorical Ballad* (an "anonymous" work attributed to Thomas Love Peacock). London: Joseph Cundall, 1843.

– ("Felix Summerly"). *Traditional Nursery Songs of England*. London: Joseph Cundall, c. 1843.

Collingwood, Stuart Dodgson, ed. *The Lewis Carroll Picture Book*. London, 1899.

Cuddon, J.A. *A Dictionary of Literary Terms*. Harmondsworth, Middlesex: Penguin Books, 1979.

Curtius, Ernst. *European Literature and the Latin Middle Ages*. Translated by Willard Trask. London: Routledge and Kegan Paul, 1953.

Darton, F.J. Harvey. *Children's Books in England: Five Centuries of Social Life*. Cambridge: Cambridge University Press, 1958.

Davidoff, Judith M. *Beginning Well: Framing Fictions in Late Middle English Poetry*. London and Toronto: Associated University Presses, 1988.

Demurova, Nina. "Toward a Definition of *Alice's* Genre: The Folktale and Fairy Tale Connections." In *Lewis Carroll: A Celebration*. Edited by Edward Guiliano, 75–88. New York: Clarkson N. Potter, 1982.

Dickens, Charles. *Hard Times*. Vol. 1 of *The Annotated Dickens*. Edited by Edward Guiliano and Philip Collins. New York: Clarkson N. Potter, 1986.

Docherty, John. *The Literary Products of the Lewis Carroll–George MacDonald Friendship*. Lewiston/Queenston/Lampeter: Edwin Mellen Press, 1995.

Donaldson, Ian. *The World Turned Upside Down: Comedy from Jonson to Fielding*. Oxford: Clarendon Press, 1970.

Duchartre, Pierre-Louis, and René Saulniers. *L'Imagerie Populaire*. Paris: Librairie de France, 1925.

Field, Louise Francis. *The Child and His Book*. London: Wells Gardner, Darton & Co., 1890.

Frye, Northrop. *Anatomy of Criticism*. New York: Atheneum, 1968.

Gardner, Martin. *The Annotated Alice: Alice's Adventures in Wonderland and Through the Looking-Glass and What Alice Found There*. London: Penguin, 1970.

Goodrich, Samuel Griswold. "Merry's Museum" and other pieces from *Recollections of a Lifetime, or Men and Things I have Seen*. Vol. 2. New York and Auburn: Miller, Orton & Co., 1857.

– ("Peter Parley"). "Prospectus" from *Parley's Magazine*. Boston: Lilly, Wait and Company, 1833.

– ("Peter Parley"). *The Tales of Peter Parley About America*. Facsimile of the 1828 edition. New York: Dover Publications, 1974.

Grabes, Herbert. *The Mutable Glass: Mirror-Imagery in Titles and Texts of the Middle Ages and English Renaissance.* Translated by Gordon Collier. Cambridge: Cambridge University Press, 1982.

Grandville, J.J. *Un Autre Monde.* Paris: H. Fournier, 1844. Reprinted in *L'Oeuvre Graphique Complète de Grandville.* Tome II. Edited by Arthur Hubschmid. Paris: n.d.

Grant, Helen. "The World Upside Down." In *Studies in Spanish Literature of the Golden Age.* Edited by R.O. Jones. London: Tamesis Books, 1972.

Gray, Donald, ed. *Alice's Adventures in Wonderland.* New York: W.W. Norton, 1971 and 1992.

Green, Roger Lancelyn, ed. *Alice's Adventures in Wonderland and Through the Looking-Glass and What Alice Found There.* World's Classics series. Oxford: Oxford University Press, 1982.

Guiliano, Edward, ed. *Lewis Carroll: A Celebration, Essays on the Occasion of the 150th Anniversary of the Birth of Charles Lutwidge Dodgson.* New York: Clarkson N. Potter, 1982.

Halliwell, James Orchard. *The Nursery Rhymes of England, Obtained Principally from the Oral Tradition.* London: printed for the Percy Society, 1843.

Hill, Christopher. *The World Turned Upside Down; Radical Ideas during the English Revolution.* London: Temple Smith, 1972.

Hoffmann, Heinrich. *The English Struwwelpeter; or Pretty Stories and Funny Pictures for Little Children.* Leipsic: Friedrich Volczmar, 1848.

Holberg, Ludvig. *Journey to the World Underground; Being the Subterraneus Travels of Niels Klim.* Translation of the 1745 original publication. London: Thomas North, 1828.

Holland, Edward. *Mabel in Rhymeland, or Little Mabel's Journey to Norwich and Her Wonderful Adventures with the Man in the Moon and Other Heroes and Heroines of Nursery Rhyme.* London: Griffith, Farrow, Kender and Welsh, 1885.

Hood, Tom. *Upside Down; or, Turnover Traits.* London: Griffith and Farran, 1868.

Howitt, Mary, " 'Will You Walk into My Parlour,' Said the Spider to the Fly." In *Sketches of Natural History.* London: Effingham Wilson, 1834.

Hudson, Derek. *Lewis Carroll: An Illustrated Life.* London: Constable, 1976.

Hughes, Thomas. *Tom Brown's School Days.* 1856. Reprint, Harmondsworth, Middlesex: Puffin Books, 1979.

Jambon, Jean (pseudonym). *Our Trip to Blunderland; or, Grand Excursion to Blundertown and Back.* Edinburgh and London: William Blackwood and Sons, 1877.

Kingsley, Charles. *The Water Babies: A Fairy Tale for a Land-Baby.* London: Macmillan and Company, 1903.

Kunzle, David. "World Upside Down: The Iconography of a European Broadsheet Type." In *The Reversible World: Symbolic Inversion in Art and*

Society. Edited by Barbara Babcock. Ithaca and London: Cornell University Press, 1978.

Lamb, Charles. *The King and Queen of Hearts; with the Rogueries of the Knave Who Stole the Queen's Pies*. London: Thomas Hodgkins, 1805.

Lax, Roger, and Frederick Smith. *The Great Song Thesaurus*. New York: Oxford University Press, 1984.

Lear, Edward. *The Complete Nonsense of Edward Lear*. New York: Dodd, Mead & Company, 1964.

Lennon, Florence Becker. *Victoria Through the Looking Glass: The Life of Lewis Carroll*. New York: Dover, 1972.

Lever, Maurice, and Frederick Tristran. *Le Monde à l'Enver; Representation du Mythe*. Paris: Hachette/Massin, 1980.

MacDonald, George. *The Princess and the Goblin*. Harmondsworth, Middlesex: Puffin Books, 1984.

– *The Princess and Curdie*. Harmondsworth, Middlesex: Puffin Books, 1980.

Madden, William A. "Framing the *Alices*." *Publications of the Modern Language Association* 101, no. 1 (May 1986): 362–73.

Mandeville, John. *The Voyages of Sir John Mandeville*. Edited by M.C. Seymour. Oxford: Clarendon Press, 1967.

Meloni, Irene. *La logica del nonsenso: Alice's Adventures in Wonderland*. Cagliari: Universita Degli Studi di Cagliari, 1990.

Mespoulet, Marguerite. *The Creators of Wonderland*. New York: Arrow Editions, 1934.

Muir, Percy. *English Children's Books, 1600–1900*. London: B.T. Battleford, 1954.

Opie, Iona, and Peter Opie. *The Oxford Dictionary of Nursery Rhymes*. Oxford: Clarendon Press, 1951.

Parker, Richard. "Conversations on the Eye." In *Juvenile Philosophy, Philosophy in Familial Conversations, Designed to Teach Children to Think*. New York: A.S. Barnes, 1850.

Phillips, Robert, ed. *Aspects of Alice: Lewis Carroll's Dreamchild as Seen through the Critics' Looking-Glasses, 1865–1971*. New York: Vanguard Press, 1971.

Pinnock, William. *A Catechism of Arithmetic*. London: printed for Geo. B. Whittaker, 1826.

– *A Catechism of Geography*. London: printed for Geo. B. Whittaker, 1820.

– *A Catechism of Heraldry*. London: printed for Pinnock and Maunder, n.d.

– *A Catechism of Optics*. London: William Pinnock, 1820.

Praz, Mario. "Two Masters of the Absurd: Grandville and Carroll." In *The Artist and Writer in France: Essays in Homage of Jean Seznec*. Edited by Francis Haskell, 134–7. Oxford: Clarendon Press, 1974.

Prickett, Stephen. *Victorian Fantasy*. Bloomington and London: University of Indiana Press, 1979.

Rabkin, Eric. *The Fantastic in Literature*. Princeton, NJ: Princeton University Press, 1976.

Rackin, Donald. *Alice's Adventures in Wonderland and Through the Looking-Glass: Nonsense, Sense, and Meaning*. New York: Twayne Publishers, 1991.

– "*Alice's Adventures in Wonderland*: An Underground Journey to the End of Night." In Donald Rackin, *Alice's Adventures in Wonderland and Through the Looking-Glass: Nonsense, Sense, and Meaning*. New York: Twayne Publishers, 1991.

– "Alice's Journey to the End of Night." 1966. Reprinted in *Aspects of Alice*. Edited by Robert Phillips. New York: Vanguard Press, 1971.

– "Corrective Laughter: Carroll's *Alice* and Popular Children's Literature." *The Journal of Popular Culture* 1 (1967).

Ruskin, John. *The King of the Golden River*. New York: Dover Publications, 1974.

Russell, J. Stephen. *The English Dream Vision: Anatomy of a Form*. Columbus: Ohio State University Press, 1988.

Sinclair, Catherine. *Holiday House*. 1839. Photo facsimile, New York and London: Garland Publishing, 1976.

Smedley, Manella Bute. "The Shepherd of the Giant Mountains." *Sharpe's London Magazine* 1, nos. 19 and 20 (7 and 21 March 1846): 298–300, 326–8.

Stern, Jeffrey, ed. *Lewis Carroll's Library, A facsimile edition of the catalogue of the auction sale following C.L. Dodgson's death in 1898 …* Silverspring, Md: Lewis Carroll Society of North America, 1981.

Stone, Harry. *Dickens and the Invisible World: Fairy Tales, Fantasy, and Novel-making*. Bloomington: University of Indiana Press, 1979.

Susina, Jan. " 'Respiciendo prudens': Lewis Carroll's Juvenilia." *Children's Literature Association Quarterly* 17, no. 4 (Winter 1992–93): 10–14.

Swift, Jonathan. *A Tale of a Tub with Other Early Works 1696–1707*. Edited by Herbert Davis. Oxford: Basil Blackwell, 1957.

Taylor, Alexander. *The White Knight*. London: Oliver and Boyd, 1952.

Taylor, Ann. *The Wedding Among the Flowers*. London: Darton and Harvey, 1808.

Taylor, Ann, and Jane Taylor. *Rhymes for the Nursery*. London: Darton and John, 1806.

– *Signor Topsy-Turvy's Wonderful Magic Lantern; or, The World turned upside down*. London: Tabart and Company, 1810.

Thackery, William. *The Rose and the Ring*. London: Macmillan and Company, 1903.

Tillotson, Kathleen. "Lewis Carroll and the Kitten on the Hearth." *English: The Magazine of the English Association* 8, no. 45 (Autumn 1950).

Watts, Isaac. *Divine Songs Attempted in Easy Language for the Use of Children*. London: M. Lawrence at the Angel, 1715.

Weatherly, Frederick E. *Elsie's Expedition*. London: Frederick Warne and Company, 1874.

Wordsworth, William. From "The Prelude." In *The Poetical Works of Wordsworth*. Edited by Thomas Hutchinson. London: Oxford University Press, 1960.

Index